T0356227

What People Are Saying About *A Girl from Busan*!

Okhui has navigated her way from despair to hope and from anger to equality, crossing a wide landscape of history and cultures. Rifling pragmatically through her multiple identities, she has nonetheless stayed true to her core self. She has won the battle and has even written an amazing book.

Tom Coffman
Author of *Nation Within:*
The History of the American Occupation of Hawaii

A Girl from Busan is unique in cultural background and story specifics, but the themes are universal. The trials and tribulations that we all experience, the feelings of solitude and aloneness, and the crossroads of whether or not to embrace our faith are all uniquely interwoven in this book. I left feeling inspired and refocused, all while learning a bit about different cultures and expectations from a unique perspective.

Jeff Timmons
Founder and member of 98 Degrees.

This out-of-the-ordinary story of a Korean American family provides deep revelations and spiritual counsel, particularly emphasizing the potency of prayer for seekers of life's truths. It unfolds an epic familial narrative brimming with hope and inspiration and is especially tailored for those endeavoring to discover solutions and support loved ones as they traverse difficult paths.

Kahu Kenneth Makuakāne
Senior Pastor of Kawaiaha'o Church

A GIRL FROM BUSAN

A Mother's Prayer

THE STORY OF OKHUI
by
OKHUI LEE

Made for Success Publishing
P.O. Box 1775 Issaquah, WA 98027
www.MadeForSuccess.com

Distributed by Blackstone Publishing

First Printing

Library of Congress Cataloging-in-Publication data
Author Lee, Okhui
     A Girl from Busan: A Memoir
        p. cm.

LCCN: 2024934705

ISBN: 978-1-64146-788-9 (*Hardcover*)
ISBN: 978-1-64146-789-6 (*eBook*)
ISBN: 978-1-64146-790-2 (*Audiobook*)

Printed in the United States of America

For further information, contact Made for Success Publishing
+1425-526-6480 or email service@madeforsuccess.net

CONTENTS

PART ONE

INTRODUCTION

"I took my troubles to the Lord; I cried out to Him,
and He answered my prayer."
—Psalms 120:1 (NLT)

IT WAS A warm summer night, and a light rain spattered across my windowpane. I must have dozed off while breastfeeding my baby girl, but not for long. I suddenly woke, drenched in a cold, sticky sweat and feeling a looming sense of danger.

My breathing became rapid, and a strange feeling came over me, a feeling that something was holding me down, sinking me into the floor. I started coughing uncontrollably as blood flew out my mouth, and I screamed. At that moment, my family burst through the door, their faces etched with shock.

My sister Okyon cried out, *"Eomma, she's dying!"*

With eyes filled with terror, my mother attempted to catch the blood gushing from my mouth with her bare hands; it slipped through her trembling fingers and transformed into gelatin.

Then, darkness enveloped my body, my consciousness slipping away.

***

MY KOREAN NAME was Mun Okhui. I grew up in the city of Busan during the Korean War. I still recall the pungent aroma of fresh fish pervading the air at the Jagalchi fish market and the chatter of villagers haggling with loud, obnoxious merchants along the waterfront. Following the birth of my first son, Jinseong, who had entered this world outside of marriage, I eventually relocated to Seoul.

I had just married an American GI, Sergeant Gordon Lee, when I was diagnosed with lung pleurisy as a result of having had tuberculosis as a child. Growing up in poverty, my family wasn't aware of the severity of the disease, and neither was I. It was just after the birth of our daughter, Marylin, when my health started to deteriorate, and according to the doctors, my lung had collapsed.

I was admitted to the 121st U.S. Army hospital at Yongsan Garrison in Seoul, Korea. Going in and out of consciousness, I could see the wispy image of my mother's face near my bed. Her eyes were closed, and I could hear her fervently praying.

Mother often reminded me that I needed to pray for my children's well-being. In her words, "Praying for the children would shape a better future." But to be honest, I never understood how prayer worked until later in my life when my firstborn son struggled with substance abuse, and I began to understand the importance of prayer.

But at this moment, I faced a medical emergency. Military hospitals in Korea lacked the necessary facilities to perform the required surgery. Consequently, I found myself being airlifted to Denver, Colorado, United States, in late 1966, where I underwent the crucial operation.

After my release from the Denver hospital, I was greeted by two smiling faces—my husband and my three-year-old son, Jinseong, who had recently been adopted by Gordon. While awaiting further medical procedures, my husband and I expedited my mother's emigration from Korea to live with us in America.

By the spring of the following year, my health improved in time for my mother and my daughter to arrive at our new suburban home in Montebello, Colorado. There, I gave birth to my third child, Patrick, and we became a family of six.

I knew I had to earn a living, but my job prospects were limited because I spoke very little English. Mother, on the other hand, wasted no time making herself at home in America. She searched local stores to buy *won bok* cabbage to make *kimchi*, and then, upon realizing the spices were not available, she took the initiative to plant her own garden to ensure she had everything she needed to make *kimchi*.

Despite the brisk, cool air coming from the surrounding snow-covered Rockies, she never had a problem with her harvest. When the fruits of her labor ripened, she would pick green cucumbers and red tomatoes for dinner. Mother often complained that Gordon was always lazing about and kept his shoes on in the house. While playing her *hwa-tu* cards, we'd converse in Korean. I explained to her that teaching Americans to learn Korean manners was like pulling bad teeth out by yourself.

Eventually, our conversations would veer into our financial situation and the difficulties of maintaining our mortgage as a one-income household. Gordon had to go on a second tour in Vietnam to increase our income.

But her more persistent topic of conversation involved telling me to send the kids to a Korean church. "They should learn about our culture," she said. "Learn about our heritage and about God." And most of all, she reminded me to pray for my children's well-being.

"Because that's what a good mother should do," she'd say. The irony of this statement wasn't lost on me.

What could you possibly know about being a good mother? I thought. She was never there for most of my childhood. It would take many years for me to understand how her faith had changed her and how it strengthened her resolve to protect our family and keep us together as we emigrated from Korea to America.

MOTHER PONG

MOTHER WAS A bright, spunky child who was strong and held her own against the boys in the neighborhood. But little girls were expected to grow into docile wives and child bearers—nothing more. Schooling and other such things were out of the question for a young woman whose main function was to produce a male child to carry on the family name. It was said that too much intelligence made a woman *undesirable*. As a child, Mother never fit into the mold set for her, and by the age of thirteen, her situation grew worse.

In the mid-1800s, China was caught amidst a rampant drug trade. Their last emperor, a boy under Japanese control in the puppet state of Manchukuo, did nothing to stop it. Japan was building up their imperial strength and felt that if they could weaken China by importing drugs, they could subjugate the Chinese military. And Korea, wedged between the two countries, subsequently became the middleman in their drug trade.

As members of the elite Korean gentry, Mother's parents could afford to purchase heroin. A concubine introduced it to my grandfather, and both he and his wife quickly developed a taste for it. Grandfather Haksong used the drug for leisure, but Grandma Boksae, who suffered from abdominal ulcers, took it to ease her pain.

The responsibility fell upon Mother to prepare and administer the drug to her parents, and its effects were immediate. She believed it was medicine . . . just harmless medicine, as she watched her parents' faces change from stern, authoritative masks to euphoric grins. At the same time, they used another drug, which came from poppy plants—opium, which their servants harvested and prepared for my grandparents to smoke.

Interestingly, when Mother Pong told these stories to her children, her style of recitation was difficult to grasp. Sometimes, she'd start at the end, then work her way toward the beginning. And, at other times, she'd start somewhere in the middle, interject a correlation about her current life, and then hop between the beginning and the end to wrap it up. Nonetheless, I believed every story she told about her family and her childhood allowed her to better understand her own life.

I recall one particular story she told fondly. "Once, on a hot summer afternoon," she began, "while reaching for a bag of rice from the top of the pantry, my grandmother—your great-grandmother—was bitten by a large snake!"

With excitement, she continued, "In her stern anger, my grandmother instructed her servants to catch the snake and cut it up. This, of course, went against our Korean tradition of respecting the spirits of animals. Large animals inside your house were a sign of good luck—luck that would be reversed if, say, a servant had been ordered to kill it with a sword, hack it to pieces, and burn the remains by the river."

With a thoughtful glaze in her eye, Mother paused to recall the lesson she'd wished to impart. "Instead of turning the snake loose into the wild, as a good Korean who respected life should have done, Grandmother killed it!" Dismayed, she continued, "Ever since, every generation has reaped the seeds of the bad karma that she sowed!"

With our full attention fixed on her, Mother would finish her story by wagging her finger in the air with a look of disapproval, as if we had killed the snake ourselves and caused our family's bad fortune. I kept in mind that she'd been telling this story long before becoming a Christian, back when she'd still followed ancient Korean beliefs. Although I personally never believed in those animistic fables, I couldn't deny the curse that sprang forth and continued to haunt our family.

Mother Pong was the oldest child in her family. She had one younger brother and three younger sisters, including my Aunties Deoki, Jeonghi, and Okhae. They were raised comfortably in an upper-middle-class home in the Korean countryside of Daegu, on a fine parcel nicknamed Apple Farmland for its lush fields of delicious Fuji apples.

By the time Mother turned seventeen, she had come dangerously close to being ineligible for marriage. Due to the Chinese opium war that pervaded much of Korea, both of her parents had become addicts. And who would want their son to marry a girl from a family of opium addicts?

Fortunately, my great-grandparents knew a family by the name of Mun who had recently relocated to Japan, a wealthy ruling family of higher status. This meant they were *yangban*—Korean nobility. The Nampyeong Moon family property in Inhyong Village has since become a historical landmark and a popular tourist attraction in Daegu, South Korea. At the time of our immigration, the Americans spelled our family name as "Mun" instead of Moon, and that was how we rendered it legally, though we use both spellings interchangeably.

Mother told us she was allowed to marry Father because of a scandalous situation in his family. My father's mother, Seokbuni, was left a widow just before he was born. According to Korean customs, a widow could not leave the house for one hundred days after the death of her husband, and it was considered shameful in Korea for her to remarry for at least three years, especially if she was *yangban*.

Mother told us Grandma Seokbuni defied customary tradition, not just by remarrying, but by marrying a disreputable playboy, therefore shaming the entire family. As a result, her relatives swindled her out of the deed to the family property. As an impoverished outcast, she and her new family were forced to move to Japan.

My father, Mun Myeongsu, now the man of the house, enthusiastically traveled to Daegu to pick up Ponghui as his new bride. And Mother was not at all disappointed. In fact, she was pleasantly surprised to see such a handsome gentleman at the door. Myeongsu greeted her with a warm, gentle smile, and she could tell right away he was shy and meek. Dressed in a sleek western-style business suit, Myeongsu kept bowing to her even though they had already completed their initial introductions.

Each step he took into the house required another bow. With a light chuckle, Mother told us he looked like a chicken plucking rice from the ground. Though he appeared well-mannered, Mother wasn't certain that he would make a strong husband who'd work hard for his family.

On the other hand, she understood that a good girl must do as she's told. Therefore, Ponghui determined that her greatest effort as his wife would be to domesticate this bowing chicken. Perhaps life in Japan would become a grand adventure.

***

I WAS BORN in Nagoya City, in the prefecture of Gifu. Living in Japan, I was given a Japanese name, Tomiko, but at home, my Korean name was Okhui. My siblings and I were required to use our Japanese names in public because, during the Second World War, the Japanese government would not allow Koreans to publicly use Korean names. My brothers told me it was because they were trying to take away our language and, subsequently, our culture.

I was the seventh of nine children, with two older sisters, four older brothers, and, at this time, one baby brother. Mother used to tell us that having many children was a good wife's duty, regardless of whether you loved your husband or not. It was her duty to look out for her family.

My oldest sister, Oksoon, was a bright and fiery girl of fifteen during the last year of the Second World War. After Oksoon was Okyon, who, at fourteen, took on more than her fair share of responsibility. Next were my four brothers: Jeongho, Yeongho, Gyeongho, and Yongho, and then me. I was followed by my baby brother Ikchan, who sadly did not survive infancy. Lastly, my youngest brother, Changho, was born years later after our family relocated back to Korea. In fact, Changho was the only sibling born on Korean soil.

During the last year of the war, my family counted forty-nine straight days of earthquakes accompanied by horrendous winds and storms. Along with the military strength of imperial Japan, it felt as though the weather itself was coming undone.

Then, on August 15, 1945, life in this tumultuous world changed into quiet trepidation. The Japanese called for *Gyokuon–hoso*, the Imperial Surrender, referring to the speech by Emperor Hirohito. The Second World War had finally come to an end.

Not everyone could afford to have a radio in their homes, so our family invited our Japanese neighbors to listen to the emperor. His regal Tokyo accent quivered as he spoke, and our guests bowed their heads as a symbolic expression of gratitude. Out of respect for our neighbors, my father bowed, too. When the emperor concluded his speech, our neighbors shook with a tearful whimper. Then, they thanked my family and left in a peaceful manner.

The war was over.

NAGOYA STATION

GRANDMOTHER SEOKBUNI TOLD us that Japan's surrender was a sign for us to return to Korea, as she believed her soul could never rest unless she was buried in Korean soil. Despite my parents' protests, Grandmother would not change her mind. So, we packed everything we could fit into our three *bottari,* or cloths used to wrap our belongings, and seven suitcases. We either sold or gave away whatever we couldn't take with us and then embarked on our journey back to our ancestral home, Korea.

Nagoya Station was packed with people shouting, pushing, and shoving from every direction to board their train. We were surrounded by many Korean expatriates who were excited to share in the hope of a bright new future by returning to the motherland. Though I was only three years old and much too young to remember the journey, my older brothers and sisters would talk about our adventurous trip in the years to come.

As soon as we arrived, Mother and Grandmother counted the heads of my brothers and sisters every few minutes. At one point, amid all the hustle and bustle, one head went missing—five-year-old Brother Yong—but we had already boarded the train.

"Tatsuo! Tatsuo!" Grandma Seokbuni frantically shouted out his Japanese name. Just as the train was about to move, a heavily bundled Korean man shoved Yong through an open window. For the rest of our half-day journey, we all huddled around him, never letting him out of our sight as we headed west toward Shimonoseki port.

Grandma Seokbuni held him in her lap while the train carried us through Hiroshima. Although I was too young to remember seeing the city's destruction, Okyon later told me what she had seen out of the train's window that day—every building had been destroyed by the atomic bomb. Hiroshima, once a large, thriving city, was buried in a heaping pile of ash under a thick layer of billowing smoke.

"I saw one chimney," Okyon said, "a single, lone chimney standing amidst the rubble. It was all that was left."

From the train station to Shimonoseki port, we boarded a refitted coal ship that would take us to the Korean mainland. After eight hours on the open sea, the city of Busan came into view. Excited, Okyon was the first to hurry portside to take a look, but the long-awaited moment was bittersweet. As my entire family gathered on the deck, we were shocked to see the once-green mountains completely stripped of foliage. Not one tree was left standing; only red dirt and jutting rocks remained. My mother explained that the countryside was so impoverished that the entire mountaintop had been stripped of its natural resources.

Okyon recalled seeing an army of defeated Japanese soldiers boarding an empty cargo ship as it prepared to head back to Japan. She heard the booming melody of a live American band playing music on the dock as the soldiers departed. Chinese passengers who had immigrated to Busan during wartime boarded the next ship headed north.

***

DURING OUR FIRST few weeks in Korea, Grandmother Seokbuni decided to move in with her eldest daughter, Soonja, in Chollado, while Father settled the rest of the family in Busan, where Aunty Deoki, Mother's younger sister, agreed to take us in on the condition that our stay would be temporary.

Aunty Deoki had spent most of the war as a "comfort woman," a euphemism for *maechunbu*, or prostitute. These women were forced into sexual slavery during the Japanese occupation, purportedly to prevent rape crimes and hostility in occupied villages.

While other trafficked women were sold to procurers serving Japanese soldiers, Deoki had been sold by her drug-addict parents to a Chinese tavern, where she learned to be resourceful and manipulative. This tavern was a front for prostitution, so by working as a barmaid and "comfort woman," she accumulated enough money to buy some men's clothing from a Japanese soldier, which she used to disguise herself and escape her captors.

Returning to Busan after the war, Aunty Deoki applied her earnings toward a simple two-story Japanese-style house for us to live in. Under the black arched entryway, the musty straw smell of *tatami* was a familiar comfort that reminded me of the home I knew in Japan.

***

ONE WINTER NIGHT, sister Okyon came home clutching little Brother Ikchan close to her chest; both were sopping wet and shivering. There had been a fire at a neighbor's house, and Okyon lingered while our baby brother insisted on watching the "firemen." These civilian firefighters sprayed the house with putrid water they had collected from the nearby canal. Without warning, one of the hoses burst, dousing Okyon and Ikchan with its polluted water. Okyon recovered, but Ikchan developed a rattling cough that worried Mother.

Two weeks passed. Then, one day, I peered around the open screen door of the *tatami* room and saw my parents huddled together, clinging desperately to a motionless bundle.

I knew the worst had happened. Father remained still, but Mother wandered into the yard and looked out above the mountaintop as her eyes welled with tears. Sometime during the night, Ikchan's spirit had departed.

My entire family mourned, but Okyon took it the hardest. She blamed herself for Ikchan's death, believing the unclean water had caused him to develop pneumonia. He passed away just one week shy of his second birthday.

SINGING WITH
THE CHRISTMAS CHOIR

ONE MORNING, UPON waking, the house was filled with the delicious smell of cooked rice. Mother was preparing vegetables called *namul*, which she wrapped with the rice and placed in a lunch box covered in a white cloth.

Mother exclaimed, "I heard you coughing all night; we should go pray to Yongwagnim, the Prince of the Ocean, for healing."

She then took me outside to a rocky area by the seashore. I clung tightly to her skirt since it was high tide. I constantly feared that the waves would whisk me away.

I watched Mother as she unwrapped the lunch box and placed it on a platter. She poured gasoline on a rolled-up paper bag and lit it with a match, and then she held it up to the sky with outstretched arms. Mother told me she learned bits of an old Shamanic religion as a child, before Buddhism and Christianity became more popular in Korea. She believed she could talk to ocean creatures to heal me.

When I was a child, Mother never engaged in organized religion. It wasn't until one day when Brother Yong, who socialized with the neighborhood kids, took me to a Baptist church that I was even exposed to the idea. This church had been built out of an abandoned school during the Japanese occupation.

At the age of seven, I'd often wondered about other children who were privileged enough to attend church, and I envied them. I also longed to be inside this large, inviting building that emanated an atmosphere of gentle peace. My heart brimmed with joy with that thought. Though unfamiliar with the concept of this higher power, I could sense profound goodness radiating from the prayers uttered within those walls.

Upon entering, I was overwhelmed with excitement. The service was held in a large, square room with a high ceiling. The air was cold, and as I sat beside Yong on a long wooden bench, I rubbed my hands together to keep warm.

I could hear a rattling wooden window frame that had been gradually eaten over time by termites, but otherwise, the room appeared tidy with a fresh wintery morning smell. Over the central altar, I noticed a cross depicting a wooden carving of a shirtless man wrapped in a loincloth. His head tilted to one side as it hung downward, revealing a sorrowful face with His mouth agape and His eyes remaining closed. A crown with spikes rested on His head, its points pressed into His skin, and His face was adorned with streaks of red paint, a sight unfamiliar to me.

Upon closer examination, I observed that His arms were stretched wide along the horizontal beam while His legs and torso were pressed against the vertical beam. My attention was then drawn to the unmistakable sight of metal nails piercing His hands and feet, securing Him to the cross.

Acknowledging my curiosity, Yong leaned closer and whispered, "That man is *Yesunim*, known as Jesus Christ to Westerners." I dared not voice my questions out loud, yet many questions flooded my head: *Why is He nailed there? Why does He look so sad?*

I presumed that this must have been an honorable death by the way this church was worshipping Him. While the hymns filled the air, I listened attentively and came to understand that He had been sent to assist children like myself.

The pastor's sermon went on and on with no end in sight, and I didn't understand everything he was talking about. However, when a group of older girls stood up and positioned themselves at the front to sing, I couldn't help but fix my attention on them.

A choir awaited with eager anticipation. Their song began with a slow and hypnotic rhythm before transitioning into a powerful, heart-racing beat. Though they sang in Korean, they mixed in some unfamiliar proper names in English. Happily, I was able to make out the words "Ee-man-you-well" and "No-El," but I still had to ask my brother to explain their meaning.

After the service, Yong introduced me to the choir director. When she heard me speak, she told me that I had a melodious voice and asked if I'd be interested in joining the Christmas choir. With an excited grin, I immediately replied, "Yes!"

As a child, I had always loved to sing at home, and I could hardly wait to sing with the choir. There were ten members ranging from age seven to early teens. We practiced late into the evening, two nights a week, and I learned all the traditional Christmas carols in Korean. I also learned to harmonize on a gentle lullaby of peace songs, such as "Silent Night" and "O Little Town of Bethlehem," blending in with their voices. I sang with fervor, and my heart overflowed with joy. I felt as though I truly belonged. Their voices ignited my love of music.

***

A WEEK HAD passed since the New Year's Eve church service, and as I made my way home, an eerie sensation enveloped me. Walking past the neighborhood houses, the familiar scent of black bean soup filled the air, triggering memories of those rare occasions when Mother would prepare it for us on New Year's Day, but only when we could afford it. I took a deep breath and ran home.

Upon reaching the front door, a single rusted hinge gave way, crashing onto the porch with a resounding clank. Pushing open the door, my gaze immediately fell to the sight of my mother standing by our charcoal stove, diligently stirring a pot of black bean soup. Yet, an unsettling feeling welled within me, as if something was profoundly amiss.

In the corner of the room, I spotted Mother's *bottari*, a bundle of personal belongings tied up with a cloth. She seemed distant, lost in her own thoughts. Overwhelmed by a sense of devastation, I rushed toward her and embraced her tightly, unwilling to let go.

Her tears fell into the soup as she gently stirred. I pleaded, voice trembling. But her lips remained sealed.

"Why are you crying?" I asked. She didn't answer.

On the kitchen counter, I noticed a row of mochi cakes. According to tradition, black bean soup and mochi prepared on New Year's Day would bring longevity, good health, and prosperity. But her brooding eyes and her solid blue blouse, which clung to her skin from perspiration, made me doubt that.

As her voice stammered, Mother told me she had to leave for an indefinite amount of time; she had decided to work with Auntie Okhae at her restaurant in Daegu. After that day, I had to rely on my older sister, Okyon, to take care of me.

But in truth, Okyon hardly ever did. Constantly in and out of the house, my sister claimed she was too busy for me. During her busiest days, she would drop me off with Father and my brothers at their new home in Chorangdong, but they would go about their business as though I didn't exist. Even though Okyon lived with me, I felt as though she were far away, not just physically but in her heart. It made me feel that much lonelier.

FIRST GLIMPSE OF
AMERICAN CULTURE

NOT WANTING TO stay at home, I spent many afternoons wandering the streets by myself. Surrounded by the bustling throng, yet isolated, I learned to be strong and embrace my own company, often singing to myself as I walked.

On one occasion, I strolled by the Munhwa Theater and gazed up at a fresh billboard standing proudly next to the glowing marquee. Mesmerized, I found myself locked in a gaze with the captivating countenance of an American woman on the billboard. Later, I learned her name was Greta Garbo, a famous American actress. I couldn't believe how someone could possess such breathtaking beauty. Her mysterious eyes seemed to track my every step as I passed by. Fascinated and captivated, I spent countless afternoons gazing up at these beautifully crafted American movie billboards.

***

WITH THE CONCLUSION of World War II, the profound influ-ence of Western culture on Korean society became unmistakable. I found myself utterly delighted by everything American—be it the music, greeting cards, or, above all, the allure of American movies.

Okyon often brought home American magazines, and I, the wide-eyed enthusiast, would park myself in the kitchen for hours, entranced by the pictures of those fair-skinned faces. With my finger, I would gleefully trace along their round eyes and plump, ruddy lips as if I were performing a finger ballet of admiration.

Those magazines and movie posters were my first glimpse of the Western world and its entertainment. I was curious but confused when Okyon used a new American phrase I'd never heard before—*movie stars.* After that, like an unruly child, I bombarded Okyon several times a week with pleas to take me to the theater.

***

MONTHS PASSED WITH all the back and forth before she finally agreed to take me into town to see my first American movie. To my delight, she eagerly dressed for the occasion, donning a gray flared skirt, a new flower-printed silk blouse, a white scarf, and high-heeled shoes. These were the most fashionable clothes at this time, and it made me happy to see her so nicely dressed, especially since I only owned one pair of worn-out shoes, a wrinkled, tattered skirt, and a blouse. Smoothing out my outfit with the palms of my hand, I felt proud to be walking down the street with my pretty, grown-up sister.

The street leading to the Munhwa Theater was muddy and unpaved, but we finally made it inside, where my heart fluttered with excitement. Unexpectedly, an American GI approached us. He startled me back to reality. Stunned, I watched him greet my sister with a tight embrace. He was obviously her boyfriend.

Since my sister was in her late teens and no jobs were available, dating an American was one of the few ways to support one's family. The American GI looked at me with an inquisitive gaze until my sister said something to him in a foreign language that sounded like an apology.

I paid little attention to my surroundings, too consumed by excitement. Having only seen pictures of nameless, beautiful movie stars, my imagination had already woven a vibrant tapestry of the world they inhabited.

In my mind, they lived in a world of fantasy and glamour, where dancers glided effortlessly, and melodies brought enchantment, laughter, and boundless joy.

The room was simple, consisting of twelve rows of nine chairs—but to me, it was enormous. When the lights dimmed, a musical overture began, and images were projected onto the screen. It was a grand adventure to witness American movie stars on the big screen for the very first time. Just thinking about it filled me with a bubbly excitement.

I could not read the names on the title cards, but I would later learn that they were Fred Astaire and Ginger Rogers. The dialogue was translated by a man hidden behind a side curtain. The projector made a loud buzzing and clicking noise as the reels spun. Yet, despite its imperfections, simply having the opportunity to sit and watch those dancing movie stars inspired me.

My heart raced up toward my throat at the sight of their weightless feet carried by smooth, almost magical rhythms. Captivated, I found myself falling in love with dancing as the movie progressed.

From that day forward, my mind became transfixed on becoming part of the glamorous American world of entertainment. However, with each subsequent visit to the movie theater, I would watch the final image fade to black and let out a melancholy breath when I realized it was time to go back to real life, to days with no reason to sing or dance.

***

OKYON HAD GROWN into a pretty young lady, yet she openly resented me, making it crystal clear that I stood in the way of her social life.

By 1949, both my sisters were in their late teens and worked as taxi dancers at Hwangkwa Dance Hall, located in the middle of the city. Men would buy tickets to dance with them, and my sisters would earn a small commission for every dance ticket they collected.

One day, Okyon dropped me off at Aunty Jeonghi's front door. Since Aunty had married a North Korean and settled with him in Busan, Okyon figured she was in a better position to take care of me. Unfortunately, it did not take long before Aunty found an excuse to throw me out like yesterday's trash.

After a few short days, I stumbled one morning while in the kitchen and dropped a dish. Aunty heard the shatter, and when she entered the kitchen, she let out a disgusted squealing noise when she saw me standing over shards of her broken china.

"You broke my favorite china dish, you dim-witted girl!" she wailed in anger. She grabbed a nearby pencil, hastily moistened the tip with her tongue, and began scribbling a note.

She was so upset that she broke the pencil tip, yet she managed to continue with a blunted stump. The veins in her forehead bulged from the fumes of her temper. Aunty Jeonghi swiftly picked up the note and read it out loud to me. "Sister Deoki, you are better off than me, so you should be taking care of Okhui."

Hearing those words, my heart sank, and tears welled up in my eyes as I protested, "I don't want to go to Aunty Deoki!" But despite my plea, Aunty Jeonghi ignored me.

"I don't quite recall her address," Aunty Jeonghi spoke while I cried. "There is an old wooden bridge everyone around here knows about. Once you cross that bridge, there's only one path that leads up the hill. You won't miss it. Now, no more fussing! Get going!"

Aunty hurried me into my bedroom, instructing me to pack my cherished white *bottari*. As I exited the house for this unexpected journey, Aunty swiftly closed the front door behind me, not even uttering a goodbye. Her sudden actions made me feel dejected and alone, as though I were as fragile and fractured as Aunty's shattered china.

I vaguely knew where Aunty Deoki lived, so I should have been able to find her house by myself. My tummy rumbled since I hadn't eaten much at Aunty Jeonghi's. I sprinted until I reached a long, old bridge that sagged in the middle because of termites.

This bridge looked familiar; I recalled crossing it during my mother's last visit to Aunty Deoki's teahouse. With my hopes high, I let out a deep sigh of relief and marched over the wooden slats.

Looking up, I saw that the sun was positioned directly overhead, and I realized it was noon. Steadily continuing up the hill, I studied my surroundings, looking in vain for another recognizable landmark. My *bottari* was now dirtied and hung heavy.

Exhausted, I tried my best not to cry. Everything looked so distant. Along the way, I passed a farm with a small fishpond surrounded by moss-like shrubbery.

I approached the pond and noticed how dewdrops had collected on the leaves. As they dripped into the pond, they created little ripples; I stopped to watch the circles grow larger and larger. Then, I plucked out a pair of leaves and tossed them upon my reflection.

When the water calmed, my reflection emerged. My eyes were tired and swollen, reflecting the pain in my heart. I was left alone, with a whole day's worth of sweat and dirt sticking to my exhausted body. My clothes were dirty, and my uncombed hair was tousled in a mound bigger than my head. I hadn't bathed in days, and I smelled like dirt—but that wasn't the reason I felt such sadness.

"I wish," I whispered to my reflection, "that somebody wanted me." I let out a tired breath and threw in a twig, watching gloomily as it disrupted my reflection.

PRETTY GISAENG
TRAINED IN MUSIC

IN THE FAR distance, I saw a wooden mansion with a familiar roof. Twelve uneven stone steps led up to Aunty Deoki's *yojeong,* her teahouse. Searching for the note Aunty Jeonghi had pinned to my clothing, I realized I had lost it somewhere along the way. Luckily, I had memorized it.

After escaping from the life of a "comfort woman" during the war, Aunty Deoki applied for work in a *gisaeng* teahouse as a madam, or more accurately, an owner and manager. *Gisaeng* was officially sanctioned in Korea in the tenth century as a way of entertaining men through music, dance, conversation, and poetry. Though the Gabo Reform of 1895 had upended their high-class status, the *gisaeng* business still existed.

Before I stepped on the first stone, I used my hands to comb my matted hair and straighten my clothes as best I could. Bravely, I trudged up to the entrance, ready to knock on the door, when

Aunty Deoki opened it. Jolted, I looked up at her and held my breath, not knowing if I'd be staying or leaving.

I felt as though I might throw up.

Her face was stoic and a little older than I remembered, but she still held the regal beauty that I had often admired. The small spattering of freckles on her face was noticeable against her fair, milky skin. She glared at me in deep contemplation, knitting together her thick, animated eyebrows—the same kind Mother and many other women in our family had. It seemed to be our defining trait.

I greeted her softly, swallowing the shame of my appearance with humility. We stood there staring at each other for what felt like hours. Then, she dropped her gaze and ushered me inside without saying a word. I set down my stained *bottari* in her living room.

"Look at you!" Aunty Deoki said, clucking her tongue. "You look like a twig. You need to eat more. There's some food in the kitchen. Ask the kitchen maid."

She took me to the end of the hallway. Aunty had added more rooms since the last time I had visited with Mother, and when we approached the first room, she blocked my path. "This is the makeup room for my *gisaeng*," she said. "So please stay out. And the second room, too; I just had it extended so my girls can rest."

She said nothing about the third room, so I peeked inside. Half a dozen colorful *hanbok* were hanging on the wall above a large table covered with jewelry and hairpieces. I took a deep whiff, breathing in the powdery air, and thought about all the pretty *gisaeng* that had passed through.

It made me feel excited.

Aunty led me to my bedroom, where I put down my *bottari*. She left me alone to explore the house further. Making my way to the backyard, I walked down a stone pathway that diverged into a well-groomed Japanese garden, which looked a lot nicer since my last visit. The willow tree was ready to sprout, and its branches swayed low, dropping its tiny green leaves into a little pond. I sat there, astounded by the serenity of the garden.

***

UPON WAKING THE next day, I began exploring the hallways, which led me to a spacious central room. Entering through a Japanese-style *shoji* door, I noticed a long table covered with a white cloth and three bottles of rice wine, the same *cheongju* my father often drank.

On a *tatami* mat along the wall, there was a *janggu* drum and *gayageum*, a stringed instrument similar to a Western harp. This was the room where tea was served. I stayed in the room for an hour before the first *gisaeng* arrived, carrying her *bottari*.

"Hello," I began immediately. "My name is Okhui. Deoki is my aunty." The young woman's eyes widened, surprised to see me.

"Okhui," she repeated. "What a cute name. My name's Nari. So, how old are you?"

I showed her with my fingers.

"Seven!" she exclaimed, then pinched my face. "What an adorable face you have."

I giggled, happy to have made a friend.

That evening, Aunty Deoki stationed two *gisaeng* at the front entrance to greet a sharply dressed man stepping out of a fancy car. The ladies told me to sit by the *shoji* door and keep out of sight, but that didn't stop me from peeking through a slit in the door.

A trio of beautiful *gisaeng* glided from table to table, conversing with customers, dancing, and serving food. Two girls, Moran and Unhae, sat abreast in front of eight men at a rectangular table covered with food. With a polite bow, Moran started a beat with her *jangguu* drum just as one of the men joyfully shouted, "*Ulshigu, Jotta!*"

In the midst of all this, none could match the enchanting allure of Nari. As she graced the room with a traditional bow, her dance movements held a delicate elegance akin to a butterfly in flight, gently fluttering upon a tree branch. Never before had I witnessed such grace, a beauty that emanated with a softness, evoking a bittersweet sensation deep within. Though I couldn't comprehend every word of the melodic song, I could sense its essence—a tale of a girl's love entangled with the pain of betrayal.

After her performance, the girls daintily settled between the men, their delicate hands pouring rice wine into their cups and delicately feeding them morsels with practiced precision, utilizing a pair of chopsticks.

I often observed their refined mannerisms with keen interest, absorbing their every movement and gesture. Then, in a mischievous escapade, I would sneak away into the tranquil Japanese garden, attempting to mimic their dance moves, twirling and swaying as if I were a part of their graceful troupe.

On some nights, when the crowds were slow, Nari would take me into the makeup room and teach me how to dance. "*Hana, dul, set, net,*" she counted, showing me how to move my arms like Aunty's willow tree.

Demonstrating the dance, she raised her shoulders slightly up, then down, and beckoned me to follow her movements. She then moved to her *janggu* drums and played a beat. I danced along. With every step, I felt like a feather carried by the wind. My heart filled with joy.

That's when I noticed Aunty watching me. It was one of the few times I managed to make her smile, but it did not stop her from criticizing me.

"Beauty is a commodity," she said. "And to have that, you need to put more meat on those bones." Aunty Deoki often compared me to Nari, who had a much rounder face and body. Nonetheless, I continued to learn how to dance, hoping someday I could dance just like her.

***

WITH THE PASSAGE of time, I began to shed the appearance of a little Korean doll as the natural course of growing up took its toll. My two front baby teeth bid farewell, leaving behind a noticeable gap in my mouth. Slowly but surely, the attention I once received from everyone, including Aunty Deoki, started to wane. To make matters even worse, Aunty Deoki adopted a baby girl, a child connected to one of her *gisaeng* acquaintances.

On one particular day, I unintentionally caught a snippet of Aunty Deoki's conversation with Nari, where she uttered words that stung deeply. Aunty Deoki proclaimed that I lacked the beauty required to be groomed as a *gisaeng*.

The weight of her words crushed my spirit, leaving me feeling utterly rejected and unwanted. Shortly thereafter, she dispatched a letter to Okyon, urging her to arrange for my pickup within the upcoming week. When my sister arrived, she whisked me away from Aunty's abode, guiding me outside into the drizzling rain.

The steady sound of raindrops brought me some comfort as we embraced the journey that awaited. I was hopeful for a future where my worth would be recognized and cherished. Once again, the same words slipped from my lips, "I wish somebody wanted me."

***

OKYON TOOK ME to live with my father in Dongsallee Amidong Valley. Living with such a large family, food was always scarce. With Mother gone and Father not making enough money to feed us, we often went hungry for up to three days; the pain of hunger became a constant companion.

On one such third day, sister Okyon made *chook*, a Korean version of rice soup. She took a handful of rice and added a gallon of salt water. Unfortunately, our stomachs had been empty for so long that we ended up vomiting it all up later that afternoon. Our digestive systems simply couldn't digest any food. For years afterward, the mere sight of *chook* made my stomach turn.

Fortunately, Mother dropped off some money the following week so we could buy food and clothes. My brothers all got decent haircuts, and she left a full bag of rice on the kitchen counter before she went on her way.

THE ROAD TO THE KOREAN WAR

FOLLOWING THAT EVENTFUL summer, a significant change occurred in our lives. Mother returned from Aunty Okhae's residence in Daegu, where Okhae had been operating a restaurant out of her home and illegally selling homemade liquor. Along with her return, Mother brought news of our family's relocation.

So, we bid farewell to our old home in Dongsallee Amidong and embarked on a new chapter in Yongdusan, Nampo-dong—a charming house nestled into the side of a hill. While moving often brought upheaval, I didn't mind this transition because it meant we would remain together as a family.

As we traveled to our new abode, Mother arranged little brother Chang atop the rented *kuruma*—a broad and straightforward wooden wagon—carefully situating him between two bundles of *bottari*. I observed Father as he loaded more *bottari* onto the *kuruma*, determined to pull the wagon himself. But it soon became clear that steering the wagon with such a heavy load would be incredibly difficult.

Brother Yeong was caught between his love for his artwork and the job we needed him to do. He reluctantly left his drawings and joined the rescue. It was funny watching him try not to draw while dealing with such a difficult task.

Brother Gyeong, true to his impatient nature, couldn't resist taking matters into his own hands. He leaped up and blocked Yeong's path, dramatically placing his hand on Yeong's chest and declaring to Father that Yeong was too slow. The irony wasn't lost on anyone—the one who had initially paused his busy artwork was now being accused of sluggishness.

Meanwhile, our oldest brother Jeong held onto his own belongings while Mother nagged him quietly for not helping. He insisted he didn't want to get his clothes dirty. Apparently, he cared more about his appearance.

As things got more chaotic, Yeong shoved and shook the stuck wheel. The wagon tilted dangerously until a disaster happened: the pile of our belongings, with Brother Chang sitting on top of it, wobbled and fell forward.

Luckily, Mother reacted quickly. She moved swiftly to catch little Chang before he got hurt from falling. Amazingly, she defied gravity by balancing Chang's fallen *bottari* on her head without any trouble, keeping everything perfectly steady.

Mother's swift thinking saved the day. As Father and Brother Gyeong worked to put the *kuruma* upright, we patiently sat on the ground, recovering from the mishap. Taking a moment to relax, I reached into my pocket and pulled out a mochi rice cake that Mother had given me earlier. Just as I was about to devour it, Brother Yong whispered slyly in my ear, "I can make you a star out of that mochi rice cake."

Intrigued, I challenged him to show me how. He took the mochi from my hand and skillfully nibbled away at the edges, molding it into the shape of a star. However, his enthusiasm got the better of him, and he ended up biting off too much, leaving only a tiny piece behind. With a grin, I relinquished the tiny star-shaped mochi to baby brother Chang, who eagerly accepted the unexpected treat.

Once the *kuruma* was ready, our brothers continued pushing the cart, singing Japanese songs in harmony. These were the only songs we'd learned as children, but our parents didn't mind. We were all happy that the *kuruma* was moving again. Singing and laughing together made our journey that much better.

***

THE PERIOD AFTER World War II, just before the start of the Korean War, was a decade-long victory celebration for the Americans. Foreign and local businesses associated with Korean nightlife were booming. While big bands gave way to jazz and rock-and-roll in America, the GIs stationed abroad continued to dance boogie-woogie and swing with Korean girls. Americans routinely poured money into Korea's open hands while danger lurked behind the scenes as Communists grievously stalked the streets at night.

That word—communist—sounded unsettling whenever anyone spoke about them, but personally, I did not know what it meant. I first saw the term on posters of Korean caricatures holding swords. They were plastered on every wall, layered on top of one another, and on thousands of leaflets being dropped from planes flying overhead. Their message contained the same ominous mantra: "Soon, the whole world will turn to Communism."

Being a child, I did not understand why people were fighting over that word. It was just a word. But it was clear to me it meant something bad—something that was coming toward us. Late at night, I trembled as I pulled my blankets over my head and worried about how my siblings and I would grow up in this changed environment.

***

BLACK SUNDAY OCCURRED on June 25, 1950. North Korean leader Kim Il Sung invaded South Korea to unify the peninsula under Communist rule. We called it "Black Sunday" because black symbolizes death.

Within three days, the army of the North occupied the capital city of Seoul, and South Korea's elderly president, Syngman Rhee, declared Busan a temporary capital. "There is no need to worry," he announced to citizens in his raspy, senile voice. "We are safe."

I was about to turn eight and had just started attending Dong Kwang Elementary School when the war shut it down. South Korean foot soldiers swarmed the streets, and talk of war became more prevalent. I really enjoyed going to school, but my time there was brief.

Brother Jeong was only seventeen when he was drafted into the army. Basic training was held in Nonsan in Chollado Province, a little north of our coastal city. Mother was angry when he got the draft notice, but according to the government, if a young man was old enough to hold a gun, he could be drafted as a *hukdobyong*, or military student.

Over the next ten years, all four of my older brothers would end up serving in the military, even after the war was over.

FIRE IN BUSAN

THE BUSAN PIER Fire occurred on September 29, 1950. Just past midnight, a huge explosion shook my family's house. Through the fog of sleepiness and confusion, I heard Mother screaming. My siblings jumped up in alarm while Mother ran toward the window with my baby brother Chang in her arms.

My siblings and I ran outside toward the edge of the hill, overlooking a panoramic view of flames below. The massive blaze had engulfed both piers, which had been vital to the central supply headquarters of our country. These docks were the only place military supplies could be unloaded for both American and South Korean armies.

"Damn Communists," Father muttered, his face lit bright orange by the fire. I teetered over the edge of the hill and watched the flames rise to the sky, releasing plumes of dense black smoke. Gas explosions reverberated through the air. Even from a distance, I could feel the heat of the blast on my face. A wet warmth interrupted the dry heat as a trickle of urine dribbled down my legs, and my teeth chattered uncontrollably.

The fire burned during the night and continued to burn over the next few weeks. When it was over, nearly one-third of Busan had burned to the ground. Our home was safe except for the charred holes in our ceiling, which had let in some of the smoke from the burning city. Fortunately, the Americans helped us rebuild, and increased American presence brought more of their culture into our own.

By October 1950, China had sent millions of soldiers to join the conflict in support of North Korea. This intervention by China significantly impacted the course of the war. United States General Douglas MacArthur launched a counterattack, deploying troops at Inchon and breaking through the North Korean lines, forcing them to retreat. Both halves of the country were separated by an intersection of the peninsula at the infamous circle of latitude: the Thirty-Eighth Parallel.

Standing in the face of the oncoming enemy, the formidable North Korean army advanced toward us, supported by China. The combined forces of the American and South Korean armies fought valiantly but, in the end, met defeat.

Over two thousand soldiers perished in combat near Nakdong River in Gimhae, near Busan. That would be the first wake-up call for the South. They worried the North Koreans would take Busan the way they had taken everything else.

The conflict ended on July 27, 1953, with the Korean Armistice, which created the Korean Demilitarized Zone, separating the North and the South. Since no actual peace treaty was ever signed, both sides continue to fight the war.

The Korean War was indeed one of the most destructive wars of modern times, resulting in a significant loss of life. It is estimated that approximately three million people, including military personnel and civilians, perished during the conflict.

THE HOMELESS GIRL
UNDER THE BRIDGE

DURING THE WAR, a temporary school was set up along the hillside of Nambumin-dong. The makeshift Nambumin Elementary School was cleverly concealed by the hill, posing a challenge for any student trying to find their way to it. My mother tirelessly roamed the village, seeking directions to the school's administration office. This was no small feat since the school itself was not a traditional building but a sizable white tent with sheets serving as walls. With scarce resources, we lacked school supplies and furniture, leaving us to sit on the bare dirt floor.

Our teacher, Miss Micha, stood before us on the first day, a youthful and attractive woman with a surprisingly high-pitched, child-like voice. She emphasized the importance of sharing the limited number of books available. As one of eight siblings accustomed to sharing, I didn't mind.

Our third-grade class was composed of four boys and six girls, but among them, one country girl stood out. She wore a faded green *chŏgori* blouse paired with a small *chima* skirt that seemed a tad too tight for her. She appeared to be around ten years old, slightly older than me. Her chestnut-colored hair cascaded unevenly down her back, presenting a scraggly appearance that was common among girls from rural areas. But it was her pretty brown eyes that caught my attention, perfectly matching her hair, and a notable mole graced her upper lip.

As Miss Micha instructed us to introduce ourselves, we took turns sharing our names and places of residence. When it was the country girl's turn, she introduced herself as Mina, yet she remained tight-lipped about revealing where she lived.

Puzzled, I assumed that she was probably shy, but when we stood up and sang the Korean national anthem, I could hear her sweet, melodious voice above the rest. A voice that prompted me to trust her.

Over the next two weeks, we became close friends, and she finally asked if I wanted to visit her house after class. "My house is not too far from school; there's a shortcut through the open market."

Describing the directions to her home, Mina mentioned a long bridge near the river. At noon, the marketplace streets were lively and filled with a dissonance of voices. Rambunctious shoeshine boys ran past us, shouting, "Shoeshine! Shoeshine!"

I felt apprehensive about cutting through the crowded marketplace, but Mina held onto my hand and guided me through. Halfway through the market, we saw a Korean military truck pass by, filled with soldiers heading north. The soldiers sang a familiar Southern patriotic song with the lyrics, "I shall die for my country."

As the soldier's voices faded into the distance, Mina and I continued down the red dirt road, where the air hung over us like a thick, heavy blanket. She stopped at the edge of a riverbank and pointed to a stone bridge at the edge of a steep, rocky cliff. As I focused, I could see a few shacks in the distance.

Mina pointed to the shelters under the bridge. "You see the second shelter, the brown one? That's my home."

Just then, I saw an old, gray-haired man standing atop the bridge. Strangely, he tossed down what appeared to be some sort of white animal, which I first assumed was a cat. I tugged at Mina's arm, urging her to follow me to investigate. We hurried to take a closer look. To our horror, the white furry creature was a little dead rabbit.

Mina probed its plump, limp body with a stick. "We should give it a proper burial so that its spirit can go to Heaven," she said, then paused. "Do you know what *Heaven* is?"

"It's where we go when we die," I replied. "My brother Yong told me that's where my younger brother Ikchan lives."

Mina lowered her head and smiled, then told me her definition was the same. I steadily dug a hole by the river while she made a cross using two strips of wood and planted the cross in the dirt. Mina prayed over the rabbit and ended with the sign of the cross.

"My father and brother live underneath this bridge," she said. She did not say anything about her mother. Saddened, I imagined it must have been something tragic, so I didn't ask.

We walked toward a row of low-lying hovels under the bridge, their walls made of rice bags held in place by rotting pieces of timber. In front of a dull brown shack, a wrinkly-faced man smoked a long bamboo pipe. I could tell that he was blind by the way he fumbled around to stir a pot of soup hanging over a stone firepit.

"*Appa!*" Mina called to her father. She approached him and tugged on the man's pant leg. "This is my new friend, Okhui."

The man smiled in acknowledgment. Then, as if on cue, a younger man—whom Mina told me was her older brother, Donggwon—appeared at the top of the bridge, carrying a wooden pole on his shoulders. Two buckets of water hung from ropes at either end.

Even though we could hear a few bombs exploding in the distance, Mina's home appeared safe as she led me inside. Mina shifted her gaze toward me, brushing tears aside. "My mama died last year. She used to take me to the Catholic Church where she worked. She got sick after her boss's family was killed by the North Koreans. They—they killed them just because they were C-C-Catholic. Then, my father nearly went blind from an explosion at work."

From the corner of the room, Mina took out a small, termite-eaten black box. Inside was a necklace made of wooden beads with a rusted chain she called a *rosary*, a word I had not heard before. "This belonged to a Catholic girl who was executed by the North Koreans," she told me before whispering, "In the name of the Father, the Son, and the Holy Ghost." She raised the rosary to her lips and kissed its cross pendant.

Mina turned to me and smiled, "When I grow up, I want to become a nurse. I want to help sick people. Even though we're poor, I plan to go to nursing school. I have faith that I will."

"Faith?" I asked. "What's *faith*?"

Mina nodded slowly as though she had answered this question many times. "Faith means believing that something good will happen even if it doesn't look like it will. My mother told me that God wants us to have faith so that He can bless us."

Although I did not quite understand the concept, it obviously meant something special to her.

As we stepped outside, Mina gazed up at the gray sky. "I love a gentle rain," she remarked, "we can gather it in buckets and enjoy a bath. Just have to be cautious, though. If it turns into a downpour, we might end up getting swept away."

***

SINCE IT WAS getting late in the afternoon, I knew it was time for me to leave. Mina kindly gave me an old, worn-out Korean Bible, which I carefully wrapped in my *bottari*. Then, she put the rosary in my hand and whispered one word, "Faith."

When she saw me struggling to put on my worn-out shoes, she took off her own shoes and gave them to me. They were slightly bigger, but I found them easy to walk in. I roved through the pathways back to the village, but as soon as my home was in sight, I broke into a sprint like a wild stallion toward the front door, which had been left unlocked as usual.

My return was met by my mother dashing out of her room. Upon seeing me, her face changed to a blind rage. She grabbed me by the ears like a rag doll and greeted me with a resounding slap on the forehead.

"Where have you been? We searched high and low for you!" my mother shrieked.

With a crooked face and tears flowing down my cheeks, I managed to answer her. "I was just visiting my friend who lives under the bridge." Oddly enough, it felt good to see my mom both worried and annoyed.

Quivering and sobbing, I endured my mother's angry outburst. She bellowed, "You were wasting your time with beggars?" Her gaze shifted to my slightly stained *bottari*, evidence of the dirt floor at Mina's place. Before I could explain, my mother snatched it from my hands and sprinted up the hill behind our home.

In a panic, I chased after her.

"It's filthy!" Mother yelled as she flung the *bottari* over the cliff. I let out a horrified scream as I realized Mina's rosary and Bible were in there, gone forever. Too stunned to cry or protest, I realized I could never retrieve what was lost. Yet, amidst the devastation I felt, I also learned a valuable lesson. Despite Mina and her family's humble circumstances, their compassion made them strong.

Unfortunately, the very next day, an unexpected thunderstorm ravaged our village, forcing the makeshift schools to close. When they finally reopened, Mina was nowhere to be found on our tented campus. I wondered about the fate of her home after the storm, but nobody had any answers when I asked.

Sadly, Mina never returned to school, leaving me with a heavy heart and a mystery surrounding her whereabouts.

THE WAR AT HOME

BY NOW, THE war had dragged on for two years, and my older sisters were in their early twenties. Okyon, the sweet, hard-working daughter, chose to follow her American GI boyfriend north toward the border of the Demilitarized Zone. She frequently sent us money as a generous attempt to support our family from afar.

My other sister, Oksoon, remained at home—without a job and no desire to have any real connection with our family. She did, however, spend an awful lot of time with our next-door neighbors, Song Daelyup and his wife, Kay. Both were involved in show business, working at the U.S. military nightclub. Thus, the wife had taken an American name.

Daelyup was a singer, and Kay was a dancer. They appeared to be a nice, average couple with a daughter about my age whom I had noticed accompanying them to work. They often dressed her in a pretty Western dress, making her look like the Shirley Temple I'd seen in American magazines.

But the truth behind her parents' lifestyle was not so innocent.

After overhearing a conversation between Mother and Oksoon, I was horrified to discover that this show business couple had been supplying my sister with heroin. Oksoon denied ever taking the drug and argued that Kay was only teaching her to dance.

Oksoon was constantly rude and petulant around me, so I avoided her at every chance. Though Mother tried her best to keep a peaceful household, everything came crashing down when, one evening, I walked into the middle of a violent argument in the living room.

Grabbing Mother by the shoulders, Oksoon pushed her against the wall. "Where's my stuff?" she screamed.

"I threw it in the trash!" Mother snapped back. "I know what you're doing. Your grandparents had the same problem! Now you're a junkie, too! It's our family's curse!"

Oksoon squeezed Mother's neck harder, causing her to cough profusely. When she let go, she pushed Mother toward the ground and stood over her with balled-up fists and hate-filled eyes. Then, she turned and furiously stomped out of the house.

Mother didn't get up, not even after Oksoon left. She wept, her chest heaving and her arms spread out on the floor. From then on, Mother's heart weighed heavily with grief each time Oksoon left our house.

Years later, Mother told me that Oksoon had nearly died on the same day they'd had that fight, having fallen off an American Jeep earlier in the morning. That explained why she wore a long-sleeved blouse—to cover the scars on her left arm, mutilated by the tire when it got caught under the Jeep. Shortly after she healed, she moved in with her American boyfriend near the Demilitarized Zone.

Eventually, my parents purchased a house across from Aunty Deoki's new house to get a fresh start. Although my sisters Oksoon and Okyon hardly ever came home, and Brother Jeong was still on active duty, I found our new house delightful.

Unfortunately, that feeling did not last.

Late one night, I was promptly jolted awake by the sound of Father coughing in his bedroom. His cough worsened as it continued, getting louder and harder. Then, I heard Mother's voice, followed by Father's; both sounded very serious. I wrapped myself in my blanket, pushed my ear up against the wall, and listened closely.

"Yes, I agree you should have a new woman in your life," Mother told him. "I'll never be the right wife for you . . . What we need is complete separation."

The frankness of her words was terrifying. I didn't understand it at first, but I suddenly recalled a specific memory from a week before, something I hadn't paid much attention to at the time. I had seen Mother coming out of a *makgeolli* restaurant with another man. Now that I thought about it, she had been smiling differently than how she normally smiled at Father.

Mother continued, "You're not getting younger, Myeongsu. You need someone to look after you. You do not deserve this. Think of our children!"

My head buzzed with shock; her words stabbed deep into my chest. I could only imagine Father's pain. His response sounded unsteady and hesitant, "I don't see any reason for us to separate. How would that solve anything? How will that help our children?"

That's when his words triggered her. In the typical fashion of irritated Korean women, Mother's voice rose an octave higher. "Our children are old enough to take care of themselves, but I am taking baby Chang with me," she said firmly. "I've waited all these years. It's time for things to change!"

As their voices settled into a dull silence, I thought about all they had said, and I wondered if they were even looking at one another. I started wondering if they had even loved one another in the first place.

After a long pause, Mother spoke again in a lowered whisper, "After our separation, you and your girlfriend should take Yong and Okhui with you."

I gasped. My eyes burst wide open, and I wanted to scream, *Not me! I don't want to go. I won't!* But no words escaped my mouth, and I definitely didn't want them to hear me. My face became red hot; I felt the blood rushing to my head. Our family had only recently been reunited. We had all survived the war together, and now Mother was throwing it all away.

How could this be? I wanted to scream, but Father spoke up.

"Why Yong?" Father asked, sounding as though he had just lost a war and was now being offered reparations.

"Yong is the most handsome," Mother said. "Your second wife will be delighted to have him as part of your new family."

"Maybe," Father began. "But I won't be able to take care of a little girl."

Mother let out a breath. "Fine."

At that point, I stopped listening and focused on the thoughts running rampant through my mind. I wanted to cast away this entire conversation as a product of my imagination—in no way did this feel real to me. The nonchalant manner in which my parents were throwing away our future was enough to make me cry. Or vomit.

But I did neither.

There was another long pause, followed by the sound of footsteps walking out the door.

A few days later, Mother announced that she and Father would be splitting us into two families. Father settled in with his new girlfriend, and Yong stayed with him. Shortly afterward, Mother transferred her share of the house deed to Father, leaving her side of the family without a home.

Luckily, Okyon had rented a room in a mid-sized house after breaking up with her GI boyfriend. She had also found a hostess job at the Baekjo Nightclub, so we moved in with her.

Whenever I spent time with the children in this new neighborhood, I noticed many families where both parents stayed together. In my case, the presence of either my mother or my father felt fleeting. Our family structure had completely changed, and I felt as though I were standing on shaky ground, about to fall.

THE DAY MY SISTER TRADED MY FUTURE FOR HEROIN

OKYON'S COMPACT ROOM became a central gathering place for the rest of the family. Brother Yeong eventually left for Seoul to pursue a career as a theater billboard artist, while my other siblings moved in and out of our home so rapidly that I rarely saw them. The only one who stayed to care for me was Sister Okyon—but now, there was an edge to her, a fierceness I would see more frequently. I admired her for that.

On the other hand, Sister Oksoon's visits became increasingly rare, but when she did show up, it made everyone uneasy. Early one morning, I bumped into her while she stood quietly in the middle of the room. When she turned to glare at me, I gasped.

Her skin was rough and yellow. She was dressed in torn, shabby clothes and still carried her old faded brown handbag. Her eyes appeared empty, soulless.

She turned away without saying a word. I tried to brush off the disconcerting feeling, but every time I passed her by, I could still feel her eyes following me.

Later that day, I heard Okyon ranting about some clothes that turned up missing. When I asked her what was wrong, she told me Oksoon had taken them to pay for drugs. Since Okyon was paying for our food and my schooling, she couldn't afford new clothes for herself.

Furthermore, Okyon couldn't find a decent job, and Mother had left us months ago. Our resources were dwindling. I once had to go three days without food living with Father; I'd hoped I'd never have to go through that again. Now, I realized my hope was in vain.

***

THROUGHOUT MY CHILDHOOD, I attended three different elementary schools. By 1954, I had completed enough schooling to graduate from Toseong Elementary and moved on to middle school in Namyeojung, across Yeongdo Bridge.

On that sunny first day of spring semester, the refreshing scent of chilly spring filled the air. As I made my way toward the main building, my attention was drawn to a plump young girl sitting on the front step, completely absorbed in her studies with a notebook on her lap. Intrigued, I approached her.

With a friendly smile, she welcomed me to sit down beside her and introduced herself as Park Yeongja. Immediately, her warm and inviting nature made me feel at ease. We started sharing stories about our friends and our studies, but our lively chatter was interrupted by the presence of another student passing by.

Though she couldn't have been much older than either of us, she was thinner and strikingly beautiful, making her appear more mature. Yeongja smiled when she saw her, but the girl never acknowledged us. Yeongja leaned over and whispered to me, "That's Yee Adae. I heard her cousin is Yee Gyeonghui, the movie star." When I turned to look, Yeongja nudged her elbow into my rib.

I whispered, "She's very pretty." I noticed how her upturned face thoughtfully studied her surroundings the same way my childhood friend Mina had. There was a depth in their eyes, insightful and optimistic. I'd find out later she was an aspiring artist and writer.

A few months later, I competed in a school-wide poetry contest and won first prize. On the same day my name was posted on the bulletin board, I bumped into Yeongja and Yee Adae in the cafeteria. They were the first to congratulate me.

After that day, Yee Adae started hanging out with us, and we all became good friends.

***

DURING MY SECOND year of middle school, I was sitting on the front steps of the building, finishing my literature essay, when I was unexpectedly called into the principal's office. The old crank didn't even greet me when I sat down, looking at me through his thick, black-framed glasses. He firmly asserted in his droning, monotone voice, "I'm sorry, but your tuition is overdue. I need to speak with your parents."

His words landed like a brick, and I sank into my chair. Mother was no longer around, and Father couldn't care less about me. Moreover, Okyon could barely feed the two of us, and there was no one I could ask for money. Did the principal not understand that?

The heat of bitter tears stung the corners of my eyes; a little ball of discouragement formed in the back of my throat.

"How am I going to finish school?" I whimpered. The principal simply repeated his statement. I growled with frustration, jumped out of the chair, and never bothered to say goodbye. Nor did I close the door behind me.

When I told Okyon, her face transformed from frustration to fury.

She shouted, "Mother's never around! And Father only cares about his new girlfriend!"

"But I'm his daughter!" I cried.

"You're right," Okyon agreed. "Jeong just completed his tour of duty and is helping Father. They are making good money now. Father needs to take some responsibility." She arched her eyebrow, her fierce resolve returning. "You know what? I'm going to go find him and make him pay your tuition. Today!"

With that said, she marched out the door.

***

WHEN OKYON RETURNED home, she took a cigarette from her purse and lit it up, her face contorted with rage. I didn't feel very hopeful.

"We live here in this dump, struggling for your tuition," she grumbled, "while your father sits all afternoon drinking *makgeolli* wine in a restaurant. When he saw me coming, he barked at me— told me he wanted to live his life like a normal person."

I let out a breath, expecting the worst.

"He said, 'Neither you nor Okhui are my responsibility. You need to take care of yourselves.' I would have kicked over his table if his friends weren't sitting there. Then, he cursed Mother for his hardship!"

As she continued, her voice rose two octaves, "I stormed off to his hardware store where stupid Jeong was standing, picking his teeth. That idiot tried to run away, but I grabbed the back of his shirt. He only yelled at me, saying he won't invite me to his wedding because when people see my cheap painted face, it will make him look bad."

Without waiting for my response, Okyon ran to her bedroom. I watched her through the doorway as she wiped a tear from her eye before slamming the door shut. I realized that although she had grown to be strong and fierce, she was still the same sensitive Okyon I had grown up with.

Giving in to her last resort, Okyon borrowed money from a well-known loan shark in town, Lim Ajumma, to pay off my overdue tuition.

***

DURING THE SUMMER before my fifteenth birthday, Grandma Seokbuni died. A black hearse with a gold stripe across its middle arrived to take Grandma away. Okyon was still upset at Father for not helping with my tuition, so she refused to attend the funeral. She sent me to my father's house by myself.

Keeping with the traditional Korean send-off, Father picked up Grandma's favorite porcelain bowl and threw it behind the black hearse while it slowly moved toward the cemetery, where Grandma would be cremated.

"Farewell, Mother!" Father shouted. "Take all our bad luck with you!"

That same evening, Father, Jeong, and Yong arrived home with a small wooden box wrapped in a white cotton cloth. Inside the box was an urn, which Father and his girlfriend set on a homemade shrine in the corner of the room beneath a framed photograph of Grandma to prepare for *jesa*, where we commemorated the dead using ceremonial incense. The smell of incense would linger several months after the daily burning ceased.

***

ONE DAY, OUR youngest brother, Chang, appeared at our door with no shoes and tattered clothing. He told me that Mother had left him with one of our relatives, but he ran away and ended up living on the streets. I welcomed him inside with tears in my eyes, thrilled he had finally returned home.

Shortly afterward, I offered to babysit my neighbor's infant to earn some money for Brother Chang. Though the job didn't last long, I saved up enough that Chang and I could see the Kim Kil Cha musical at the theater.

Returning home, we collected magazines and cut out the faces of famous Korean actors and dancers, as well as Hollywood movie stars. We then mounted them to our bedroom wall with sticky cooked rice. The two of us would dream about becoming like them someday. I would draw pictures of myself standing on the stage, performing for crowds of hundreds.

It was the first time I made my dreams clear to myself and my brother.

BUSAN WOMEN'S
HIGH SCHOOL

THE MUSICAL SHOWS in Nampodong were beautiful. Actors in elaborate makeup danced as though their bodies were made of water, and they sang with the voices of angels. These actors would steal my heart every time, and sometimes Brother Chang and I would hide under the chairs to sneak into the next show.

But all the fun times with my brother would come to an end when Mother visited with her boyfriend, Yim. A homely man in his early fifties, he had deep wrinkles that looked like dark, dirty crevices carved into his face. I had to hold my breath to avoid the smell of alcohol on his breath.

I wasn't the only one disgusted by this troll of a man, but Yim did attempt to make peace by giving us an allowance. After the musical shows, Brother Chang and I used the money to sign up for dance classes. We took jazz dance and ballet until the money ran out. Learning to dance invigorated me with a strong desire to become a dancer for years to come.

However, amidst this newfound passion, there was a growing tension within our family. Despite Yim's financial help, his presence was extremely disturbing. Sister Okyon constantly argued with Mother about this strange affair until finally, Okyon snapped.

"Why are you wasting your time with this drunk?" she shouted. "You take no responsibility for your own children. You should take care of at least one!"

And with that, my mother left with my baby brother. But what hurt me the most was that she didn't even attempt to help me with my schooling. My heart was heavy with sorrow, but I couldn't hate her. Even though she'd abandoned me once again, she was still my mother.

***

OKYON AND I relocated to a quaint cottage in Busan before my middle school graduation. She worked tirelessly to repay the loan shark while I focused on applying to Busan Women's High School. The anticipation grew as the selection process began in mid-March, and the names of the chosen students were posted in April.

Outside the auditorium, I scanned the faded yellow paper on the bulletin board, searching for my name. When I finally spotted it, my heart skipped a beat and filled with joy. Excitedly, I shared the news with my classmates, only to realize that my friends Park Yeongja and Yee Adae hadn't made the list.

On graduation day, as we crossed the Yeongdong drawbridge together, we shared one last laugh, aware that our paths would diverge from that point forward. It was a bittersweet moment, filled with nostalgia and the realization that our shared journey had come to an end.

***

"I GOT INTO Busan Women's High School!" I exclaimed to Okyon shortly after I returned home, showing her the paperwork. Okyon, however, appeared upset. I had hoped my acceptance would cheer her up, but her eyes were full of frustration and sadness.

I winced, giving her a confused stare.

"I knew you'd get in," she said. "I saved a lot of money for your tuition, but those two junkies stole it."

My mind went blank, and I wanted to scream. By *two junkies*, she meant Oksoon and our Uncle Ilnam, who had begun showing up at our home these past few weeks. Okyon revealed that Uncle was Oksoon's dealer.

Those two useless, decrepit zombies took my tuition money? My blood boiled with rage. Utterly devastated, I ran into my bedroom, where I cursed Oksoon and Uncle. Gradually, my anger reduced to a simmer, and I felt numb and cold. Once again, Okyon had to borrow money from Lim Ajumma to pay my tuition.

***

DURING MY SECOND year of high school, a group of doctors and nurses visited our classrooms. Sent by the Board of Health, they tested all of us for tuberculosis. Since we had all been given polio shots the previous year, I wasn't looking forward to receiving another shot. I lined up in the auditorium with the rest of my class, waiting for that dreaded needle to go into my arm.

Our class had been informed that if a bump appeared after getting the shot, it meant you tested positive for TB. Sure enough, in a few days, a little round ball of skin blew up on my arm like a balloon.

How could I have been so lucky? I thought sarcastically. The nurses told me to report this to my parents right away, but unfortunately, Mother wasn't home, and I had no idea when she would return. I told Okyon, but she ignored me without even trying to understand how serious it was. Despondent, I cried in the corner of my room. I had no idea whether I had infected Okyon or if this would cause problems for me in the future.

In addition to all my worries, it took four weeks for my arm to heal.

***

TOWARD THE END of my senior year, Mother returned to our house with Brother Chang—and Yim. Though I felt grateful that Mother was staying with us, it didn't last long. One rainy day, Okyon saw a bruise around Mother's eye, and she immediately threw Mother and Yim out the front door, along with their belongings.

Then she turned on my brother and me. "Why am I stuck here with you?" she voiced out loud. "My life is miserable! I can't even get married because of you guys!"

"Don't blame us," I retorted. "You only date married men!" But she wouldn't listen and continued venting variations of the same theme over and over again.

***

LATER THAT NIGHT, I cried in my sleep. "Where did Mother go?" I asked out loud. Just then, I remembered something she'd said to her boyfriend as they walked away from the house. She'd mentioned something about moving to Masan, a fishing village.

The next day, in the early morning, Chang and I packed a pair of knapsacks with some clothes, caught a bus from Busan, and went for a ride along a stretch of bumpy dirt roads toward the countryside. We had no clue how to find her, but I knew Mother and her boyfriend liked to hang around *makgeolli* houses.

Chang and I walked through the Masan fish market, which was busy with swarms of people coming in and out of the waterfront. We searched for Mother from one street corner to the next, hoping to find some clues. After fruitlessly searching for one day, we had no choice but to return home.

As the day started to fade, I knew we had to hurry to catch the last bus. Brother Chang and I walked along the pier, hand in hand, watching the sun set into the sea. In our imaginations, we pictured a gigantic stage with the horizon as the backdrop. We sang old folk songs as we waited for the bus to arrive, lost in the beauty of our make-believe world.

From that day on, I never returned to school. Not just because of my absent mother but because of our dwindling finances. I was only three months shy of graduating, and I didn't want to give my school any more excuses.

Although a high school education wasn't mandatory in Korea at this time, I would feel the scars resulting from my derailed education in years to come. The constant hurt and despair lingered for many years—a wound that would never heal. I swore that if I ever had children, I would never let them suffer the same way.

LOVE IN BUSAN'S
FINANCIAL DISTRICT

SINCE BECOMING THE first president of South Korea in 1948, Syngman Rhee led us through three years of war, but the conflict didn't end with the armistice of 1953. The rest of the world recognized him for bringing independence back to Korea, but the Koreans knew the truth. Though he publicly spoke of democracy, he was a tyrant who ruled with an iron fist. At the ripe old age of seventy-three, his policies grew more ruthless as his presidency stretched on, enabled by his staff of cronies, including his stepson, who kept him in the dark so they wouldn't lose power.

In 1960, student protesters rose all over the country, demanding a new government. Rhee's regime began to crumble. Brother Yong marched with the protesters. One afternoon, I saw him riding in the back of a truck with his fellow youths, shouting, "Down with Rhee!"

I had just turned eighteen. I noticed that as more protestors filled the streets, the more blood the government would spill. In the middle of the night, I would lie on the floor trembling with fear, jolted by the rumbling of explosions below.

In time, Rhee's aggressive efforts to stamp out the protests proved futile. After a military coup led by General Park Chung Hee in 1960, Rhee's republic was overthrown. He fled to Hawaii, and the country tried to become a democratic nation under General Park.

Our new leader considered himself a Puritan, and as part of his "purification" efforts, he shut down many nightclubs, including the one where Okyon had been working. As a result, Okyon could no longer afford as much food, and with Brother Chang living with us, our food supply quickly dwindled. In time, Mother decided to rejoin the family after breaking up with her boyfriend. But it wasn't until we sat down to dinner on her first night home that I noticed Mother now wore a small rusty cross around her neck.

As the evening unfolded, I saw her kneel on the floor, close her eyes, and murmur softly. Her words were heartfelt; she was talking to someone who must have meant a great deal to her. Perhaps she was talking to herself.

I walked away and didn't pay any further attention.

***

ONE EVENING, I found myself lost in contemplation, and my thoughts drifted toward the uncertainty of my future.

"Okhui," my sister's voice interrupted. Her face expressed a mix of weariness and concern. "It's time for you to find a job. You have to begin earning a living to support yourself."

I let out a breath. Fortunately for us, Aunty Deoki came through after learning of a small trading company operating in Busan's financial district—and they were currently hiring. In fact, she told me I wouldn't even need an interview. Her referral was enough to convince the president of the company to hire me since Aunty Deoki had run a successful—yet secret—business for years in Busan.

In early November, I was hired as a messenger girl in a fancy upscale office and quickly became accustomed to the acrid tang of freshly brewed coffee in the morning. As humble as my job was, I gladly went about my daily tasks of wiping off desks and preparing the day's paperwork with an overwhelming sense of pride.

I closed my eyes, taking a deep breath as I touched the freshly polished corner of one of the desks. I envisioned myself being promoted and sitting confidently in one of these chairs, and I felt like I truly belonged.

Every morning, I would greet my fellow workers with a smile, bowing respectfully whenever our company president, Mr. Cheon, would pass by. Routinely, as the president passed me, he would smooth down his thinning gray hair with his hand while his beady eyes ogled my body. By my late teens, I had already become aware that men were looking at me differently; I had to learn to ignore them.

One of my work assignments was to deposit money at the bank at least three times a week. One day, while on such an errand, I bumped into a well-groomed gentleman standing directly in front of the bank entrance. When he opened the door for me, I found that I could not take my eyes off him. He was a good-looking and outwardly dignified man with a wide chest and light-brown skin. His youthful face and jet-black hair made a lasting impression on me, as most bankers in this branch had gray hair and always looked exhausted.

"*Annyeonghaseyo*," he greeted me as we walked inside. "My name's Kim Gwangyeong. You may not know me, but I've seen you quite often at our bank." After a pause—perhaps waiting for me to respond—he added, "I'd like to get to know you. Would you like to go out with me?"

My face turned as red as a beet. This handsome man just asked me out!

I answered in a hesitant voice, the words stumbling awkwardly out of my mouth, "W-w-well, I'm not sure."

I turned away and made my deposit. My hands shook during the process. As I was about to leave, Kim blocked me, and I found myself frozen. I stood there as Kim closed the distance with an elegant flair. I couldn't help but smile.

"Oh, Miss!" he exclaimed a bit too loudly. The crowd turned their attention toward us. Kim paused, then said to me, "I—uh, was just coming back from lunch, but perhaps you'd like to join me for an early dinner."

"Well, I'm officially done for the day," I announced, though that was a blatant lie. I actually needed to head back to the office, file reports, and punch my timecard, but I didn't care. I didn't want to miss this opportunity.

As we strolled through the Jagalchi fish market, the scent of fresh fish filled the air, strong but oddly comforting. He held my hand tightly, and in that embrace, I felt a profound sense of safety and happiness.

We walked into a quaint Chinese restaurant near the wharf, where the staff warmly greeted us in Korean but with Chinese accents. A friendly, hefty waiter guided us upstairs to a small private room.

"I waited all day to ask you out properly," Kim said with a warm smile. "I'm sorry if I was too forward."

I graciously chuckled. "No, you weren't."

He appeared sincerely delighted to hear that. During our dinner conversation, he wanted to know more about me. I openly shared all the complex details of my schooling and my family history, and my stories lasted well into the evening.

He listened attentively, occasionally adding a note of empathy without derailing the subject. I relaxed; the Chinese plum wine must have added to the enjoyable atmosphere of the evening.

To my surprise, he admitted he was only nineteen years old. I was taken aback by how deeply entrenched he already was in the business world. It made me wonder if he possessed exceptional intelligence or if he simply had influential family connections.

When the restaurant closed, we stepped outside into the night air. An icy breeze wrapped around us, and the neon lights of the neighboring stores made the streets glow. Kim held me close and gently kissed my forehead. At that moment, I heard my heart thumping.

But Kim made no further advances. In fact, he acted like a perfect gentleman, wrapping his arm around me as we walked down the street. His warm, boyish smile indicated that he was considerate and caring. He even paid for my cab fare home.

After that evening, we went on many more dates, enjoying afternoons at the teahouse or evenings at the music hall and movies. The following weekend, we took a long, sweaty hike in the mountains, where Kim serenaded me with a Korean pop song, "Red Shoes Lady," by popular crooner Nam Il-hae.

He belted out the tune with his arms wide open as though he were singing at an opera house. Afterward, he told me he had practiced this song for a local contest held for bank employees and won first place.

"But I don't want to be a professional singer," he said. "In fact, I'd rather become an actor than work in a bank for the rest of my life."

With a lighthearted laugh, I brought Kim home to meet Mother; she squealed in delight. Any man who worked in an office, even foul-smelling after a long hike, was welcome in any parent's home.

***

ONE WINTERY DAY, I quit my job when Mr. Cheon gave me a Christmas gift of embroidered underwear. Disgusted by that man, I decided to go with my backup plan and apply for the job I actually wanted.

When I had been sent on bank errands, I often passed by the Mihwa Dance Studio. Because of the many pleasant memories of training with Nari at my aunty's teahouse, walking past this studio would reignite my passion for dancing every time.

Since I now had the time, I immediately stepped inside to ask for an application and got hired without hesitation. Mihwa, the owner, was delighted to have me working there and informed me about her upcoming showcase touring Europe by the end of the next year.

I definitely wanted to be included, but I wasn't prepared for the coming months.

***

WHEN MARCH ROLLED around, Kim and I visited Yangsan Tongdosa, a Buddhist temple nestled in the mountains. I was overjoyed to see the cherry blossoms blooming along the temple's stony path. The snow on the rooftops was partially melted, and there was a gentle breeze nipping at our cheeks. The cool, fresh scent of early spring made us giddy.

Approaching a nearby river, I picked up a shiny polished stone and, without aiming at anything, tossed it toward the flowing water. But instead of landing in the river, it launched directly into a stone lantern on top of a ten-foot pagoda by the side of the temple.

"Oh! How did that happen? That pagoda is about eighteen feet away from us!" I shouted.

Kim chuckled. As we moved closer to the pagoda, I noticed the engraving below the lantern inscribed, "If you wish to conceive a son, throw a stone. If it lands inside the lantern, your wish will come true."

We laughed out loud at the silly superstition and continued our stroll through the temple garden, enjoying its beauty and one another's company. We rented a cabin and spent the next few nights together. The sweet chirping of birds greeted us every morning, and we could hear the monks chanting—a low, steady rhythm kept by the beat of a small gong.

In the months that followed, I noticed that my breasts were swelling, dark rings were appearing under my eyes, and from time to time, I would experience nausea and vomit for no reason.

I recognized the signs from what my mother once told me—I was pregnant! Surprised by the sudden realization that we now had a family, Kim and I got engaged. Although this meant I'd have to quit my job as a dance instructor and drop out of their European tour, I believed our upcoming marriage to be the start of a brand-new life.

I couldn't have been more wrong.

Mother suggested that I get an abortion since we weren't married. On the other hand, Kim's family strongly opposed terminating the pregnancy, and because Kim was their only son, they were eager to have an addition to their family. Kim's mother, Bokdong, wasn't hesitant to communicate her intentions.

"Even though you are not married to my son," she told me, "For the sake of your unborn child, please move in with our family."

Conservative as she was, her insistence felt genuinely sincere. After several family dinners, I accepted her invitation and moved into their home in Jeoki, known around the countryside as Cow Stable Village. Their family home was a typical Korean house with thin wooden walls and a concrete floor in the main room. The kitchen had a dirt floor with a stove made of clay, and they used chopped firewood to cook their food and warm the floor in the wintertime.

Kim's father ran a tiny hardware store next door, and I occasionally offered to help clean the store. The old man continually refused my help, but I did it anyway. While at home, he kept to himself, though I would soon discover that he was much more hospitable than his wife.

MY MOTHER-IN-LAW

OVER THE NEXT few weeks, Kim's mother transformed from a friendly, kind woman to the wicked stepmother one finds in fairy tales.

According to Korean superstitions, it was the spirits' right to have the first taste of freshly prepared rice. Many Korean families shared this belief, but Bokdong took this tradition much too far. Whenever I cooked dinner, she would scold me if I failed to feed the spirits.

She would scoop up some rice from the *gamasot*—a black iron pot—and cast a few grains over her shoulder. "I feed you well today, my dear ancestors," she would say, then wave impatiently at me to repeat after her while she continued, "Please bring us a healthy baby boy and good fortune."

One evening, after I finished preparing a pot of rice, I helped myself to some of it. Suddenly, Bokdong appeared behind me and snapped, "How dare you feed yourself first?"

I snapped back, "I don't care about your imaginary ghosts! You're making me waste food for no reason. *I* am a real person. *I* need to eat!"

Her eyes bulged. "You will be haunted by our ancestors forever!" she shouted, her face inches from mine.

Angrily, I put the rice paddle back in the pot, stirred vigorously, scooped out more rice, and ate it right in front of her. In an instant, she raised her hand and slapped me hard across the face. The paddle clattered on the floor as a chunk of rice flew out of my mouth. I gasped, glaring into her eyes, but she didn't blink.

After a long pause, she shook her head and walked away.

***

ABOUT A MONTH into our cohabitation, Kim's behavior started to change. One night, we decided to see *Breakfast at Tiffany's* at the Munhwa Theater, starring my favorite actress, Audrey Hepburn. Unfortunately, halfway through the film, I felt a strong tug on my arm.

"Front row, third guy!" Kim growled and probed me. "Why are you looking at him?"

"What are you talking about?" I asked. "I'm trying to watch the movie."

His response was incoherent as he continued to interrogate me with irrational questions, gradually getting louder. My heartbeat accelerated when he pulled on my arm and dragged me out of the theater. I was furious because now I'd never know how the movie ended.

On the way home, his fury continued, which led to a fistfight. I attempted to throw a punch, then slipped and fell to the ground. That's when I felt the baby inside me kick, and I screamed from the pain. Recognizing my condition, Kim picked me up off the ground and apologized, but the emotional damage had been done. At that moment, I started to doubt whether he cared for our baby or for me.

We walked the rest of the way home in silence.

MY FIRST-BORN SON

AT THE AGE of twenty, I prepared to welcome my first child into the world. That following January was cold and dark, and I was plagued with discomfort as I neared my due date. It wasn't unusual for women to give birth at home, but no one could have prepared me for the reality of childbirth. I cried out in excruciating pain with each contraction, like an iron grip on my torso.

When evening came, I lay on the floor under an empty bookshelf, holding onto its legs, gripping tight as contractions mercilessly continued. Bokdong informed me that it would be another hour before the local midwife arrived.

A gray-haired woman holding a black leather case eventually appeared at our front door. I screamed as I nearly passed out. The midwife guided me, comforted me, and instructed me on how to breathe properly. I forced myself to focus on her directions instead of the contractions until I looked down and saw a tiny black head coming out of my body and felt the sensation of soft, tiny feet kicking out from under me.

"It's a boy!" Bokdong shouted.

At that moment, Kim ran into the room and stopped mid-step with a dumbfounded expression. Immediately, I saw dread, confusion, and uncertainty on his face, giving way to a joyful smile. My arms flailed weakly as I tried to wipe away my tears. Cheerfully, Bokdong knelt, picked up my baby, and began to wipe his body with a handkerchief.

Following Korean tradition, Bokdong gave my baby his name.

"Jinseong," she said emphatically. "That will be his name." It literally meant "Long Great Wall," which signified a long and prosperous life.

Though I'd been entirely unprepared for motherhood, I felt comforted by the waves of love that immediately washed over me. No words can fully explain the feelings of a woman after her first childbirth.

"When the baby is born, so is the mother," the midwife said.

How right she was. At night, my baby cried on and on for my swollen, tender nipples. In my weariness, I reminded myself that he was an innocent child who needed milk for nourishment; he had never asked to be born. His helplessness put me in a melancholy mood—until one night, I was startled out of my sorrow by a voice singing over a radio somewhere in the neighborhood.

Listening closer, I recognized the song as *Ave Maria*, a Catholic hymn played on a *pyeongyong*, a stone chime instrument. I thought of Mina, my childhood friend who lived under the bridge; it had been her favorite song. And even though I had only an inkling of who Mother Mary was, at that moment, I felt that someone, somewhere, was watching over me.

***

TWO WEEKS LATER, when the snow fell heavily around our house, Mother arrived to pay me a surprise visit. Seemingly calmer and more complacent, she was now dressed up in a red velvet *chima,* though her face appeared wearier, lined with age.

As soon as she took one look at my Jinseong, however, her face lit up, and the years melted away. She happily clicked her tongue at him and shouted, "*Hanunim Kamsahamnida!*"

This meant, "Give thanks to God." I had heard her exclaim this before, but this time, it felt more real. But I didn't understand why.

"Okyon moved to Daegu City with her boyfriend," Mother began updating me. "We are renting a new house in Chorangdong near the railroad by the Sangho paint shop with your brothers Gyeong and Chang." She took a breath. "You should visit us sometime," she suggested.

Bokdong quietly crept in and eavesdropped on our conversation. While Mother held baby Jinseong, Bokdong never took her eyes off her. I could tell Mother was growing uncomfortable with Bokdong's silence, so I walked Mother outside.

She leaned in close and spoke in a low voice. "Your sister Oksoon wrote me. She's planning to marry a GI but has yet to beat her drug habit. She's in a drug treatment program in Seoul, and I'm going there to see if I can help. Just thought that you should know." She forced a small smile, staring past me at Bokdong, who was still listening from the living room.

"I promise I'll visit again," Mother declared before walking away.

***

MY EARLY SUSPICIONS about the rottenness in that house were further validated months after Jinseong was born. Kim frequently exploded when we were in the presence of other men; he would automatically assume I was looking at them. This behavior happened nearly every time we were in public, and I found it very unnerving.

The respect and love he once had for me had now turned into doubt and mistrust.

In spring, after Bokdong returned from a trip to her hometown, she sat on a floor mat in the main room and said, "I met a healthy young lady from the countryside near my family's home. She seems like a good fit for my son and our family."

My eyes widened in shock, and I asked, "What about me and my baby?"

She gave me a surprised look as if my question was absurd, but she replied, "You can live anywhere you want, but leave the baby with us."

I may not have liked my living situation, but I never imagined that she would take my son away and throw me on the streets like an obsolete piece of furniture. Something inside me snapped. I turned on her with fury.

"This woman—? Good for your family?" I snarled. "You don't want a daughter-in-law. You want a slave! I don't belong here. I'm not even treated like a human being! You think you have a great son? This man is insane. You can have him back! In fact, the devil can take you all!" I ignored her icy stare as I stormed past her, packed my few belongings, and headed for the door.

"You'd better wait until my son comes home," Bokdong threatened. I picked up baby Jinseong and tied him to my back with a papoose.

Without rising from her mat, Bokdong snarled menacingly, "You are not leaving this house with my only grandson! Don't you dare take Jinseong with you! You have no legal claim on him."

I avoided her gaze, but when she realized that I wasn't going to stop, she quickly stood up and blocked the door. "The baby belongs to our family," she hissed like a snake. "He is *our* flesh and blood. I forbid you to take him away!"

She reached for my hair, but I dodged her and hit her square across the face with my open palm. Like a freshly cut tree log, she dropped onto the doorstep with a loud thud, then casually rolled to one side and stood up, promptly heading for the kitchen, where she sat down and stretched her legs out across the floor.

In her insane, unhinged manner, Bokdong began to pound the floor. "*Aigo! Aigo!*" she wailed. "Ancestors, hear me! That tramp has brought bad luck to our family."

I snapped at her, waving my fist in the air. "Bad luck? I wish good luck to you and your damned ancestors in dealing with your psychotic son! You are going to need it!"

With that, I dashed out the door with my baby in tow. I could still hear her irritating voice screeching her pleas, so I ran faster and faster, struggling to keep Jinseong balanced on my back. I continued down the road until her screaming sounded like a distant foghorn. Fortunately, my baby had fallen asleep by then.

A . . . new life . . . I mused through waves of emotion. *A better life . . . That's all I want.*

I believed I was now a stronger version of myself, but as I trudged onward, feelings of doubt continued to build—sorrow, frustration, and anger stacked upon one another.

Though exhausted, I couldn't break down. I had to stay strong for my little baby.

NEW BEGINNINGS

RECALLING MOTHER'S DIRECTIONS to the railroad, I made my way toward her new home in Chorangdong with my baby still tied to my back. There was a little paint shop on the third street going west toward a house with a broken wooden door, just like she had described.

Somehow, Mother must have already heard my voice asking for directions. I was still a few feet away when she opened her front door.

The doorway was set extremely low, so she had to duck to come outside. Mother didn't even ask why we were at her doorstep. She didn't need to. I saw her face light up as soon as she laid eyes on my baby. She embraced him right away.

"This is a blessing!" she shouted joyfully.

Upon entering the house, I was extremely appalled by Mother's living conditions. At least three windows were missing. Mold and mildew grew wild on the walls, and there were no closets. My brothers hung their clothes on three-inch nails hammered into the walls. In one corner, I recognized Chang's clothes tossed on the floor.

Before I could ask, Mother answered, "Chang ran away—again. Brother Gyeong's looking for him right now, but we haven't heard anything good yet."

I was disappointed and hurt since Mother had never told me about any of this during prior visits. I let out a breath and hoped, wherever he was, that he was safe.

***

THANKFULLY, I WAS able to find a waitressing job at a *dabang*, a coffee shop. Mother took care of the baby so I could make some extra money. Strangely enough, Kim came back into my life. Only now, he appeared to have changed for the better.

Over the next two months, he visited me at Mother's home and made several half-hearted attempts to convince me to return home with him. After everything he and his mother had put me through, I refused every time. Kim was saddened by my continuous rejection, but he managed to remain humble and calm. He'd simply bow and leave every time, and after several weeks, he stopped visiting. Then, one day, his brother-in-law appeared at my doorstep, claiming that Kim was very ill, and begged me to come visit.

Troubled by this sudden news, I didn't know how to react. Yet, after watching me pace the length of the room, observing the turmoil within my head as I mentally debated with myself, Mother encouraged me to go.

"You need to end this once and for all," she said.

Fortunately, the bus ride to their house was a short one. But as soon as I entered Kim's living room, I noticed a thick, metallic smell. The walls were scribbled with what looked like red paint. Upon closer inspection, I realized it was blood, and not just random scribblings, but Korean writing: *Okhui, my love forever.*

I found Kim lying under a blanket in the middle of the bare wooden floor. When he saw me enter, he threw it off and embraced me with his cloth-bandaged hands. Startled, I took a step back and gaped at the bloodied fingertips under his bandages. He had bitten them with his teeth to write on the walls. This practice was called *heulsuh*, a traditional Korean way of expressing passionate love.

Before I could say a word, Bokdong appeared behind me, but she didn't raise her voice. In fact, her eyes were much softer and shone with sadness.

"He quit his bank job and then went on a hunger strike. His doctor told me he may have paranoia." She lowered her voice and said, "I tried to take him to the University Medical Center for psychiatric treatment."

"I am not crazy, Mother!" he interrupted with a maniacal grin. "I am fine. Just fine."

Feeling disturbed by this entire situation, I backed up against the front door. Even though I'd long made up my mind to leave that family, it was truly painful to see him broken like this. Knowing I could not help him, I said my goodbyes and then walked away.

FAREWELL TO BUSAN

IT WAS THE summer of 1963 when I decided to say goodbye to Busan, the city of my childhood. My aunty Jeonghi, the same woman who once kicked me out of her house, had a change of heart and began to visit our home regularly.

"If you have a child out of wedlock," she told me, "No Korean man will marry you."

She was right—I was considered damaged goods. My chances of marrying a Korean were slim, but I didn't mind marrying an American instead. Doing so could even help my mother and siblings gain a better life should we move to America to escape the poverty of Korea. It would also give my baby boy a chance to have a new life.

Aunt Jeonghi advised me to look for a job at the U.S. military compound since I had already learned some English in high school. Given the circumstances, that wasn't a horrible idea. According to Mother, Oksoon was about to move to America, so we decided to go to her home in Seoul. I thought maybe my sister could help us start over.

The next morning before dawn, we waited patiently for the train at Busan Station. Mother held little Jinseong in her arms while I held his baby blanket and papoose. Brother Gyeong carried our two *bottari* over his shoulders while we waited for the black steam engine train to pull up in front of us. With our bulky *bottari,* we stepped inside a narrow aisle of passengers, where we were quickly pushed into wooden benches by the sheer force of the incoming crowd.

I discreetly nursed Jinseong under a blanket while gazing out the window. The train picked up speed, rocking and roaring rhythmically. Up ahead, I could see a small village surrounded by the murky waters of a sprawling rice plantation. An elderly woman carried a large clay pot on her head while her balding husband pulled a cow and walked beside her. I heard the honking of flying geese outside the train and saw a rainbow above the farmhouses.

For a fleeting moment, Korea was not only beautiful but timeless. The remnants of wartime violence and poverty had been displaced by nature, complete with a rainbow to greet us. I believed this would be a positive step in my journey.

***

IT TOOK NEARLY twelve hours before we arrived at Seoul Station in the late afternoon. I immediately spotted Oksoon standing on the arrival platform. Now in her early thirties, she was still pretty, but her face showed the wrinkles of years of hardship. Her weariness, however, disappeared as soon as she laid eyes on Jinseong.

"Is this your little boy? Oh, he's so adorable!" She paused to observe his face. "He looks very . . . Korean, doesn't he?" Mother frowned at the denigrating tone of Oksoon's voice, but I nodded politely.

Oksoon informed us that she was living on base with her husband, Mr. Scarborough. With pleasantries out of the way, she called for a taxi to take us to a cheap motel close by. Her curt manner gave me the impression that she had no interest in further visits. Once we all arrived at the motel, we gathered for a family conference.

"Oksoon-a," Mother began. The tone of her voice changed, as though she were talking to her equal, "We don't have a lot of money to start over. Is there anything you can do to help us?"

My sister tightened her lip, and with a strained voice, she replied, "I don't have that kind of money." Restless, Jinseong would not keep still as Gyeong struggled to hold him steady. Oksoon looked over at my baby, but without a hint of sympathy, she shook her head.

Astonished by her lack of concern, none of us spoke another word as she walked out of the motel room. Mother sat down beside me on the bed and sighed.

"I am still praying for her," she said. Then the tone of her voice changed, "It was a nightmare to get her off that miserable heroin. Immigration laws would have prevented her from entering America unless she was clean and sober."

With no solution at hand, the four of us remained in the motel for another week, leaving as soon as the money ran out. Brother Gyeong suggested that we rent a house in Ojeong-ri, where he had served in the military, like Brothers Jeong and Yeong before him.

We didn't have enough money for a down payment. Fortunately, the landlord gave us a week to raise the rest of our rent. In a desperate attempt, I visited Oksoon once more. At the military gate, I had to wait an entire hour before she came out to see me. Strolling leisurely to the gate in an elegant, freshly ironed Western-style dress, she appeared oblivious to the urgency of our situation. I implored my sister for help.

"Please, help us. I'll repay you as soon as I find work. Our money is running out, and my baby's future is at risk," I pleaded all in one breath.

After a brief pause, she mentioned a name—Hoja Ajumma. I couldn't shake the feeling that she was putting on an act like she often did with Mother, but she wrote down the name and address of this woman living in Sinchon Village, who supposedly needed a tutor for her daughters.

"By the way," she added. "If you really need quick cash, I can introduce you to my husband's good friend."

"What for?"

"What do you think?" she said, then added with a wry smirk, "Everybody's doing it."

I knew my options were limited, but I didn't want to think about that. First, I needed to go see this Hoja Ajumma.

After Oksoon left for America, our family settled in Ojeong-ri. Gyeong secured a job in the construction industry while I prepared myself to become a tutor.

THE VILLAGE OF SINCHON

AFTER SOME DELIBERATION, I finally got up the nerve to head to Sinchon. I believed that tutoring would be a good line of work.

It was common knowledge that most people in Sinchon made their living off the U.S. military bases since it was a small, simple village. It was from Sinchon that the United States helped rebuild Korea and kept peace between the North and the South.

In the afternoon, I got off the bus and followed a narrow road, passing through rows upon rows of small shops, clubs, and houses. The windows of the clothing stores were filled with black satin and leather jackets embroidered with multicolored dragons. I looked at the address Oksoon had written on a small scrap of paper and approached the owner of one of the shops. He paid little attention to me; he was more interested in whatever deal he was making with two GIs holding a pile of jackets. Continuing, I spotted two young women exiting a nightclub, sporting tanned skin and messy, red-dyed hair.

I walked past the club and eventually found a large wooden door matching Oksoon's description. Its iron ring-shaped handle looked rusty. Opting to knock, I received no response.

Peeking through the keyhole, I spotted an abandoned garden in a vast yard, with clothes hanging on a line and a water pump. The garden was surrounded by a series of doors arranged in an arc. As I leaned in, I heard approaching footsteps, and the front door suddenly swung open, startling me. The woman appeared to be in her early forties, with jet-black hair and sharp facial features. She wore a black one-piece dress and heavy makeup, giving her the appearance of a scary Korean witch. She scrutinized me and spoke in a gruff, throaty voice.

"Call me Hoja Ajumma," she said. "I've been expecting you. Just not so soon."

Following Hoja Ajumma, I couldn't understand why anyone would want to raise children in such a location.

Not good. How did I end up here? I struggled to speak, managing only my sister's name. Hoja bombarded me with confusing questions, and my mind wandered. "Are you listening to me?" she asked.

"Yes," I replied, snapping back to the present. "What subjects will I be tutoring your daughters in? Math or English?"

Hoja Ajumma arched her dark eyebrows and looked at me, puzzled. There was a long silence before she spoke again, "Naïve girl, follow me."

When she led me inside, she pounded on her chest and then shook off the minor pain with a cough.

"Excuse me, forgot to take my pills this morning," she said. Hoja Ajumma took me through the main house and into a small room toward the rear, where there was no furniture other than an old bed, dead center.

"This is your temporary bedroom." She then muttered under her breath while instructing me, "It doesn't take too long to get used to this work."

Frustration built up inside me, and I couldn't help but growl in annoyance. Deep down, I had convinced myself she only wanted me as a tutor. I angrily tossed my handbag aside, plopped onto the worn mattress, and stared up at the ceiling, my heart shattered. I let out a long sigh filled with dread.

Memories of my high school years flooded my mind; I distinctly recalled receiving an honorary award from Busan Women's High School. Now, a profound sadness surrounded me as I felt like a piece of meat for sale. In the present moment, I had to provide for my little baby, but the weight of those childhood memories burdened my heart, and a sense of unease made my skin crawl when confronted with Ajumma's true intentions.

"But I really need money!" I whispered just softly enough for her not to hear.

Hoja Ajumma stood in the middle of the doorway and said, "Your sister told me to advance you." She handed me a thick wad of Korean *won*, then pointed her bony finger toward the kitchen and told me to help myself.

I wasn't hungry.

***

THAT NIGHT, HOJA Ajumma brought me a set of fresh towels and bed sheets, and I laid them at the foot of the bed. My body sank into the mattress. *What kind of world have I entered?* I asked myself.

"Expect your first client tonight," Hoja Ajumma informed me. I hardened my heart but fell asleep near the eight o'clock hour, believing he was not going to show.

Half-awake, I noticed a shadow of a man creeping across my bedroom wall, approaching my room. He knocked on the door, which had been left ajar. I could not understand a single word he was saying. Standing closer, I could see his blue eyes illuminated by the streetlight through the window. He was wearing a military uniform.

"*Saba saba*," he said. I had no idea what that meant, but I assumed it referred to sex. Later, I would be told it was American GI slang for "screwing."

I was petrified. I picked up my bag and dashed out the door while he stood there, befuddled. I saw no one else that night.

***

DURING DINNER IN Hoja Ajumma's kitchen the following night, I met her nephew Joe, a young rugged Korean scoundrel. He presented himself with a tough Western persona, complete with a black leather jacket. Suddenly, he aggressively grabbed my arm, his bloodshot eyes glaring at me, sending a shiver down my spine. His unanticipated behavior left me shaken and uneasy.

"Heard you ran out of the room last night," he said with a snarky laugh. Shaking his head, he added, "You better start earning. We can't be keeping dead weight around here, bitch!"

Then he growled at me, "We gave you money. To you *and* to your damn sister! You get smart, or I will hurt you!" In a contemptuous motion, he backed me into the corner and shoved me against the wall. My back slammed against a nearby shelf, sending a pair of ceramic *kimchi* pots crashing to the floor. With a loud growl, he walked away.

At the same time, a tall young girl entered the kitchen. Speaking with a low, gravelly voice and a compassionate demeanor, she introduced herself as Junhwa and told me about her struggles during her first year in the house. Apparently, Hoja and Joe were also drug dealers, and many of their girls fell into addiction. But Junhwa stood her ground and refused to bow to their demands.

"We won't be doing this forever," she added. "You won't be stuck being called a 'GI whore.'"

I chuckled nervously, worried about the whole situation. Then, she brought up my sister Oksoon, claiming she was lucky for getting clean and hitching up with an officer. I kept my mouth shut, thinking, *Lucky? That's an odd way to put it.*

***

THE NEXT DAY, I hopped on a bus to Ojeong-ri, and the driver gave me a friendly grin when I got off. With a bag of groceries in hand, I strolled down the long dirt path, longing to see my baby. As soon I approached, I could already hear him calling for me from inside the house, "Um-maaa . . ."

At the door, Mother greeted me with a radiant smile and a wet towel around her neck to beat the summer heat. She handed me the towel to wipe my face as she took the groceries. Excitedly, she shared Jinseong's new talent: recognizing my legs under the door and pointing at them. My heart melted, and I burst into joyful laughter.

While I held Jinseong close, feeling an unusual amount of warmth from his body, Mother fetched a bucket of fresh water from the backyard well. Concerned, I asked, "What's wrong with the baby?"

As Mother started pouring water into the bucket, her tone noticeably changed.

"He had a fever last night," she said. "His breathing stopped, but Brother Gyeong knew CPR. After a couple of breaths into his mouth, the baby threw up some milk from his nose and burst out crying. We took him to the doctor, and . . . Oh, thank God, I thought we were going to lose him."

After a pause, she continued, "My prayer was answered. His fever went down."

I held my baby close to my chest as she spoke. Mother then mentioned that Gyeong had started a new job with a construction company near Inchon but would be around for a while to help take care of Jinseong.

Later in the afternoon, we took a walk through a rice farm and listened to the birds chirping around us. Mother tried to balance the wiggling baby on her back. When we crossed a narrow dirt road, Mother pointed out a quaint wooden church across from the rice farm.

"When I attend service there with baby Jinseong," she said with an embarrassed laugh, "the parishioners think he is my son."

I chuckled. "Lately, I've heard you frequently calling out the name, 'Yesu.' Didn't you worship Yowangnim, the Prince of the Ocean? What made you convert to the Western God?"

She took a long breath and told me, "The day Okyon kicked me out, Yim and I went to Masan, hoping for a new start. But Yim's drunken rage left me battered and bruised. The next morning, I left him to visit your Aunty Jeonghi, and she took me to church the next day. The pastor was gentle and kind. He offered to say a prayer for me. And when his hands touched my head, I felt calm. And the tears flowed down my face like a waterfall. I felt a release, a cleansing. Like somehow, I knew my soul would be at peace."

She paused, then looked up to the sky, appearing relieved to have told me this story. I had never seen such a serene expression on her face. Seeing her like that made me feel a little more at peace.

When the sun dropped behind the mountain, I kissed my baby's chubby cheeks and hurried to catch the bus back to town.

Back to work.

***

JOE'S CLUB WAS a typical, straightforward name for a nightclub, and Hoja Ajumma instructed me to report to her nephew upon arrival. It was a place exclusively for American servicemen, referred to as GI Joes. As the sun set, the entire village came alive with a lively blend of lights, music, and loud foreigners laughing and shouting in English.

The inside of Joe's Club was huge, resembling eight living rooms cobbled together, with a massive revolving chandelier filling the room with a dazzling light display. A colorful jukebox played a diverse selection of American songs, from old-school crooners like Bobby Vinton and Tony Bennett to contemporary rock and roll.

American GIs and local girls occupied side booths, enthusiastically jumping onto the dance floor when their favorite songs played. I made my way to the bar, trying to maintain a smile while waiting for my first customer. Since I was in a bind and owed Hoja Ajumma the money she had advanced me, I couldn't just quit at this point. I had no other choice but to push forward.

At that moment, a Korean bartender sporting a thin mustache and a boyish smile approached me. He appeared to be in his mid-twenties. Feeling anxious, I ordered a drink, telling him to put it on my tab. I foolishly assumed that liquor would distract me from my gloomy mood. Unfortunately, three shots of Jim Beam were enough to make me drop to the floor, where I crouched and vomited.

I tried to lift my head, but the room would not stop spinning. While battling this stupor, the legs of men and women closed in all around me, although some of them carelessly walked right over me. The room faded to black.

Just before I blacked out, I caught a fleeting glance of the bartender lifting me off the floor and Hoja Ajumma carrying me into my room. Over the next few days, I kept throwing up thick yellow mucus mixed with blood. While I recovered, Hoja Ajumma told me I had become a liability.

Very quickly, I became much sicker as my body temperature rose higher and higher. Every time I lay down, I heard a rumbling in my right lung. Night after night, I woke up in a cold sweat, and I could not stop coughing. Some nights, I vomited blood, but there was no way I could afford to go to a hospital. Luckily, Junhwa lent me the money to see a general practitioner in the village.

***

THE DOCTOR LIVED and worked in a simple one-story house three blocks away. Inside were pictures of a middle-aged man in a white gown, surrounded by African children. He must have been active in charity work, I thought.

The same man from the picture, looking a little older, came into the living room and greeted me with a warm smile. He did not have an assistant or a nurse—just a single bed in a corner, covered with a thin white sheet.

I described my symptoms to him as he listened to my heartbeat with his stethoscope. In just a few minutes, he diagnosed me with lung pleurisy, likely stemming from childhood tuberculosis that had never been treated due to our family's limited knowledge of such matters.

"You should go to a hospital in Seoul," the doctor said. "They have better medical facilities there. This is more than I can handle."

Before releasing me, he gave me a penicillin shot and some medication. He charged me very little for the visit. Unfortunately, I could not afford further treatment, so following up with a trip to Seoul was definitely out of the question.

The rest of the week, my face was covered with red blisters. I had lost so much weight that I could have easily been knocked to the ground by a gust of wind. When Ajumma saw me, she described me as a scarecrow.

"What a mess," she exclaimed. "Go to the clinic and get some medicine for your skin." Fortunately, after a few days of taking the prescribed medications, I felt much better.

MY FIRST TUTORING JOB

CLOSE TO MIDNIGHT, I went to the community water pump for some relief from the night's heat. While filling a small metal bucket with cold water, I heard a faint moan. Curious, I followed the sound and found a pregnant woman sitting alone against a wall, appearing to be on the verge of giving birth. Despite our limited acquaintance, I recognized her distinctive hairdo—a bright red beehive-style.

This young girl had slender ankles and an extraordinary fashion sense, even during pregnancy, with high heels and multicolored slacks. Her gold chain necklace held a large dangling cross. While I had seen her around town and she would wave to me, we had never spoken before.

I froze, too afraid to move, until the shrill voice of an older woman shook me back to the present.

"Judy! Sorry, I'm late!" That voice belonged to a neighbor, Mrs. Chee.

We lifted and carried her into her house. Mrs. Chee then ran to wake up the village nurse, and the three of us helped Judy deliver her baby.

"I can see its head," Mrs. Chee shouted. Judy screamed her pain-filled response.

Then the nurse shouted, "It's a girl!"

Unlike Judy, the baby was born with light brown hair. But her face was the spitting image of her mother. I stayed with Judy through the night and visited over the next few days. Her young fiancé, Joshua, stayed at the house for several days until he had to return to base. Because they were only in the process of getting married, Judy was not allowed the medical benefits afforded to a military wife.

In the morning, Mrs. Chee made seaweed soup for Judy and kindly shared some with me. I noticed the décor in Judy's house—distinctly American, and it smelled of Western furniture polish. I couldn't help envying her since everything she owned had come from the United States.

Her refrigerator was filled with food, and her couch matched her coffee table. Even her kitchen cabinet was filled with a set of American coffee cups, while my siblings and I used to share the few cups we had. In my family, such household items were a luxury.

While she breastfed her baby, Judy and I chatted about our jobs, particularly mine.

"You don't seem like the type to work for her," Judy remarked. "How did you end up in that position?"

"I was hired to tutor her daughters in English and math," I replied.

"Wow," she said, surprised. "You can read and write in both Korean and English?"

"Yes," I confirmed, though I hadn't completed my education. Back then, a woman with a high school diploma was quite impressive to Judy, who asked if I could teach her the basic English alphabet before she moved to America.

She even let me stay with her until I could afford my own place. The next day, Judy paid me a wad of *won*, with which I paid Hoja Ajumma. Naturally, she was shocked that I had gotten the money so fast.

"I won't be a sex slave," I insisted. "Give me some time, and I'll come up with the rest of the money."

I quickly returned to my old room and gathered my belongings. When she saw me leaving, she screamed, "How can you leave without my permission? You still owe the house a lot of money!"

"You can't control where I live!" I shouted back.

At that moment, Ajumma's anger erupted; she grabbed me by the arms. With the force of a hurricane, she slapped my face. I felt a painful sting, but I met her gaze. She buckled.

"Why do you treat me like this?" her voice wobbled, unsteady. "I risked my name, put my reputation on the line, yet you accuse and claim your debts are fine."

I held my composure, took a deep breath, and told her, "I have honored my debt. I want nothing more to do with you."

As she turned her back, I took my leave, walking away to break free.

A week later, Hoja Ajumma's nephew, Joe, was arrested on a drug charge, though he was quickly released. Like any other illegal business in this village, bribery was quite common. Shortly after, I paid off the rest of my debt to Hoja Ajumma. No longer bound by her, a new path beckoned—a brighter day.

Three weeks later, Junhwa informed me that Ajumma had a stroke and needed medical attention. Her husband came to take her back to the countryside, where she received the necessary treatment and care for her recovery. Although I had no connection to her medical condition, I couldn't help but feel a twinge of guilt.

Meanwhile, my friendship with Judy flourished, and I assisted her with housework while she cared for her baby. Seeing her with her precious little infant reminded me of how much I missed my own baby boy. I longed to have Jinseong come live with me in Judy's home.

On my twenty-first birthday, Judy gifted me an expensive makeup set from the military post exchange (PX). Having noticed my limited wardrobe, she decided to buy me new dresses and taught me how to apply makeup.

Since I needed a job, Judy introduced me to her group of recently married Korean friends, all of whom had American GI husbands. When these women told me they were illiterate, I began tutoring them in both Korean and English.

Unfortunately, after six months, Judy and her husband Joshua had to move closer to Seoul for his tour of duty. Before leaving, she generously gave me two months' rent in advance and left most of her furniture with me.

Then, we bid our farewells.

Our short-lived friendship meant a lot to me, especially the compassion she showed me. Like Mina, the girl I knew from my childhood who lived under a bridge, Judy's genuine kindness left a lasting impact. I have learned that compassion begins with kindness, and it's indeed a powerful and truly impactful force.

LIEUTENANT RON HOLDEN

HAVING A PLACE of my own, I was overjoyed that I could now cook in *my* kitchen. I immediately went to the farmer's market to buy the most colorful vegetables I could find—lettuce, *namul*, and red peppers. I started shopping at this open market quite often, without realizing one particular morning would change the course of my life.

I was buying rice early in the day, and a vendor picked up a square wooden box and pretended to fill the bag. When he charged me for three full scoops, he claimed he was being generous, but I rolled my eyes at him. Rice vendors often scooped rice quickly, leaving a bubble of air at the bottom, so customers would unknowingly receive a less-than-full box of their order.

While there, I also picked up some herbs and cuttlefish. Awkwardly plowing through the end of the marketplace, I heard voices of GIs passing by in an army Jeep. At first, I paid no attention since those vehicles often drove straight through the market.

"Hey, beautiful!" One of them stopped, pulled up to my side, and asked, "You need any help?"

Beautiful? I thought with a smile. No one had ever called me that before. Perhaps it was Judy's makeup.

With subtle curiosity, I turned toward the soldiers flirting with me. Inside a compact Jeep with a tent covering its cargo were two American GIs. Both were fair-skinned, but I noticed the stripes on the driver's uniform—he was a sergeant. In complete shock, I froze.

The other GI murmured, "Ain't she a beauty?"

At that moment, while staring closely at the passenger, I saw that he was a very handsome young man. On his chest was a silver bar denoting the rank of lieutenant, an even higher rank. "Do you speak English?" he asked me.

I held on to my grocery bags and answered, "Yes, a little."

"Hold up," the lieutenant told his driver as he hopped out of the Jeep.

"My name's Ron," he said, extending his hand, "Ron Holden."

With a slight smile, I chuckled under my breath. His name was Holden, like one of my favorite actors, William Holden. I put the bag of rice on the ground. Then, I shuffled my groceries under my left arm as he took my right hand.

We both paused, unsure how to proceed. That was my first handshake with an American. People passed by and stared at us, but I ignored them.

"Um," he said with a gentle smile. "What's your name?"

I nearly choked, then thought for a moment. Since his name reminded me of William Holden, I gave myself an American name associated with him.

"Suzie . . . Suzie Wong." Suzie was the name of the Chinese lead in *The World of Suzie Wong*. I thought my decision and name choice were cute and funny. Predictably, neither of these men questioned why a Korean woman would have a Chinese name.

"Where are you heading?" I did not understand the word "heading," so I did not answer. The driver whispered something to the lieutenant, and then he corrected himself. "Oh, we can take you home."

I daintily returned a smile. Lieutenant Ron quickly made some space in the rear compartment, then gestured like a gentleman to welcome me into the Jeep. Because they seemed sincere, I complied. Ron gently took my grocery bags, put them in the rear compartment, and helped me into my seat.

With my best English, I asked him, "Where you come from?"

"Wisconsin," Ron replied, then continued slowly, like a shy teenage boy, "I'm very pleased to meet you, Suzie. Your English is very good."

"Oh, no," I contradicted him, "not so much." I did not want to admit that I tutored English since I didn't feel comfortable conversing in a foreign language.

I looked at his friend in the driver's seat. He pointed to his name tag and mouthed, "Duane."

I bowed and thanked him for the ride. It didn't take more than fifteen minutes before we arrived near my house. Since there were no roadways for vehicles to continue further toward the houses in my neighborhood, I told them to let me off at the corner. Duane turned to Ron and said, "Let's invite her to our party this weekend."

Ron got out of the Jeep and took out my groceries. I tried to take them from him, but he politely insisted on carrying them.

"And if you've got a friend, bring her along," Duane said as Ron walked me down the pathway to my house. Having a man do this for me made me feel secure. Korean men never behaved like this.

While we casually walked down the pathway, I could see my neighbors peeking through their windows, but it did not bother me. When I got to the front door, he leaned in and kissed me on the cheek. For the first time, I felt a flush of warmth saturate my face.

"If you're not busy tomorrow," he said, "I'd like to see you again."

I nodded like a schoolgirl. "Your friend said you have party?"

"Actually," he said, "I never liked those parties. I was thinking of having lunch tomorrow—just the two of us."

I told him, "Yes."

***

RON WAS WAITING for me at the front gate of the military base. When he saw me, he waved. I bashfully walked up to him, and we embraced. When we entered the gate, the guard promptly saluted. Beaming, I felt proud to be walking with him.

Ron held the door to the mess hall open for me. Other soldiers were already eating, and the smell of meat made my stomach growl. I noticed some of the GIs staring at me with curiosity, but their wives sneered and tried to redirect their attention.

Is it my long eyelashes? My overly exposed skinny legs? My miniskirt? These nagging thoughts scrolled through my head. Nervously, I tugged at my clothes, not sure if I had dressed appropriately. Ron seemed totally unaffected and pulled out a chair next to a seated lady GI. Her head had been buried in her newspaper, but when he moved the chair, the stern-faced woman looked up at me and grimaced.

"I'm sorry," Ron said, sounding a little panicked. "Was this seat taken?" The woman shook her head and returned to her paper.

Ron smiled awkwardly with a boyish grin, which I found charming. He asked me what I wanted to order. I told him that I wanted a large hamburger and a bottle of Coca-Cola. Having dined at the mess hall before with my friend Judy and her fiancé Joshua, I knew they served large portions of food, and I could not wait to have another burger.

Ron ordered two icy bottles of Coca-Cola, two large burgers, and french fries. The instant the food was set before us, my mouth began to water. Before Ron even picked up his burger, I had already taken a bite out of mine and chewed enthusiastically.

"Mmmm! Taste so good!" The warm, greasy juice from the meat dripped all over my fingers, which I licked off as I continued to gobble it down. Containing his obvious embarrassment, Ron stared in awe, then looked around to see if anyone had seen me eating like a common construction worker.

"Take it easy," he said. "Y'know, if you chew slowly, you might be able to taste it."

"Oh, I grow up in large family," I told him in the best English I could muster. "So, I always ate quick before my brothers grab off my plate." Just then, a piece of meat slipped out of the corner of my mouth, which I pushed back in with my finger. And that was when I noticed everyone else had been eating in silence. I slowed down, suddenly feeling ashamed.

I changed the subject and told him about my baby boy and my mother. He seemed surprised that I had a son but didn't comment on it. He then told me a little about his family, but I couldn't understand most of it because he used a lot of unfamiliar English words.

"Let's walk around the compound," he said. I complied.

Ron escorted me outside, where enlisted soldiers saluted him as we walked by. Pausing beside a stately pine tree, I found myself entranced by the depth of his azure eyes, their gaze locked onto mine. Spontaneously, as we leaned against the pine's sturdy trunk, I embraced him, and he pressed a tender kiss to my cheek. My face flushed, and the rhythm of my heart seemed to echo in my ears.

A few days later, I dined with Ron at the village café and decided to invite him home to see my place. I was excited to show him all the American furniture Judy had left for me. When we got to the house, Ron noticed the décor right away. I told him how my former roommate loved Americana, and her appliances made daily living much easier.

We spent the rest of the evening having dinner, which I cooked, and then we relaxed watching television. Unfortunately, he had to leave before 10 p.m. due to his military curfew. That's when I felt a pang of sadness.

With Judy gone, I was left with less income, and I definitely did not want to rely on Ron's paycheck. Though he began visiting often, bringing me food from the commissary and helping me pay the rent, I wasn't about to continue taking advantage of his generosity. I had to think of my family and how much it would cost to move them into this house. Eventually, Brother Gyeong agreed to contribute part of the rent, so that was a relief.

***

AFTER A MONTH of traveling between cities, I noticed my baby had already learned to take his first steps. My heart melted when I saw how fast Jinseong was growing. In the meantime, Ron brought gifts of Gerber's baby food.

Over the next few weeks, Mother moved out of Ojeong-ri and into my new place, so I invited Ron to meet my family. On the drive over, Ron asked me to teach him how to pronounce some Korean names and phrases so he could properly greet my family.

"What's your son's name?"

"Jinseong."

"Jeen Sahng?" he attempted to get the pronunciation right. "How do you say, 'How are you? Glad to meet you?'"

"*Annyeonghaseyo* would be enough," I told him. He tried to repeat it several times before he finally gave up. As we approached the house, he got a little nervous.

Just then, Mother spotted us and came out to greet us with my baby. She held both of Jinseong's hands while he practiced walking. When he saw me, he got so excited he kept babbling and squirming out of her grasp to run down the dirt path to embrace me.

"White man?" my mother said, taken aback to see this tall Caucasian man. But I was sure she wasn't surprised. Walking into the house, she whispered to me in Korean, "Don't you think he's too young?"

"I am young too, Mother."

"But you already have a child," she argued politely. "You need an older man who can accept that you have a son. This man looks like a statue. Acts like one, too."

I scoffed at her, wanting to explain that this is simply how foreigners behave. Before I could say another word, Ron leaned over and whispered, "I don't think your mother likes me."

I didn't respond but instead turned to my mother and told her, "Ron loves little children."

"Can I show your baby the Jeep?" he asked.

He picked up my baby while I walked with them back toward the Jeep. He let my baby sit in the driver's seat and play with the steering wheel. Ron honked the horn, which made Jinseong jump with laughter.

**

BY SEPTEMBER, THE week before the Autumn Lunar Festival of Chuseok, Koreans traveled to the cemeteries for *jesa*, a celebration where families get together and visit their ancestors, leaving food and bowing at their graves to honor their spirits.

Around this time, Ron and I decided to go on a hike. We walked past the railroad, up a hillside outside of town, and through the middle of a forest. During the early days of autumn, the tops of the trees revealed sprinkles of red, gold, and brown. I took a deep breath of the clean mountain air and smiled. We lay on the grass between the trees and looked up at the sky. I could hear crickets chirping. Ron rolled over, picked a wildflower, and gave it to me.

"When I was freshman in high school," I began, "I used to collect leaves and flower petals from the hill near my house. I dried them, then glued them onto paper for my science project."

His smile grew, and our eyes locked in a meaningful moment. Then, Ron reached into his jacket pocket and revealed a red velvet box. Inside lay a pearl necklace that he tenderly placed around my neck. With a boyish, nervous smile, he asked me to marry him.

Before I could respond, he revealed his desire to take me to America—the American Dream. I gasped at the thought. Ron continued excitedly. "I want to announce our engagement to your family. Can you set the date?"

I remained silent, taking a moment to process Ron's proposal. Undeterred, he forged ahead, expressing his desire to start the paperwork for my immigration regardless of my decision.

At that moment, I stood speechless. To me, Ron looked just like one of the movie stars I'd only seen in foreign movies—and he wanted to marry me. But I also felt a pang of fear over marrying an American GI.

Over the next few weeks, I took some time to think about his proposal, asking myself if this was what I really wanted. One of my English students, Linda Seo, shared her own story of marrying an American GI. According to her, it wasn't a bad thing.

"You get to visit the PX and go see all the American movies you want," she said. "And you get to eat lots of American popcorn."

On the other hand, GI brides were treated as lower class, and the Korean community often held a negative view of women who married white foreigners.

As we conversed, Linda shared her experience of registering at a travel agency, where she requested an interpreter to translate the paperwork. She suggested having Frontier Agency handle all the necessary documentation for our marriage and travel, including booking our flight.

Early the next morning, I took a taxi downtown and located Frontier Agency near the American Embassy in Myeongdong's finance district. My excitement mixed with nerves as I entered the agency, taking a deep breath. Inside, a mousy-looking, middle-aged man greeted me with a polite smile.

The agent explained the required documents: my birth certificate, Ron's American birth certificate, a family consent form due to our ages, my medical records, and a Support Affidavit. He handed me a thick stack of papers to prepare. My dismay was evident, and he empathetically informed me that the process was complicated because I had a son from a different father.

With a frustrated sigh, I walked down the flight of stairs from his office, papers in hand. When I reached the bottom of the staircase, I was distracted by an older woman who stopped in the walkway just before me. Clad in a well-tailored business dress, she accompanied a familiar-looking man carrying a briefcase; both were coming out of an indoor café.

When the older woman bowed her goodbye, the man turned around and unintentionally bumped into me, nearly knocking me over and sending my papers falling to the ground. When I bent over to pick them up, I got a better look at the man's face.

I froze.

It was my former lover, Kim Gwangyeung. His face turned red, and his eyes looked as though he were about to produce tears.

"Okhui!" he exclaimed. "Do you know how long I've been looking for you?"

I quickly stuffed the papers into my handbag. "What are you doing here in Myeongdong?" I asked. Kim mumbled under his breath. He admitted he was a little shocked to see how much my appearance had changed.

"My job transferred me here." He gestured for me to come into the café with him. "Come, have tea with me!"

For some odd reason, I agreed. Perhaps I was hoping for closure.

Kim spoke excitedly the entire time we walked to our table. "That lady in the suit? She's one of the producers of a movie I'm financing through my bank." I honestly did not understand what that meant. Why was a bank doing business with a movie producer?

I took a seat by a window while he sat across from me. He ordered two cups of ginger tea, then took out a booklet of loose-leaf papers from his briefcase.

"This is the script they gave me," he explained.

On the cover, I noticed the movie's title *Sungyoja*, "Martyr." He flipped through the pages, stopping at a section that appeared to be a business plan. The name Kim Jin-kyu was prominently displayed at the top. He was the biggest movie star in Korea during the 1960s, but I still didn't understand what this was all about.

Kim tapped the papers on the table enthusiastically. "The director is Yu Hyun-Mok, and I'll be acting in it. I'm playing one of the pastors who gets thrown in jail, and I go crazy. I even get to die in this movie."

I simply nodded, not showing any interest. But this conversation did answer a question that I had for a long time when we lived together, something I'd never brought up before.

"I remember a few times I caught you posing in front of the mirror," I began. "So, all that time, you were practicing your acting?"

Kim chuckled, though he looked disappointed that I wasn't more impressed. Hence, he didn't say another word about the movie while we drank our tea. When it came time to say goodbye, he gave me a hug and told me, "Our baby is the strongest knot between the two of us, and it will never break apart."

His words took me aback. Kim smiled, let out a breath, then looked me in the eye. "I knew I'd see you again."

I let go of his hug gently, feeling like I wanted to say, "I'm sorry, I'm not the same person you remember." But I didn't say anything and just kept smiling. He turned and hailed a taxi for me, giving me money to pay for the ride. As the taxi drove away, I looked at him in the mirror and saw him waving until he faded onto the dusty roadside. His body melded with the wind, and I bit my tongue to hold back the tears.

That night, I told my mother that I had run into Kim in the finance district. Surprisingly, she was happy to hear it.

"You should get back together with him," she said. I shook my head. I had already made up my mind about who I wanted to be with.

Sungyoja was released in 1965. Kim had become an actor, but that was a part of his life I would never know about.

***

LATER THAT WEEK, I met Ron for lunch on base after half of the immigration paperwork had been processed. When we approached the mess hall, he stopped, took a long breath, and sat me down on a bench. The worried look on his face made me feel something bad was about to happen. There was a dreadful silence.

"Suzie," he began. His voice quivered as he choked over his words, "I've been talking to my folks, and today I got a letter from . . ." His eyes filled with tears. "You see, I'm not yet twenty-one. I need consent from my parents."

I stared, confused. He dropped his gaze for a moment. "And my parents won't approve of our marriage."

My eyes did not leave his, and I nearly choked on my words. "I don't understand."

Ron took a breath, his voice cracking as he spoke. "Suzie, you don't know my family, especially my mother. She's very much against . . ." He stopped himself.

"Against what?" I snapped, my anger boiling over.

He blushed and hesitated. "I told them I wanted to marry you, and—"

"You're ashamed of me!" I interjected, my teeth gnashing. I immediately assumed he was like other American GIs, looking down on me because I'm Korean.

His eyes widened in shock. "No, I would never let them hold that against you!"

My frustration surged, and I screamed at him, "You're no different from those other GIs. I'm just another whore to you!" He tried to hold me by the shoulders, shaking his head in disagreement, but I couldn't bear it. My heart pounded in my ears as I shrugged off his grip and walked away.

Nobody was home when I arrived, and I was grateful. I sat alone in my room, staring at my reflection in the mirror while sipping an unsweetened cup of American coffee. Taking in the last drop, I held the porcelain cup in my hand and stared at it for a second before flinging it against the mirror. It shattered my reflection to pieces, leaving behind a few jagged chunks in the frame. One of the fragments of glass fell to the floor; another piece fell an hour later. Feeling absolutely devastated, I did not bother to clean it up.

***

THE FOLLOWING WEEK, more bad news came out of the blue, suddenly and unexpectedly.

"I'm going to be deployed to Vietnam," Ron informed me. "Um . . . I was ordered to go, and I'm going to be shipping out soon." Before he left, he told me he would try to persuade his parents to change their minds about our planned marriage. I was stunned at how quickly this was happening.

When Mother overheard our conversation, she put my crying baby on the floor and entered the room. Likely, she did not understand what we were saying, but she could tell I was upset. I told her about Ron's deployment.

"I saw this coming." She said nothing else. Perhaps she had been right all along about Ron, that he was not the right man for me. That night, I couldn't help but wonder if he had requested deployment to get away from me—that he was simply creating an excuse to walk away.

It made my heart ache terribly that I would never find out.

***

MY BROTHER GYEONG moved to another town to take a construction job, which made it harder for me to keep up with the rent. But more tragedy loomed on the horizon. One afternoon, three weeks before Christmas, I looked out my window and saw an American soldier approaching my house. He was a large man with a thinning crew cut and a protruding belly. The first thing I noticed was his extra-large leather jacket decorated with sergeant's stripes, lower in rank than my Ron.

He smiled as he passed my barking dogs, Coco and Chichi, whom I had recently adopted from a neighbor. He had one hand deep in his jacket pocket and held out the other to shake mine. Then, he smiled at me, exposing a missing molar in his mouth. Before I could ask the purpose of his visit, he held out a letter, but I was too afraid to take it. His smile disappeared quickly as though he were self-conscious.

"My n-name is Gordon," he began with a slight stammer. "Ron and I worked in the same unit."

He repeated his name, "Gordon." He was so nervous that his forehead beaded with sweat despite the cold. "You're Miss Suzie Wong?"

When I nodded, his eyes were downcast, and his face looked grim. "I'm sorry to be the bearer of bad news. This letter is for you."

He handed the letter to me once more, and I took it this time. When I opened it, a handful of dried flower petals fell from it. This "Sergeant Gordon" didn't react and kept a somber look on his face.

"Ron sent it to my military P.O. box."

The sergeant then let out a breath. He didn't have to say another word. My heart shattered, my chest caved in, and my body crumpled. Gordon rushed to my side to keep me from falling. When I sobbed, he kissed me lightly on the cheek.

Then, he immediately let go and left as quickly as he had come. The letter had been dated four weeks ago:

Dear Suzie,

I'm not very good at expressing myself, so I'm writing a letter to explain. I'm standing in the middle of hell writing you. I don't know what we Americans are doing here in Saigon in the first place, but I feel like I left behind a large part of myself when I left Korea. Now, all I have are the memories of the two of us walking through the woods.

I miss those long walks.

When we passed the railroad in the countryside and walked up to the mountains, when I asked you to marry me and hung a pearl necklace around your neck . . . that memory will live with me forever.

My eyes, heavy with tears, could not continue reading. Gordon later told me that Ron was reported "Killed in Action in Saigon" the week before the letter arrived. I could not hide my tears from Mother. She didn't say anything; perhaps she felt guilty for the way she had treated Ron. Out of sympathy, Mother poured me a cup of tea and then headed back to her bedroom.

That night, I sat up in bed and looked out at the stars from my window. Emotionally, I was drawn into another world deep in shadows—a world of darkness and grief. In the middle of the night, I slipped the letter under my pillow, closed my eyes, and said a prayer for the dear departed husband whom I had never married.

SERGEANT GORDON LEE

IN THE WAKE of Ron's death, I carefully observed the world around me, but nothing acknowledged his absence. Life continued its merciless, ceaseless motion—and I still had work to do. With the increased number of family members in my household, I had to rethink my finances. Working as a tutor didn't make enough to feed my entire family, so I asked my students for favors.

Some of them had married American GIs, and they were willing to give me American coffee, cosmetics, and electronic equipment from the PX so I could sell them at the local market. This allowed me extra cash to buy food since everything from America was considered a luxury, and Koreans were willing to pay higher prices for such items.

Later that week, Gordon stopped by my house again and asked if I would join him for lunch. I accepted his invitation, happy to have some company.

***

THE WEATHER WAS bitter cold that day as I waited near the Itaewon Military Gate. The guard stood at attention, moving only to salute Gordon when he came out to greet me. Strangely, I remarked at how Gordon always stomped his feet when he walked; he explained he needed to keep his blood circulating, which I found quite amusing. Nonetheless, he took my hand and led me inside the compound. Despite the cold chill, he was sweating profusely.

I noticed we were approaching the same mess hall where Ron had first invited me for lunch, where I'd enjoyed that delicious hamburger. There was now a string of colored lights in front of the building, and the pine trees outside were decorated with colorful ornaments. The scent of those trees made me feel at peace, even today.

As we sat at a table in the mess hall, Bing Crosby's "White Christmas" played on the jukebox, which turned my thoughts to Ron and my last Christmas date with him here.

Gordon broke my train of thought. "Tell me about yourself," he said. "Do you have any children of your own?"

"Yes, one little boy," I blurted out. "Jinseong. He is Korean. I take care of my son and the rest of my family. How about you?"

"Oh, I'm from a small town called Pocatello in Idaho," he replied. "My folks own a diner called Rand's Café, right off the 86 Freeway. I plowed through two years of college in Salt Lake City, Utah."

He gulped down half his cup of coffee and cleared his throat. "Heck, I was even married once."

Awkwardly fumbling through his shirt pocket, he pulled out a worn leather wallet and showed me photos from his Idaho home. The first thing I noticed was the lack of money inside. Instead, it was filled with identification cards, the edges of which looked as though a mouse had nibbled them off. Then, he showed me pictures of some posters he had painted. One was a portrait of Jesus with a halo over his head. I was impressed.

"They're so beautiful," I declared. "You paint all these posters?"

He blushed. "Yes, I did. And thank you." He told me that he was a Christian—of sorts.

"My parents are Mormon," he added. I nodded, pretending to understand. I didn't know the difference, and he never paused to offer an explanation. I only understood they followed Jesus Christ.

***

OUR LUNCH DATE extended well into the evening; we played Bingo at the NCO club, followed by a trip to the Army movie theater to watch a film about some British spy. Before the movie started, Gordon mentioned that he had seen Ron and me together on occasion, but I simply nodded and chose not to respond. It was still too painful to talk about him.

Halfway through the movie, Gordon gently put his hand on mine. Although he was not as handsome as the actor on the big screen, I did not mind at all. By the time we got out of the theater, the temperature had gotten colder. Gordon took off his jacket, wrapped it around my shoulders, and put his arm around me affectionately. My teeth were chattering from the cold, but inside, I felt warm and secure.

***

IT TOOK SEVERAL weeks to gather up the courage to invite Gordon to meet my family. His enthusiasm was sincere. "I'd love to," he told me.

"*Annyeonghaseyo!*" Gordon greeted my mother with a slight bow. Right away, I pointed to his shoes, which he took off without hesitation. From prior experience with Ron, I learned to ask foreign men to remove their shoes upon entering.

To make it simpler for Gordon, I asked him to call my mother "Oh-ma" as it was easier for the Western tongue to pronounce. Mother smiled and bowed politely. She seemed to like Gordon's good, kind nature. She winked and whispered in my ear, "He is a better fit for you, more of a husband type."

Slightly annoyed by Mother's quick judgment, I rolled my eyes and introduced him to Jinseong, whom he picked up immediately. My dogs got used to Gordon very quickly. Coco would jump up and try to lick his face. But best of all, my baby took to him without hesitation, laughing with his eyes aglow as Gordon held him high.

The next day, he brought my baby a record player and an LP titled "Mary Poppins." Jinseong appeared to enjoy listening to the music from the record whenever I played it. We even danced together during that song with the really long title, which didn't sound like real English words. The way this gift made my baby smile, I knew right away that Gordon would make a good father.

***

LIFE GOT EVEN better after we received a surprise visit from Brother Chang. He admitted that he'd been living on the streets this whole time. This family reunion was made possible through

Aunty Deoki, who had been in touch with all my brothers during their absence from home.

Later that year, I received a letter from my sister Okyon. Having just broken up with her boyfriend, she wanted to move in with us. When she learned of my new relationship with Gordon, she told me she wasn't happy that I was dating an American soldier.

"Okhui," she said, "out of all us sisters, I thought you would be the one to have a normal life."

"I do have a normal life," I told her. "Besides, I love Gordon. He took care of me when my fiancé was killed."

Okyon didn't pursue the matter any further. While living with us, she saw firsthand how well Gordon took care of Jinseong.

Even Mother breathed a sigh of relief. "Being together once more," she began, "means a new future will be emerging for our family." I imagined Mother wanted to make up for all the years she was not there for us. Even so, I never held any desire to contradict her. For once in my life, having my family together made me feel whole.

About a week later, Gordon brought Jinseong a children's book and taught him the English names of animals. My baby was overjoyed to learn some words in English.

"How would Jinseong like to have an American name?" Gordon asked.

At first, I wasn't sure how to respond; I had no reason to object. American names sounded very distinguished to me, so I agreed. Raising a bilingual child was a source of joy and pride.

Jinseong was a hyperactive child—and a bit of a rascal. At times, he would try to climb the curtains like a spider, leaving handprints that Mother would clean up afterward. Gordon decided to name him Dennis, after the comic strip *Dennis the Menace*. I told him I had no knowledge of this character, but I liked the sound of the name. Gordon took a napkin, drew a rough sketch of an American boy with his tousled blonde hair, and showed it to me.

"Denn-niss," I said out loud in English, laughing at the caricature.

"Great," Gordon said with a gleeful smile, "Dennis it is."

***

ONE DAY, MOTHER decided to make an American meal while Gordon watched television with my baby. While I set the table, Mother brought out a delightful plate of Western-style corned beef and cabbage. It smelled absolutely delicious, and the four of us could barely wait to "dig in," as the Americans say.

After Mother and I finished ours, I gathered the dishes and carried them into the kitchen, but while placing the dishes in the sink, I noticed several empty cans of dog food on the counter.

That's odd, I thought. In Korea, we only fed Coco and Chichi leftover scraps. Then, the realization hit me with a sudden jolt. I immediately ran to the living room to discreetly confront Mother.

"Mother!" I whispered in Korean. "Don't tell me our dinner was made out of dog food!"

Mother knocked at her head in frustration. I knew she could not read English, but I could never have anticipated something like this! Mother had no idea that there was such a thing as canned dog food. Gordon must have bought these cans from the commissary but never felt the need to tell us. Mother asked me to save her the embarrassment and not tell Gordon, and I agreed.

Unfortunately, my bilingual son kept repeating "doggy, doggy" while he and Gordon were finishing their dinner. Panicked, I tapped his head to shut him up. The next time we made corned beef and cabbage, I made sure it was real corned beef.

MY CHAPEL WEDDING

SEVERAL MONTHS LATER, Gordon came into my room with a shopping catalog in his hand and a big grin on his face. "My mother's so happy I'm marrying you!" he exclaimed, handing me the booklet. Just as happy, I took the catalog from him.

"What is this for?" I asked.

He laughed. "So, you can choose your wedding ring."

I was pleasantly surprised and thrilled at the thought—I had never been given a diamond ring before. I immediately leaped into his arms, jumping up and down with joy as I embraced him.

Dennis entered the room and eagerly cuddled with us on the couch, browsing the catalog with me. Flipping through the pages, I saw a ring that I especially liked, complete with a large diamond in the center surrounded by six tiny diamonds set in a circle.

Three weeks later, Gordon presented me with that same engagement ring. "I now give you this ring," he said, his voice quivering as he put his hand deep into his pocket. Out came a small velvet box.

In my excitement, I nearly tore the box in half, staring with wide eyes at my new ring.

"It's beautiful!" I gushed. But that was an understatement. This was the first diamond I had ever owned, and I felt extremely ecstatic.

Gordon put the ring on my finger. I was so excited that my hand could not stop trembling. I moved toward the light to watch it sparkle. Gordon kept smiling as he watched me dance around the room.

"Will you marry me?" he asked.

I was thoroughly entranced by my ring but managed to look up long enough to reply, "Of course, you can marry me!" Gordon laughed. This awkward-sounding response stemmed from my lack of understanding of American marriage rituals, but I meant it just the same.

Later that spring, just when I thought that my life's dream was already fulfilled, there came another happy surprise. On the day we processed our marriage paperwork, Gordon took me to a military doctor for a checkup.

At the end of the examination, the doctor turned to me with a smile. "You're going to have a baby!" he said. Completely overjoyed, I leaped from the hospital bed and gave Gordon a warm embrace—I even hugged the doctor. He told us how far along my pregnancy was, but we decided to keep our wedding date in June, knowing I would be in my second trimester.

***

BY JUNE 1965, I was nearing my twenty-third birthday, and Gordon would turn thirty-two in just a few months. We planned a simple wedding on the base with a few friends and relatives.

On the night before the main event, I couldn't sleep from excitement. Mother, equally thrilled, woke early to pray in her room. Okyon and Brother Chang volunteered to look after Dennis while Mother and I went to the beauty salon. A hairdresser styled my hair like an upside-down ice cream cone, and an esthetician applied three layers of foundation on my face, following the current wedding fashions.

A tailor then presented me with a beautiful white gown embroidered with lace flowers. Both Mother and I were mesmerized by its beauty. It hit me that this was a significant moment. Mother, witnessing all of this, had tears in her eyes. As for myself, the anxiety made me sweat, and being six months pregnant, the gown barely fit around my waist.

I dropped the veil over my face and headed toward the front of the chapel, where Gordon and I convened to have our portraits taken against a clear blue sky. Inside the chapel, a young man introduced himself as Gordon's co-worker, Private Lawrence Adams. With a gentle grin, he let me know that he would gladly walk me down the aisle to "give me away."

Okyon held the back of my gown, and we proceeded to walk down the aisle. As Lawrence walked me toward the altar, I gradually turned toward Mother, desperately trying to keep Dennis steady on her lap. I had to turn away. Suddenly, a feeling of guilt welled up inside of me for having Dennis out of wedlock.

I tried to shake the feeling while I watched my siblings take their seats in the front pews. Behind Mother, my brothers looked on in amusement while Lawrence and I walked by. This American ritual of "giving away the bride" sounded funny to them when I'd previously tried to explain it.

I took a deep breath.

The chaplain greeted the guests, but all I could hear was my little boy's laughter echoing throughout the chapel. At the altar, I stepped toward Gordon, ready to be received as his wife. Joyfully distracted, I could barely focus on the chaplain's mumbled English or the oversized suit Gordon was wearing. But one thing I did notice when I looked at my husband-to-be was how much he was trembling—he was so nervous that I thought he would faint.

Luckily, I was able to say, "I do," on cue, as did Gordon.

When the chaplain pronounced us "man and wife," I immediately flung myself into my new husband's arms. For the first time in many years, I actually felt whole.

I now had a complete family.

MY BROWN-EYED GIRL

IN SEPTEMBER, BARELY three months after our wedding, Gordon transferred to the United States. To avoid any risk of complications carrying our baby, we felt it would be safer if I remained in Seoul. Before he left, Gordon assured me that he would find a permanent home so that he could bring Dennis, our new baby, and me to the United States.

My daughter was born on December 6, 1965, at the military hospital in Seoul. When the doctor held her upside down by the ankles and gave her a hard slap on the buttocks, a tiny squeal burst forth from her little lungs, and my heart swelled with joy.

The nurses moved me into another room with a garden view and handed me my baby girl. Oh, how precious it felt to finally hold her. My fingertips pressed her tiny little nose and her large double eyelids. Her skin was fair, and the small cluster of hair on her head was a shiny golden brown. Though I was overjoyed, I also felt a profound sadness, wishing Gordon could have been there with me to share this precious moment.

Okyon and Mother were the first of my family to see my baby girl through a glass partition outside my room. They told me she appeared more Caucasian than Korean, like the child of an American movie star—that sounded pleasing to me.

Therefore, I named her "Marylin" after one of my favorite actresses, Marilyn Monroe. Unfortunately, when I signed her birth certificate, I spelled her name M-A-R-Y-L-I-N, the way it sounded phonetically.

After I returned home from the hospital, Mother prepared *miyeokguk*, a seaweed soup that can be boiled with beef, fish, or other kinds of meat. It was traditional for new mothers to eat *miyeokguk* after childbirth to cleanse the blood. Mother fed it to me for a whole month, and though the soup was delicious, it made my body smell like seaweed.

***

EVENTUALLY, I DECIDED it would be best for the family to move to Itaewon, the Yongsan District in Seoul, so that we could be close to the American Embassy. Shortly thereafter, we hired a neighbor to help transport our belongings, including our dogs, to our new home. It was a humble house, nothing extravagant.

All our dishes were kept on wooden shelves next to a wooden pantry. Though the shelves appeared new, the cabinet itself looked as if it had been cobbled together with scraps from a local junk pile.

A sliding door made with a single panel of Oriental paper separated the kitchen from the living room. The clay walls were painted gray, and the hard dirt floor was covered with a thick wax paper called *ondolbang*, which enabled the heating system to warm the floor during the winter months.

Our house was set below street level, which allowed the damp, musty city smell to pervade the interior. With Gordon in America, I made every effort to stretch the money he sent us from his military pay as far as possible.

Later in the week, Aunty Deoki wrote to tell us that Brother Yong had started working nearby as a martial arts instructor. Mother often visited him with little Dennis in tow. Yong was overjoyed that I now had two children, and Mother eagerly welcomed him back home. Our entire family enjoyed having a new baby, and Marylin was such a happy girl.

***

IT WAS THE beginning of the summer of 1966, and I was lying down on the *ondolbang*. My body suddenly tensed up, unable to move, and my breathing became rapid. In a gravelly voice, I called out for Mother, but she did not answer.

It felt like a large weight was pushing me down, sinking me into the floor. Again, I called out for Mother—this time, she heard me and brought some blankets. Propping me up on a pillow, Mother wrapped the blankets around me to stave off the cold.

Sometime later, I awoke to Mother's voice calling for the rest of the family. I lay in bed, helpless and paralyzed, while they looked on, wide-eyed, from the doorway. Brother Chang tried to come inside, but Mother held him back.

Mother stared at me, frightened, then shook her head. I looked at my skin—pale and gray. Suddenly, I heaved in a large gulp of air.

Brother Yong gasped in shock, quickly picking Marylin up from the floor while Okyon held out a washing pan to catch my bloody vomit. Mother grabbed the pan from her and held it under my chin, wiping gobs of blood from my mouth. The blood I coughed up thickened like gelatin.

"*Juyo, Juyo!*" Mother shouted, "Make the evil spirit go away!"

I coughed uncontrollably. My head felt dizzy, and when I opened my eyes again, I could no longer see clearly. The room looked warped, elongating in different directions. I immediately felt lost and confused until someone whispered to me, "Everything will be okay."

I jolted in my sleep, then woke up in a warm sweat. I began to feel a little better, if only briefly. The very next morning, I was admitted to the American military hospital, where half a dozen doctors examined me. After a lot of poking and prodding, they could not agree on a diagnosis. Apparently, my condition was far more serious than a local hospital could handle.

Before long, the doctors ordered that I be airlifted to the 121st Hospital just outside of Seoul. Gradually, I faded in and out of consciousness as a loud cranking noise screeched near me. Then I felt gusts of dusty wind blowing in my face from a set of whirling blades; it was a helicopter arriving for me. Everything blurred together as I lay face up inside the helicopter, vaguely catching sight of two interns seated in front of me. They kept me on an IV for a blood transfusion, but I was too weak to stay awake. I took a deep breath, then drifted into unconsciousness.

***

WHEN I AWOKE, I lay on a hospital bed in a sterile room, surrounded by medical equipment I did not recognize. Yellow spots danced in front of my eyes, and my stomach churned and coiled. Several doctors and technicians ran about the room. One of them elevated my feet ninety degrees into the air while their voices intermingled.

"Mrs. Lee!" one doctor called out. "Don't go to sleep!"

"Can you hear me?" asked another.

"Her body temperature is astronomically high," said a third doctor.

Although I had never been taught how to pray, I did recall how my childhood friend, Mina, used her hands to draw the shape of a cross in front of her body and spoke to someone she referred to as "Our Father." Mustering up my strength, I followed her example as I folded my hands and begged God, whoever He might be, to help me make it through this pain.

"I'm only twenty-three, God," I whispered. The memory of Grandma Seokbuni and the shattered dish entered my mind. In the blink of an eye, life suddenly felt more fragile.

"Take your bad luck with you!" I recalled what Father had once shouted to Grandma's hearse on the day she passed away.

Desperately, I struggled to shout out loud, "I don't want to leave my kids and the rest of my family. I am too young to die."

Moments later, a young nurse transferred me to a tiny, dark room. Another nurse rolled me onto a cold, hard bed while a third nurse brought a dozen small bags of ice to place over my entire body. They then set up six fans around the room.

Through a window, I could see Mother standing outside, looking worried and distressed. Sometime afterward, I saw her standing over me, holding her hand above my chest, praying for me to be healed. Then, her image faded away.

My tongue was soaked in blood, and I could not speak. Tears streamed down the side of my face. Then, an orange wave of light—an orange aura—surrounded me, and warm milk began to drip from my swollen breasts. Though I was still very weak, I could hear my daughter gurgling, and I felt a cold wind brush against my cheek.

The attending doctors surrounded my bedside, but their odd, unmatching shadows hovered along the walls and passed over me. I wanted to cough, but my throat tightened.

"She was throwing up yellow mucus and gelatinous drops of blood," a male doctor spoke.

Another male voice added, "She has a history of lung problems. One of her lungs has collapsed. And she's got a high fever."

"We have to notify her husband right away," a third voice chimed in. Those were the last words I heard before I blacked out and drifted into dreamless oblivion.

When I awoke, several days had gone by, and I had been transferred to a different room. My vision had cleared up enough to see green foliage outside the hospital window. I could hear the flutter of albatross wings outside. When I finally regained consciousness, I felt like a thunderstorm had passed, but I'd survived.

A FAMILIAR VOICE

A MIDDLE-AGED AMERICAN doctor entered my room wearing a white cotton mask, followed by two interns in white gowns, their masks draped under their chins. The doctor briefly studied my chart before approaching me, then sternly stood at the foot of my bed.

"Your husband is on his way," he said. "How do you feel?"

Distracted, I did not answer. I'd been staring at one of the interns behind him—a Korean woman around my age who somehow looked familiar, but I could not place her. She was too preoccupied with her clipboard to notice me, but when she got closer, I noticed a large mole on the left side of her upper lip. There was only one girl whom I recalled with a mole just like that.

"You suffered a collapsed lung due to tuberculosis," she said in a more mature but familiar voice. "But your condition is now stable . . . Okhui."

"Mina?" I asked.

The intern looked at me with a warm smile. It was little Mina from under the bridge, now fully grown and no longer the emaciated child I'd known before. The doctor chuckled. "You two know each other?"

Mina nodded and silently mouthed in Korean that we would talk later. Her smile remained as she walked away with the medical team. True to her word, hours later, Mina returned. I noticed her once dull beige skin was now a healthy shade of golden brown, and she looked stunning in her white uniform.

With a gentle touch, Mina placed her hand on mine and said, "I thought you'd never wake up." Her coarse regional accent had vanished, and she now spoke in the standard Korean dialect. "I saw your medical records. You married a GI and have two children?"

I nodded.

"At first, I wasn't sure if it was you," Mina continued. "I had to hear your voice." Her voice choked with emotion as tears filled our eyes, and we held each other's hands tightly. But before I could ask where she had been all this time, she began to share her story.

"On the day of the storm, we heard a loud roar from the mountain. Suddenly, a massive wall of water came rushing down. Father and Donggwon quickly gathered our belongings, and we rushed to find higher ground. Remember the rosary I gave you?"

I nodded. Many years had passed, but I did not have the heart to tell her that my mother had thrown it over the cliff. She demonstrated such excitement as she spoke and even lifted her eyes upward in acknowledgment, or in communion with someone up there. I didn't want to burden her with any bad news.

"Well, my church had given me another one," she said, "which I'd kept in a box. But during the flood, the box drifted away. I tried so hard to reach for it, but it went down too fast."

Mina cleared her throat. "Father caught pneumonia and passed away one month later. I haven't seen my brother since the day Father died, but I was adopted by a nice Catholic family who sent me to medical school."

"You look so pretty in that uniform," I said softly. I meant what I said. She was beautiful, and her calm self-confidence lit up her entire personality.

Mina smiled. "Thank you." She pulled a brand-new rosary from beneath her uniform and showed it to me. It dazzled with bright orange beads. "Remember," she said, "always have faith."

I was captivated by her stories and the way she held her rosary. I shared a condensed version of my life, omitting the embarrassing parts involving Kim Gwangyeong and Hoja Ajumma. Mina's presence was comforting, and I knew she wouldn't love me any less after hearing about my past. However, the shame I'd felt before getting married still lingered inside me.

On the other hand, I admired her strong faith. As I lay in the hospital bed listening to her tell the story of her own survival, I wondered how Mina's faith had never wavered, even after she had suffered so much loss. Unlike my own life, Mina had lost everything—her parents, her home; yet somehow, she fulfilled her childhood dream of entering the medical profession. We chatted for a long while, exchanging stories and life lessons until she had to leave for an emergency and return to her duties. Before leaving, she declared, "I'll pray for your healing, God willing."

Sadly, that was the last time we spoke.

PART TWO

GOING TO AMERICA

SHORTLY BEFORE MY hospital discharge, a familiar voice inquired outside my room, "Is this Mrs. Lee's room?" My eyes lit up at the sight of Gordon carrying his Army-issued duffle bag. He had just arrived. As he entered, I noticed some changes in him: darker, puffier eyelids and a slightly larger belly. Something was amiss, and I couldn't help but wonder if he'd been drinking.

"Gordon?" I attempted to call out, but my voice came out as a strained whisper. Nevertheless, he heard me, dropped his bag, and rushed to my bedside, embracing me with a gentle kiss on my forehead.

"I came directly from the airport. I can't wait to see our daughter. How are Dennis and Oh-ma?"

Despite my lingering weakness, I managed a faint smile. Gordon, visibly relieved, took a calming breath before he spoke. "I spoke to the doctor on the phone. He said you need to go to an American hospital for further treatment. I can assist with the immigration paperwork."

With excitement bubbling within me, I felt an overwhelming sense of relief—the prospect of living in America might be closer than I thought.

Later that afternoon, Gordon went to see Mother to discuss my condition. I had a collapsed lung and required months of outpatient treatment. Unable to travel, I had to let Gordon and Dennis go to America first. As I pondered this, I realized my little boy would be the first in our family to live in America, and that brought me nothing but joy.

My visa was processed quickly. The main challenge would be the frequent hospital visits. I had three options: Honolulu, Hawaii; Denver, Colorado; and Phoenix, Arizona. I chose Fitzsimons General Hospital in Colorado. I used to listen to an American song called "Colorado Moon" in the music hall when I first met Kim. There was something about that song that always stirred a sense of romance within me.

Because of my illness, I couldn't care for my baby, so I had to leave Marylin behind. It saddened and frustrated me, but I held onto the belief that it would be worth the wait. Thankfully, Brother Yong stepped in and offered to care for her.

***

IN LATE OCTOBER, I was carried on a narrow stretcher onto a military cargo plane. The engine was extremely loud, and the wind so strong that in my exhausted and weakened state, I felt as though I'd returned to a war zone. However, what I saw on that plane was much worse.

The Vietnam War had inflicted unimaginable damage, and onboard that military aircraft, I saw some of that devastation up close. A small squadron of wounded soldiers was being transported on the same flight. My stomach turned from the pungent odor of their blood and sweat, which flooded my nostrils. Even though the medics had tried to close off the area from view, I could still see the injured men through an opening in the curtain.

One soldier had his head wrapped in gauze, and I could hear him groaning in pain throughout the entire flight. Another was wrapped from head to toe like an Egyptian mummy. Others had missing limbs with bandages that covered the rounded, eraser-shaped stubs that remained.

I'd always dreamt of flying to America, but the cargo plane flight filled me with apprehension. As nervous thoughts raced through my mind, a nurse checked my blood pressure and gave me pills with warm water. The medicine helped me relax, and I dozed off occasionally until our layover at Narita Air Base in Japan.

Soon, I would land in a brave new world, a realm of opportunity where I could provide my family with everything I could never have before. Money to spend, higher education for my children, and a permanent home for my family all danced in my dreams. My heart longed to establish deep roots in this unfamiliar land.

My children would become Americans. My mind swirled with thoughts of the future until I finally drifted into a deep slumber, carrying a sense of melancholic hope.

***

WHEN THE PLANE landed on American soil, I felt a newfound strength to stand on my own two feet after hours of lying down. My first steps outside stretched the numbness from my body as a nurse guided me toward a long, green bus on the tarmac—twice the size of any I'd seen in Korea. Soldiers from the flight followed me, led by hospital staff, onto the same bus.

The lyrics to "America the Beautiful" played in my head, and I sang softly to myself, "O beautiful for spacious skies, for amber waves of grain . . ." The skies were not just spacious but crystal blue, with rows of snow-capped mountains in the distance.

As the bus sped along the highway, I saw towering billboards advertising everything from Salem cigarettes and Coca-Cola to fast food and stylish clothing. The scent of lush pine trees drifted into the bus through the open windows, painting a hopeful picture of the new world ahead.

The bus slowed down when we passed through a small town, where I saw rows of little wooden houses painted in vibrant pinks, blues, and yellows nestled along the hillside. Above the hills were the snow-covered peaks of the Rocky Mountains. It was a scene right out of a greeting card. Finally, I understood what Americans meant when they claimed they lived in "God's country." God must have enjoyed creating this wonderful place.

***

AS THE BUS arrived at Fitzsimons General Hospital, the building's unique architecture immediately caught my eye. Yet, what truly stood out were the fiery red maple leaves dancing in the wind. After stepping off the bus, I took off my surgical mask and breathed in the fresh scent of American autumn.

This new, unfamiliar environment initially frightened me, but soon, I felt a comforting warmth, a healing sensation in the gentle autumn breeze. That night, as I attempted to sleep, the hospital room grew cooler. I looked toward the east window, and a series of images rushed through my mind: Mother's face, my little girl's big brown eyes, and my brothers, sisters, and neighbors from the village all appeared. I wondered if they were thinking of me, too.

A few days later, Gordon drove from his parents' home in Idaho to visit me with Dennis. When the nurse informed me of his arrival, I hurried through the hospital lawn toward his approaching Chevy, adjusting my cloth mask. Wearing it allowed me to go outside.

I noticed the back seat of Gordon's Chevy was filled with boxes of tools, light fixtures, and kitchen appliances, indicating he had been busy. From the passenger seat, Dennis spoke like an Americanized three-year-old. Upon exiting the car, he ran toward me, calling out in English, "Mommy!"

I embraced him, and the scent of a strawberry lollipop lingered on his breath. *He even smells American*, I thought. With curious giggles, Dennis playfully tugged at my mask as I repeatedly pulled it back into place. He thought it was a fun game. Slipping out of my arms, he toddled around, exploring the trees and grass in the courtyard.

He glanced back at me, asking, "Mommy, can I pee-pee on the grass?" It was the second time he had called me "Mommy" in perfect English. I marveled at how quickly he had learned a foreign language in just a few months. Taking him behind a tree to relieve himself, I felt immense pride in my little boy.

Unbridled joy filled me as I held Dennis's hand, but when I pulled down his pants, I noticed a sizable purple-red bruise on his buttocks. I turned to Gordon with an angry look as I pointed to the bruise.

Gordon explained, "The other day, he spilled some soda, so I had to punish him."

"He's still a baby. Why did you do that?" I kept my voice low so as not to upset Dennis. Oblivious to my tone, Dennis finished, picked a tiny yellow flower, and handed it to me with a chuckle.

"It's for my pretty mommy," he said, pulling down my mask again. "Mommy, I want to see your face!" I consoled myself with the hope that perhaps his daddy hadn't meant to hurt him. Gordon stayed silent, and I assumed he felt guilty.

We stood a few feet apart, as instructed, silently watching Dennis kneel among dandelions and wildflowers. Our visitation time passed swiftly, and I bid them farewell before being led back into the hospital.

RELIGIOUS AFFILIATION

MY DOCTORS WANTED to monitor my health closely after my arrival, so I was not allowed to visit home at first. This meant I had to miss my first American Christmas.

Fortunately, Gordon managed to visit after the holidays, and in early January, we sat in the doctor's office. The doctor and Gordon had a serious conversation, and Gordon grimly told me, "Doctor says you need a major operation."

We exchanged nervous glances as the doctor placed my X-ray film on the lightboard and turned it on. He continued to explain his findings, his voice solemn.

"Your lung has collapsed," the doctor said, trying to break the news gently as he tapped his pen on a clipboard. "We'll have to remove two-thirds of your lung, which will require six to eight hours of preparation and surgery."

He handed me a stack of medical documents for the surgery. As I glanced through the pages, I came across a line: Religious Affiliation. Initially, I left it blank, but after a moment, I proudly declared myself a Christian, hoping that declaring a connection with God on paper might help me get through the surgery. This choice was inspired by my childhood friend Mina's unwavering faith.

***

IN EARLY JANUARY, the doctors allowed me to go home for a while to be with my family before the operation. As we drove home, I noticed a field with numerous large buses parked in rows. Gordon explained they were mobile homes where people lived.

Puzzled, I asked, "Why would anyone want to live inside a vehicle?"

"It's temporary," Gordon reassured me. "I applied for base housing months ago, and we've been on the waiting list. In a few weeks, they should be ready for us to move in."

We parked in front of one of the mobile homes, and Gordon greeted our neighbor, Norman, a burly man with a Southern American drawl. I nodded politely, finding it hard to understand him. Meanwhile, Dennis came out of Norman's house wearing a red cape and proudly proclaiming himself as Superman.

My attention shifted to a crying bulldog tied to the trailer's hitch, struggling against a tight rope around its neck. I hurried to free the dog and questioned Gordon about it. He shrugged, saying it was the park's rule, but the dog, Bobby, didn't seem to mind.

I sighed and turned to inspect our new home. The exterior surprised me, but my concerns faded once I stepped inside. It had carpeted floors, unlike the clay floors with *ondolbang* heating in Korean homes. The furniture was familiar, albeit closer together in the compact space. Despite the clutter from Gordon's moving boxes, I was delighted to see a small, well-decorated Christmas tree in the corner.

Gordon introduced me to a dishwasher, which baffled me, so I decided to wash dishes by hand. I marveled at the soap-filled cabinet and the warm water from the spigot. There were machines for everything, including a washer and dryer.

Our brand-new refrigerator was stocked with food, and Gordon pulled out a "TV dinner" from the top cabinet. He explained that you're supposed to eat it while watching TV.

With all these incredible inventions, I was overjoyed to be with my family at last and hugged Gordon in gratitude. The next morning, I savored my first American breakfast outside the hospital: scrambled eggs and bacon. It was a delightful experience.

***

A WEEK LATER, I returned to the hospital for a follow-up visit. Over the next few days, the doctors prepared me for surgery, explaining what foods I could and could not eat. I would basically be put on a liquid diet.

On the day of the surgery, four nurses helped me onto a plastic bed. That's when pangs of nervous tension set in. My chest tightened, and my hands felt cold and clammy. I closed my eyes to focus on my breathing as instructed while the nurses wheeled me out of the room. I could hear a series of heavy thuds as my bed was pushed through swinging doors. With my eyes closed tightly, I sensed a row of bright yellow lights switching on overhead and shining through my eyelids. My body stiffened in the chill of the operating room.

Then, I heard the clink and clatter of medical instruments being placed on metal tables.

Feeling a sharp prick in my arm, I opened my eyes. A young intern leaned over me, appearing perplexed as he tried to find a vein for the IV. After several attempts, he dabbed my blood-flecked skin with a cloth and secured the inserted needle with tape. A warm fluid gushed up my arm and into my body. The faces of the doctors quickly melted into one, and my mind slid into darkness.

Then I saw my husband's face smiling at me.

Though it seemed like I had my eyes closed for a few minutes, Gordon told me the surgery had lasted nearly six hours. My body felt like it was rising out of a murky haze. I desperately struggled to get off the table but was immediately paralyzed by pain, as if a military Jeep had just run over my chest.

I moaned and winced as a nurse administered an injection. Tubes protruded from the gauze covering my emaciated upper torso, with more tubes connected to my ribs, draining blood into a large plastic container.

Despite this daunting ordeal, my physical recovery held a glimmer of hope. The worst part was the nightmares, which had haunted me long before my illness. During the nights, I found myself running from shadowy figures that loomed over me—perhaps my ancestors?

During my recovery, these shadows seemed more real and menacing. The pain from reality seeped into my dreams, and I could sense these dark figures closing in behind me. But a bright glow appeared in front of me, and as I rushed toward it, I saw Mother on her knees, praying for me.

Hearing her words brought me solace.

***

DESPITE MY FRAIL appearance, I could be discharged in ten days if I committed to physical exercise. I was moved to another ward for monitored breathing exercises during the rest of my stay.

Every day, the physical therapist had me blow up a balloon to strengthen my lungs. It was initially challenging, and I felt close to fainting after each half-hour session. However, I persevered, and by the final therapy session, I successfully inflated the balloon.

When Gordon brought me home, I was in for a pleasant surprise. He had relocated us to a spacious three-bedroom residence on the military base, as the housing he applied for months ago had finally become available. We eagerly planned to have additional space for Mother and Marylin when their visas were processed.

It was something truly wonderful to look forward to.

***

WHEN WE FIRST got to our house, a young blonde babysitter brought Dennis outside. She was a tiny, round-faced lady, and her head barely reached my shoulders.

"Is dot your *mutter*?" she said with a German accent. Dennis nodded. In a quaint manner, I introduced myself and thanked her for watching Dennis. My boy led me up three stone steps toward our new home.

Directly behind the front screen door, there was a kitchen. I was thoroughly impressed by how large it was compared to the kitchen in our trailer. Around the sink were rows of cabinet spaces where I could now display my pots and pans. The stove had four burners powered by gas, which I had never seen before, except in American magazine ads. Gordon demonstrated by turning a knob that released the gas, which he then lit by striking a match. A ring of blue flames miraculously appeared around the central metal disc.

I gasped, grateful that Gordon had made all this possible. Everything about America was greater than I had anticipated. Relaxing inside the house each day, I continued my breathing exercises and regularly walked our bulldog, Bobby, around the base. I also made sure to keep up with my doctor's appointments.

One day, after my afternoon walk, I received a phone call from my doctor. "Mrs. Lee, there's something I need to tell you. Your urine test came back positive."

"What it means . . . *positive?*" I asked.

"It means you're pregnant." There was a moment of silence, then he cleared his throat and said, "You're going to have a baby."

The news took me by surprise. I had just recovered from major surgery; I could never have expected to have another child so soon. When Gordon returned home, I shared the news, and he was elated. To be honest, I was not ready for another child. But he was so happy, I could not tell him that.

MOTHER PONG COMES TO AMERICA

FEBRUARY 1967. NEARLY five months had passed since I'd last seen my family, and some nights, I wept for them. The thought of Mother and my siblings struggling in Korea without my care tore at my heart, often reducing me to tears. My yearning for my baby girl was especially intense.

Gordon, understanding my pain, took decisive action. He wrote a heartfelt letter to President Lyndon B. Johnson, pleading for Mother and Marylin's case. While we weren't overly optimistic about the outcome, we believed it was worth a try.

To our immense relief, we received a letter soon after confirming that Mother had been granted her visa by the U.S. Embassy in Korea. I felt a deep sense of gratitude, wishing I could personally thank the president for this wonderful news.

On February 22, 1967, I received a phone call informing me that my mother and baby daughter had arrived at Denver Airport.

Dennis and I eagerly waited at the customs gate, wondering about little Marylin's growth and appearance.

Among the disembarking passengers, I finally spotted a middle-aged Korean woman holding the hand of a little girl in a bright red sweater. Overjoyed, I ran toward them with outstretched arms.

As soon as Mother saw me, she exclaimed, "You've lost so much weight! We were all so worried about your surgery." Marylin, in her excitement, tried to break free from Mother's grasp, so I held out my arms to take her. While I cradled my daughter, Mother shared her travel adventures, including getting lost during layovers due to the language barrier at the airport.

Almost halfway to the terminal, I shared the big news with her. "I'm pregnant."

Mother gasped, concerned for my well-being. I reassured her as we made our way to the terminal. Her worries instantly transformed into tears of joy, relieved that she had finally made it to America.

I couldn't help but express my happiness, running my hands over Marylin's smooth, plump, milky face. Marylin, noticing her older brother, pointed at Dennis with a joyful laugh. We then proceeded to the baggage claim area to collect their luggage.

As we all piled into Gordon's Chevy, Mother confided in me that she was feeling sad about being separated from the rest of our family.

"I told everyone I was leaving; I believe all of Korea knows I'm going to America," she said with a bittersweet laugh. "I contacted your father, and he said, 'Don't forget me.' And as for your brothers, Jeong is struggling with his wife and four kids; Gyeong is looking for work; Yeong just got divorced; Yong works at his martial arts studio; and Chang is living with Okyon."

"I'll have to work harder if you want me to help them," I assured her, declaring that the rest of the family would soon follow. "How are my dogs?"

Mother chuckled. "They're fine. Your Aunty Deoki is taking care of them."

Although she appeared in good spirits, her mood changed when I asked about the money from our *jeonse*—the deposit on her house—she got quiet and avoided the subject. I suspected that she had given the deposit to my siblings, but it felt pointless to press the issue further.

***

THE RIDE HOME felt endless to Mother, and the air was much fresher than our old hometown. Light snow fell as we arrived at the base, and it drifted into Mother's open car window. As expected, she was exhausted but overjoyed and amazed by our American house—its size, spacious rooms, and all the kitchen appliances.

Marylin eagerly explored the rooms, with Dennis trailing behind. Giving Mother a grand tour, I led her to her bedroom, where she hung a small jade cross on the bedpost. After her long journey, she lay down to rest and slept for most of the day.

Meanwhile, Gordon's stepfather, Patrick, and his mother, Virginia, made the journey from Idaho. Gordon treated the whole family to a fishing trip in the Rocky Mountains, where we caught rainbow trout. Additionally, I had my first experience at a drive-in theater. These moments marked the wonderful beginning of our life as an American family, tinged with a sense of nostalgia.

***

WITHIN A FEW months, Gordon and I purchased a new house in a new suburban development close to Fitzsimon Hospital. Our home was a one-story "art deco" building with three bedrooms and a two-car garage, surrounded by a red brick wall. In the rear, there was a spacious backyard, which, at the moment, lay empty.

Mother and I spent our days together, taking care of the house and the children, and we would often entertain ourselves by keeping each other abreast of anything going on in our lives.

"I thank Jesus for protecting our family." She would often talk about the Lord and His blessings in an exuberant, positive manner, even more so than she did back home. And in addition to her spiritual growth, Mother started devoting time to a new hobby—gardening.

One morning, I got out of bed to find her kneeling in a square patch of dirt she had cleared in our backyard. She tended that patch for weeks, and one day, little buds of hydrangeas and vegetables appeared.

The first crop grew quickly, aided by her patient and gentle hands meticulously yanking the weeds and tilling the dirt. Soon, vivid colors and wonderful textures filled every inch of earth. Hilariously, I once saw her give a thumbs-up to a massive butternut squash for growing so large. It was nice to see how much Mother enjoyed her new hobby.

With our dog Bobby at my side, I would get on my knees to help water her plants. We often worked together, and by the end of spring, our neighbors took notice; many came by to look at her produce and consult with her on their own gardens.

Mother would share the fruits of her labor with them and give them gardening tips, using broken English and elaborate hand gestures. But Mother's garden was not the only thing bearing fruit in our household.

BORN IN THE USA

IN OCTOBER 1967, I brought home my third bundle of joy wrapped in a blue blanket—my first American-born child. We named him Patrick after Gordon's father, and within a few short weeks, my baby's facial features began to resemble Gordon's. Like his big brother Dennis, Patrick had a contagious laugh. Unfortunately, he was sensitive to the cold and would hiccup every time I laid him in the cradle, so I constantly had to pick him up to keep him warm. This never got tiresome because I delighted in kissing his chubby cheeks.

With my medical problems fading, I considered myself blessed to be alive. The entire ordeal made me determined to find purpose in my life. At night, while I stood over Patrick's crib, I pondered my purpose in this world.

"Sleep well, baby Patrick," I whispered. "Tomorrow will be a brand-new day."

***

WHEN I LEFT Korea, I thought life in America would be much easier. I had imagined that a husband and father with a full-time job could provide for his family. More so, I had believed that a wife and mother only needed to do housework and raise the children, but I quickly learned a life like that only existed on the television shows we watched, like *Leave It to Beaver*.

Within a few months of purchasing our home, Gordon built a wet bar and refurbished our basement as a lounge with an additional bathroom for guests. Unfortunately, Gordon's salary was barely enough to feed a family of six after all these renovations. He had to take a second job as a part-time cashier at a small convenience store, which allowed us to get by, but our struggles weren't over yet.

One afternoon, a neighbor invited me to attend an Avon sales seminar. When I got home, Bobby started barking more aggressively than usual. A large moving truck had backed into our driveway, and two men in matching shirts knocked on our front door. As soon as I opened the door, the larger man showed me a piece of paper and indicated where he needed me to sign.

I could read a few words, but not enough to understand what the paper was about. It was obvious by their serious demeanor that they represented a large company. Despite my confusion, I signed the paper right away, which prompted the men to come into our house and survey our furniture. Mother sat on the couch with the children while they informed me that they were going to repossess everything due to late payments.

I gasped, trying to find the right words in English. Mother buried her head in her hands while the children panicked and started crying.

"I am so sorry," I pleaded. "I need a few more days. I tell my husband." My distress caused me to stumble over my words. "Give me please one more chance."

"I'm sorry, ma'am," said the smaller man, "but we're just doing our jobs."

The larger man looked long and hard at Mother and the children. When the smaller man turned toward the doorway, the larger man asked if he could use our phone to call his employer. After talking for a few minutes, he turned back to me. "The office manager says you got one week to make the payment, or else we gotta come back."

I nodded. "I promise. I'll pay in one week."

I felt hopelessly angry and humiliated. When Gordon returned home late that night, I snapped at him, shaking my fist in his face, "Why didn't you tell me you never pay for the furniture?"

Gordon did not pretend to be shocked. He lowered his head and grumbled under his breath. Since I had paid cash for everything in Korea, I did not understand the concept of a credit card or "minimum monthly payments."

But at that point, I did not care. "Look at me!" I screamed, but he avoided my gaze.

"I don't want to talk about it," he grumbled, then retreated to our bedroom. I followed him, but he did not acknowledge me. Overwhelmed with anxiety, I told him I was willing to look for work.

"I need to look for a job someplace where I don't need that much skill," I explained. "I can provide money for our family, same as you." But having attended the Avon seminar, I realized that sales would not work for me—not with my limited English.

Gordon muttered under his breath, "I admit it—I overspent." A frown darkened his face, and his downcast eyes were full of shame.

A few days later, Gordon delivered even more surprising news. "I signed up for a year overseas in Germany, but there's one condition—I have to spend two months in Vietnam. But the military will increase my pay."

I calmed myself, putting the thought of the Vietnam War out of my mind. "Perhaps we could accompany you to Germany?"

When I suggested it to Mother, she objected, pointing out how hard it would be to relocate with her and three children. She was right. Dennis had just started preschool and needed a stable home, so I gave in, telling Gordon, "Just go by yourself. I can look for a job while you are gone."

Sitting in his soon-to-be-repossessed armchair, he appeared helpless, struggling to respond. I wondered if he felt weighed down by our financial problems and shipping out to Germany was his solution. Or was it an escape?

In either case, I needed to learn to drive so I could function on my own. Before Gordon left for Germany, I asked him to teach me. During my first driving lesson, I hit a large tree, but thankfully, the impact did not damage the car—much. Still, that minor fender bender was enough to make it the last lesson he'd ever give me. I had to enroll in a driving school shortly afterward.

Because of the added expenses, I asked Gordon if he could ask his mother for some money to pay our bills. It took a week before he finally gave in. It was the cost of gas and maintenance on the car that convinced him.

Gordon continued working his two jobs until the day he shipped out while I searched for one for myself. The day after Gordon left for Germany, our family gathered at the breakfast table. I poured myself a hot cup of tea and sat down to browse the employment ads in the *Rocky Mountain News*. Circling the ads that looked promising, I traveled to each one via taxi, leaving applications in every grocery store and restaurant from East Colfax Boulevard to West Colfax Boulevard.

Unfortunately, my conversational English skills weren't good enough, despite having worked as an English tutor in Korea.

***

SEVERAL WEEKS PASSED since Gordon had left without a single phone call. At night, I often found Mother praying at her bedside. One time, she began with, "How are we going to bring the rest of the family from Korea?"

The anguish in her prayers over our separation from my siblings did not sit well with me. I felt as though she cared more about the children left behind in Korea than the ones living in our home, but it would hurt her to tell her that.

So, I swallowed my feelings and let her pray in peace.

THE TIKI TORCH

EVENTUALLY, I FOUND work at a Chinese restaurant called the Tiki Torch, but in truth, I only lasted one night. Before my first night, I carefully studied the menu and memorized all the foreign names of their drinks. I even practiced by walking around the living room in my dark green *cheongsam* uniform.

The restaurant was designed in a Polynesian style with a full bar next to a small stage resembling a grass shack with a fake thatched roof. I had studied how to add garnishes for their two specialty drinks. Chi Chi's required little paper umbrellas, a pineapple wedge, and a maraschino cherry, and the Tropical Itch, a slice of lime with a small backscratcher.

Unfortunately, upon serving those drinks to my first customers, my entire tray—two tall glasses, straws, cherries, limes, pineapple wedges, paper umbrellas, and a backscratcher—toppled over and drenched my first customers' heads. I was fired immediately and given a few dollars for the night's work while they called for a cab to take me home.

I waited outside for half an hour as the air grew colder. When my cab approached, I flagged him from across the street. The middle-aged Caucasian driver rolled down his window.

"Waitin' for a taxi, ma'am?" I nodded and opened the back door. My purse went in first, then I flung myself inside. The driver asked where I was headed as he flipped down the mirror on his front visor.

"Can you take me to my home, 4980 Troy Street?" I asked. The driver turned on his meter and sent the destination to his dispatcher. I struggled to conceal the distress in my voice. "It's in Montebello. I just got fired from my waitress job."

He nodded. Then, I lowered my head and cried quietly. We pulled away from the curb, and the view of the Tiki Torch slowly faded into the distance. The driver looked at me from the rear-view mirror, revealing his soft, sympathetic eyes.

"I know a few places you can work," he began. I could hear the sympathy in his voice. "By the way, call me Anthony. Any time you want a ride, just give me a call."

When we reached my home, he took out a piece of notebook paper from the glove compartment and wrote down his phone number.

"Look," he began. "I got a friend—owns this club downtown called the Body Shop."

I hesitated. "I'm no good with cars," I told him.

He laughed. "Not that kind of Body Shop. Look, you just lost your job, but you can make good money waiting tables there. For tonight, just pay me for the gas, and we'll call it even."

I nodded gratefully. As soon as he left, Mother greeted me at the door. Her expression turned sour the moment she saw me. "You smell like alcohol, but you don't seem drunk," she said as I threw my bag on the floor.

"I don't feel like talking," I snapped. "Period!" I headed straight to the bathroom. Mother followed, prying me for information.

But I had already shut the door on her.

Several days later, hunched over the "Help Wanted" ads in the kitchen once more, Mother waved two letters in front of my face. One was from Korea. The other was from Oksoon, who was living in Pennsylvania. Mother opened the letter from Korea first and asked me to read it for her.

"They need money—as usual," I told her bluntly, then explained, "Okyon wants to know when we can send some money for their immigration paperwork." I sighed. "They don't understand our situation. They think I came to America and immediately struck it rich."

Mother said, "I would like to see all of you together again."

I opened the second letter and read it. My heart sank a little.

"Oksoon is getting a divorce," I told her. "She wants to visit us before she moves to Japan."

"Hope she is still clean," Mother said. I could see the frustration in her eyes. Feeling overwhelmed, I got up and stared out the window, grumbling to myself. How could my damned sister even think of staying with us? After all these years?

"What's the matter now?" Mother asked, becoming annoyed.

I retorted, "Oksoon never did anything for the family."

I refrained from responding further. Oksoon cared only for herself and her drug habit. I seriously did not think she deserved our help.

In contrast, I felt differently about my brothers. Despite their uncaring attitudes toward me in the past, I held no resentment toward them. I understood the hardships they had endured. Even so, I simply could not imagine how I could help any of them when I was barely making a living for my own family.

Burdened by this crushing struggle, I reached into my pocket and took out the piece of paper Anthony had given me.

I told Mother, "I have to apply for a job."

THE BODY SHOP

STANDING ON THE sidewalk, the first thing I noticed was a revolving neon sign that read, "The Body Shop." To calm my nerves, I took a deep breath before walking through the thick wooden doors. The entryway contained intervals of shadow and sparkling lights, producing the effect of night turning into day. The lobby resembled the type of burlesque house I'd seen in American movies, such as *Gypsy*.

Photos of exotic dancers lined the glass cabinets mounted on the jet-black bulletin board at the head of the walkway. A central poster featured the headliner with the caption, "The Heavenly Body, The Blonde Bombshell, Tel Starr!"

Across the lobby walls, more signs had been set up: "Eighteen Scan-delicious Girls!" "Continuous Shows from 2:00 pm to Midnight!" "The Sensational Music of the Jo Jo Williams Trio!" "Gene Temple and his 'World on a String' Marionettes!"

So many exclamation marks. They must all be famous. Just then, a young Hispanic man in a black tuxedo approached me, beaming with a big smile as though he was laughing at a private joke. Although we had never met before, he spoke to me in a familiar and casual manner.

"Hey, how are you doing, *mamacita*?" he said. "Anthony told us you were coming." He looked me up and down. "He didn't lie. You're one groovy chick."

I extended my hand and introduced myself. "My name is Suzie Wong."

"Name's Martin, follow me. I'll give you an application." He continued but spoke so fast that I could not understand him, so I simply nodded and smiled, feigning understanding.

"You are hiring waitress?" I asked. We walked to the side of the main double doors into a hallway.

Martin turned to me and said, "To be honest, we don't need another waitress, but we're always short on dancers."

We circled the perimeter of the main showroom. I watched as a six-piece band set up on the right side of the stage. The red velvet curtains opened, and a thick, smoky haze floated over a colorful array of stage lights.

A curvy Black woman with her bare legs exposed sat on a high stool on the large proscenium stage. Her hair was styled in an afro, which I had never seen before except in American magazines.

I could not understand what she said, but I assumed she was doing a stand-up comedy routine since the audience was laughing loudly. I was pretty sure her jokes were especially raunchy.

"It's no big deal, dig?" Martin spoke to me as though he were giving me a sales pitch. "You go up on that stage, strut around in your high heels, and dance—that's all there is to it. If I was a chick, I'd be making money doing it, too. Say, would ya step into my office for a sec?"

Following him down a squeaky set of stairs to a corner room in the basement, I paused only to notice the crooked hinges on the office door. Martin pulled out an application from his desk drawer and gave me the phone number of a dressmaker named Carmen.

"Best costumes in town," he praised her. "All the girls go to Carmen." I had to wonder how good she really was if all the women wore so little clothing.

I quickly scanned the application and informed him that I'd need a few days to think it over. On my way out, I stopped in the back of the showroom to watch the band perform a James Brown song with an unmistakable Motown beat—I quickly recognized it from record albums that Gordon and I had bought for our children.

Despite my hesitation, Martin was correct. I could make so much more on the stage than waiting tables below it. I could even pay off our family's debts and bring the rest of my family to America. Plus, I actually had some dance experience.

Upon returning home, I skipped cooking dinner and rang up Carmen to discuss my costume. In person, Carmen turned out to be a tall, vivacious woman with strikingly long lashes and a flawless figure accentuated by her impressive legs. She generously offered to create some designs for me without any extra charges and even gave me a sneak peek at her dance moves.

"Follow my lead, *mija*," she declared. "This is how a showgirl walks." With confidence, she demonstrated a sassy strut. "Let's work on your stance, and then we'll get into some bumps and grinds." While I didn't quite grasp the exact meaning of those terms, they did sound intriguing.

"By the way, you've got beautiful hair," Carmen complimented. "You should make it a part of your act. Just bend over and flip it back, like this." She proceeded to demonstrate a sensual hair flip that resembled something out of a Rita Hayworth film.

Her graceful demonstration left me in awe, as if I were watching Rita Hayworth in *Gilda*. I chuckled nervously but couldn't help but entertain the thought that I had always dreamt of becoming a professional dancer. Carmen went on to explain how some burlesque dancers had risen to stardom, earning substantial paychecks. As I envisioned the possibilities of fame, a wide smile stretched across my face. I could see myself becoming a headlining act, opening doors to bigger stages, perhaps even American movies.

***

ON MY FIRST night at work, I was about to enter the club when a young Black man carrying a small brown bag stood in front of the door. I invited him inside, but he thumbed his cheek to indicate his skin color. I quickly realized he wouldn't be allowed in. I forgot that White Americans tended to discriminate against folks with darker skin.

"My wife, Cleo, works here," he said. "Would you please give this to her?" I nodded, realizing I would've been treated the same way had I not been working there.

I made my way inside. Behind the swinging front door, I was impressed to see Martin greeting me in a well-tailored suit. He escorted me into a medium-sized dressing room just above the stage. The makeup counter had eight seats with a long mirror framed with vanity lights. I noticed a vast array of cosmetics, brushes, wigs, a rosary, and odd props on the makeup counter.

I felt a bit nauseous from all the different mixed fragrances in the room, but I made my way toward the mirror labeled Cleo. I gave the woman sitting there the brown bag, telling her it was from her husband. She took it with a knowing smirk.

At that moment, I heard Martin calling my name from the dressing room door. I hurried to meet him, putting the disconcerting experience I'd just had with Cleo's husband out of my mind.

"You go up first, at the top of the second show," Martin said. "Eight o'clock sharp. Got that?" I nodded. "Oh, and break a leg."

I winced. "Break what?" I asked nervously.

One of the dancers, a young Mexican woman, playfully leaned into me with a cigarette dangling from her mouth and explained that it was bad luck to say "good luck" before a show, so theater folks traditionally say "break a leg" instead.

"By the way, I'm Gloria." She extended her hand.

With that, Martin left us to change.

Attempting to find some changing space, I stepped behind a wardrobe rack. Within minutes, seven other dancers occupied every available makeup station. I sat on an extra chair, awaiting my turn while taking in the diversity of this group. At the age of twenty-five, two individuals appeared almost a decade older than me. The rest of them appeared to be around my age.

On the far side of the room, I spotted the headliner—a short blonde named Tel Starr. Close up, I noticed that she looked older than her billboard photo, with makeup piled on to conceal wrinkles. Tel Starr casually picked up items from her makeup table, discussing her recent breast implant surgery performed by a Dr.

White, and even arched her back to show off the scars. Though her implants might have looked impressive on stage, up close, she looked as though she had swallowed two rice bowls.

Seeing her alterations stirred butterflies in my stomach, intensifying my nerves. I reminded myself that I was now a professional dancer and should not be nervous, but that didn't quell my anxiety. This audience and dance routine were unfamiliar territory, making me increasingly restless. Unable to sit still, I leaned against the wall and raised my left leg toward my chest to release some pent-up energy, instantly drawing the attention of the other girls.

"Lawd have mercy!" Tel Starr exclaimed. "We've got ourselves a real bona fide dancer here." Laughter filled the room just as another girl rushed in—a tall brunette with an athletic build. She stopped directly in front of me.

"Whadda-we got here? An Oriental cutie!" She remarked with a wink before promptly undressing in front of the wardrobe rack. "I got stuck pumping gas for six big rigs."

Gloria told me, "That's Tracy. She pumps gas." She then proceeded to imitate Tracy's mannerisms by flexing her muscles as she pantomimed filling a gas tank. I never knew women could be employed at gas stations.

While fully undressed, Tracy complimented how my dress highlighted the shine of my dark hair. She hastily put on a sexy cowgirl outfit and gave me another wink before heading toward the stage.

I turned away and noticed Gloria wincing when she spotted a large purple bruise on Tel Star's left arm.

"Oh, not again!" Gloria exclaimed.

"It ain't nothin'," Tel Starr mumbled audibly. She reached into her purse, pulled out a rolled marijuana joint, and lit it up.

"Don't mind us, babe," she said. I didn't respond.

***

ONCE I WAS ready to go on stage, I kept my full attention on the jazz band. When I heard the drummer launch into a solo, I made my way toward the wings and watched as the emcee, Thad Swift, made his opening remarks.

He certainly looks different from his picture in the lobby. His once-blonde hair had turned gray, appearing white under the spotlight. His cream-colored suit made him look somewhat distinguished, but the cigarette dangling from his mouth tarnished that image.

Tonight, ladies and gentlemen, prepare yourselves for a special treat," Thad announced. "When we opened The Body Shop, we wanted to dazzle with acts from every corner of the globe. And tonight, fresh off the Orient Express from the enchanting Far East, I present to you . . . the one and only . . . Suuuu-zieeee Wong!"

That was my cue. Then, the band played a flourish of instruments. "Let's make her feel extra special!" Thad declared. "Give it up for our Oriental cutie! Suuuu-zieeee Wong!"

The drummer beat loudly between Thad's announcements. "Once again!" Then, a drumroll.

The crowd started to applaud and whistle. Once I took the stage, the light hit my eyes so hard I could barely see any faces in the crowd, though I could hear the rising volume of the clapping and whistling.

I froze in an awkward position, standing centerstage in the smoke-filled theater. Then, the music began. It sounded like a simplified Chinese flower drum song, except with saxophones, though it was barely recognizable from the record album I had used for rehearsals. A dozen questions flooded my mind: *Should I launch into a ballet move? Maybe a Korean dance routine? A combination of both?*

Spontaneously, I went with the combination, starting with a tendu plié, then leaping, twirling, and segueing into a faux Korean dance. Allowing the music to carry me, I pranced around the entire space like a young colt.

While focusing on the rhythm of the music, I was able to shut out the crowd. But when the band slowed down for the final measure of the song, I realized I had failed to remove a single article of clothing.

The music stopped as I ended my dance. I had expected applause, but instead, there was complete silence. My heart began to hammer until I heard some scattered clapping. A single voice shouted from the audience, "Take it off! Take it off!" followed by a barrage of whistles.

Someone else shouted, "Hey! We didn't come here to see a ballerina!"

I must have stood center stage like a deer in headlights for only a few seconds, but under the heat of the lights, it felt like hours. My face turned red, and I felt genuinely humiliated. I thought, *What have I gotten myself into?*

That's when my dance training kicked in once more, and I returned to performance mode. I took in a long, deep breath, then turned toward the band, crooking my finger to cue them. The musicians tittered and started playing a second, slower number.

Moving toward the lip of the stage, I slowly unrolled my gloves one at a time and threw them in the direction of a man smoking his cigar, causing a raucous cascade of laughter. Borrowing a technique I had learned from Carmen, I slowed down my movements to match the tempo of the music and exaggerated the motions of undressing.

Pushing aside my shame, I slowly removed my kimono top, swung it in the air, and threw it on the side of the stage. By law, dancers were required to wear pasties, which felt uncomfortable in the dressing room, but on stage, they felt free and liberating.

The audience roared as I sashayed offstage. When I reached the edge of the curtains, Thad grabbed me by my shoulders. "You were sensational, Suzie!" he said. "Look, your first set went a bit rough, but the audience seemed to like it! You're a real natural! Keep it up!"

I nodded with a slight smile, pretending not to understand his compliments. But deep down inside, it felt exhilarating to be desired as a dancer. Still, part of me questioned the nature of this job. Plus, I knew it would have to be a secret, so I decided to keep my costume and makeup at The Body Shop. After every show, I would change back to my normal clothes before going home. Admittedly, there were a couple of times I almost got caught.

One night, Mother asked why I needed to cover the surgery scar on my back with a thick layer of foundation. So, of course, I told her my cocktail uniform was backless—she had no problem believing that.

THE SHOW MUST GO ON

A FEW WEEKS later, I dreamt I stood in the middle of my living room, looking out through a rain-spattered window. A middle-aged woman dressed in black stepped out of a long black limousine in front of my house; her face was a blur. This limo stretched over an entire block, complete with gold-plated hubcaps. It reminded me of the hearse that took Grandma Seokbuni away.

Looking closer, I somehow knew that the deceased inside was fellow dancer Tel Starr. I could see her pallid face beckoning me in front of my window.

"It's time," the woman in black said out loud. I told her I wasn't leaving, then I woke up drenched in sweat.

What an odd dream, I thought.

***

THE FOLLOWING NIGHT, when I arrived at work, I found Gloria and the other girls huddled in the dressing room. Gloria held a rosary in the middle of a silent prayer.

"May she rest in peace in God's grace," she said, and the girls responded with a heartfelt "Amen."

Curious about what had happened, I asked Gloria. Sadly, she shared the news that Tel Starr and her new husband, a man from Hawaii, had been found dead in her bedroom in what appeared to be a murder-suicide.

That evening, Thad made an announcement to the crowd, informing them that Tel Starr would no longer be performing at The Body Shop. Soon after, Martin approached me and asked if I could take over Tel's spot, which meant they needed professional photographs of me, and my headshot would replace Tel's in the lobby.

Thad privately explained to me that there was an old saying in show business: "The show must go on."

And it did.

My opening act drew more customers to The Body Shop than ever before. In my brief time as a dancer, I had suddenly become popular. Martin, pleased with my unexpected popularity, encouraged me to join the American Guild of Variety Artists (AGVA) because a union could offer me job security and higher pay. Martin's father—a talent agent—would earn a percentage on my membership once I signed with him.

Soon, I earned enough from union pay and an increased salary to clear my family's debts. I was even able to buy a brand-new American car—a Ford Mustang—and still had money to send for my sister and brothers in Korea.

When Mother saw my car, she was overcome with joy. "You must be a very popular waitress!" she exclaimed.

***

ON NOVEMBER 15, 1968, a significant milestone occurred. I finally obtained my U.S. citizenship. With this newfound status, I could finally start the process of sponsoring my siblings' emigration from Korea. Gordon told me how proud he was of me and that he would assist in any way he could. I had already acquired his signed affidavit of support, though it needed to be signed by more than one U.S. citizen. With my own signature, we were able to change Mother's visitor visa to a permanent green card.

Although immigration law stipulated that siblings could sponsor one another, that rule wasn't going to be enough to bring them over. We needed to apply for chain migration, the process in which an immigrant sponsors other family members, who then sponsor more family members. Additionally, the law required a parent to bring their own child over, so I depended on Mother to sign those necessary papers.

While waiting for my siblings to arrive, we replaced our worn-out furniture with new furniture. Our financial worries were gone for the time being, but other problems would spring up like the weeds in our front garden.

GORDON'S HOMECOMING

EARLY ONE EVENING, Mother called while I was at work to tell me Gordon had returned home. He had been gone ten months, and I was uncertain how I should tell him about my new career.

Anxious to see him, I rushed home. Sadly, Gordon looked exhausted—he had bags under his eyes and had gained at least an additional ten pounds.

"You got a new TV?" he asked suspiciously. "And new furniture?" It surprised me to hear him start off our conversation that way since we hadn't seen each other in nearly a year.

"She is waitress—good money job," Mother interrupted in broken English.

Purposely ignoring her, I took my husband aside. "What happened? I thought you were still deployed." He only grunted an unintelligible answer.

During the first two nights after Gordon's return, he kept tossing and turning in his sleep, waking up drenched in sweat. The situation escalated on the third night when he woke in a panic, screaming. Something was pulling him into a dark corner, leaving me feeling utterly helpless. I even noticed he'd shown no affection to his beloved dog, Bobby, since his arrival.

"Honey, is something wrong?" I asked, taking hold of his shivering body. He dismissed it as a bad dream and said nothing else. I asked him again why he had returned home earlier than scheduled, but he still would not tell me.

The following day, I took the initiative to speak with Gordon's doctor to gain some clarity. The doctor diagnosed Gordon with post-traumatic stress disorder (PTSD) due to his exposure to a chemical called Agent Orange during his time in Vietnam. The severity of his symptoms had led to his early return home and the need for professional treatment.

Though I was happy that he had returned safely, I continued to be concerned about my husband's condition. I asked Martin if he would allow me to take three weeks off. He would only approve two. At the same time, I found myself faced with the challenge of revealing my occupation as a burlesque dancer, which I wasn't prepared to disclose to Gordon.

Truthfully, I wasn't ashamed of dancing. On the contrary, this job afforded me the chance to make real life-changing plans. I could go back to school and pursue a degree in addition to raising three little children. I was also in the process of helping my siblings emigrate from Korea, so there was no way I would quit now. But I knew, sooner or later, I would have to be honest and tell my husband the truth.

Fortunately, or perhaps unfortunately, the choice would be made for me. It started at breakfast when Gordon sat down to read the morning paper. He had just brewed a fresh pot of coffee and poured himself a tall mug when I sat down to eat with him. Mother was preparing breakfast for the children.

As Gordon flipped through the newspaper, his gaze landed on the local section, and my heart sank as I saw it, too—the half-page advertisement for The Body Shop. It was impossible to miss. Every fiber of my being screamed, "Turn the page! Turn the page!"

But I couldn't utter a single sound, paralyzed by the fear of the truth being exposed. Gordon's face quickly turned white as a sheet. Immediately, the corner of his left eye started twitching, and the coffee cup in his hand started to shake.

I patted him on the back. "Do you need to see a doctor?"

"A doctor? Look! Look at this!" He waved the newspaper in front of me and demanded an answer.

For a split second, I froze, then faintly replied, "That's not me. Maybe somebody looks like me."

"It says right here!" he started in on me. "Suzie Wong! The name you used to call yourself! Don't tell me that's not you!"

I stood up, stunned.

"Your picture is all over the *Rocky Mountain News*. What the hell am I going to tell my family? I'm married to a goddamn stripper!"

"I'm not a stripper!" I snapped. "I'm a showgirl. I don't even take my clothes off." I paused, then added, "Not all of them."

Gordon shook his head. "How could you?"

His reaction enraged me. He had some nerve to yell at me about my job. "You remember those bill collectors?" I reminded him. "They tried to take the kids' piano and all the furniture! How else could we keep up with the bills if I wasn't dancing?"

Furious, I did not wait for him to argue back. I quickly ran into our bedroom, locked the door, fell into bed, and pushed my face into a pillow. By that time, my children must have been watching from the door because I heard Mother ushering them away, berating them in a whispered voice.

The next day, an awkward silence pervaded the house. Even the kitchen was quiet, but not empty. Mother cooked breakfast—rice with chicken broth—and Gordon sat at the table alone. His hands were folded, and he would not look at me.

"Whatever happened to the Okhui whom I loved in Korea?" he said. "The woman I nearly lost in that hospital in Korea. The day after I visited you, I went home and cried all night." Gordon let out a breath. "We need to talk about what we're going to do next."

"I don't have much choice, do I?" I told him. "We need the money."

I sat down at the table and ate in silence. Actually, I was silent— he did all the talking, but not about my job. He confessed that he had medical problems and finally admitted to suffering from PTSD. He made a remark about nearly ending up in jail but said nothing more about that. And I was too afraid to ask him.

"I feel so angry all the time," he exclaimed. "Life just isn't fair." After breakfast, he hit the wall and then slammed the door on his way out.

***

UNSURPRISINGLY, GORDON'S MOOD got significantly worse. Late one afternoon, Gordon returned home from work and discovered the antique ivory coffee table that we had brought with us from Korea was broken in two. My ever-rambunctious Dennis had been jumping on it.

"What the hell happened here!" he shouted.

Marylin said in casual fashion, "Dennis."

Speechless, Mother and I stared at each other in silence. Gordon's face turned pale, and I could hear him seething with rage. He ran out the door and down the sidewalk to where Dennis was playing with the neighborhood kids. He lifted him over his shoulder and carried him home.

Mother shouted in Korean while we both chased after him. She caught up to them and yanked at Dennis's arm until Gordon dropped Dennis to the floor and unbuckled his belt. Undaunted, Mother pounded his chest with her fists, shouting, "*Inomosekiya.* Goddamn you, you jerk!"

"He needs to be punished!" he shouted slower and louder, believing Mother could understand him that way. But Mother and I stood defiantly between him and Dennis. He unclenched the belt in his hand, then turned and sulked away, giving up.

Marylin ran to me and clung to my skirt, crying in terror while Mother sternly took Dennis by the hand. Inside the house, she picked up baby Patrick from the couch and took the boys into her bedroom, beckoning Marylin to follow her.

Gordon had disciplined Dennis before, but this time, he was out of control.

The next morning, when Mother made breakfast for all of us, the house was quiet. As Gordon prepared his morning coffee, he confessed, "The real reason I got discharged was because I gave my commanding officer a knuckle sandwich."

Mother leaned over and whispered to Dennis, "What is nuh-koro sando-wich?" My bilingual boy translated by demonstrating a punch to the side of his mouth. I held back my laughter.

Gordon glared at me. "I need to move back home to Idaho," he said. "I'd like you to come with me. I'll give you a couple of weeks to think it over."

However, I'd already made up my mind, and I didn't want to become a potato farmer.

***

THREE WEEKS PASSED. With a somber shrug, Gordon promised he would visit the kids as often as he could. Then, without another word, he went into the bedroom and packed his suitcase.

Given his determination to leave, I should have been angry at him, but I was not. There was no energy left in me to fight a losing battle. I felt as though I had already said goodbye to Gordon a long time ago. On top of that, it wasn't easy for him to leave me either. He lingered on the front porch, holding his suitcase with both hands.

Just then, Dennis approached his father and looked up at him with his eyes soaked in tears. Marylin stood at my side, staring at him in confusion with her finger in her mouth. Mournfully, Dennis turned to look at me. "Is Daddy leaving us?" he asked.

Feeling heavy-hearted, I could not answer him. Instead, I placed my hand on top of my little boy's head and fought back the tears. Gordon turned toward me, then cleared his throat. "If you change your mind, call me," he said gruffly. "After I settle back home, I'll pick up the rest of my belongings."

Clearly devastated, Dennis jumped toward his father and embraced him while Marylin clutched the hem of my blouse. Mother went to her bedroom with baby Patrick and shut the door.

Gordon looked at me one last time. "I'll call you as soon as I can," he said. Then, he walked over to his car, put his suitcase in the trunk, and never looked back as he drove away.

Standing there, I realized that he never bothered to say goodbye to Mother. But she knew he was leaving for good. When I walked back inside, Mother clicked her tongue.

"You should come to my church," she told me softly.

"Church? With those Koreans? They preach tolerance but don't like women who marry foreigners and have mixed-race children. You know, not everyone is privileged to simply come to America; some of us arrived as military wives, and we became responsible for bringing our families through immigration."

I knew Mother wouldn't respond, nor did she want to argue.

"I don't have time for the church," I told her in simple terms. She shook her head and walked away.

***

PART OF ME was relieved that I no longer had to keep my dancing career a secret from my husband, but at the same time, I wasn't sure how to keep it a secret from my mother. During dinner, she constantly asked why Gordon had left, which prompted my son to finally respond.

"Daddy got mad because Mommy's dancing," he said in broken Korean. This wasn't too damning until he started imitating burlesque dance moves. He must have seen me practice in my room.

I was surprised that my little boy had noticed my dancing, so I immediately took Dennis aside. Mother probably got a little hint, as she simply shook her head and grumbled in Korean, "Gordon was a nice person. You just lost a good man."

"Lost a good man?" I said. "Where were you when I needed you the most? Now you come to me, trying to be a mother?"

Mother walked away from me with her head down. I started to realize that she carried her guilt silently; she'd never made that clear to me before. I took a breath, regretting what I'd just said. I wished I could take it back.

MY PERSONAL MANAGER

DURING BREAKS, I often listened to our emcee, Thad Swift, recount his Hollywood acting career. Years ago, his mother was a chorus girl in extravagant MGM musicals like *Dames* and *42nd Street* during Hollywood's Golden Age. I shared my childhood admiration for those movies from my time in Korea.

Whenever I talked about my dreams of going to Hollywood, Thad would smile and say that lots of people wanted to be famous there. I thought he wasn't really paying attention until one night, he came up to me and said, "Suzie, do you want to work in Hollywood?"

"Hollywood?" I repeated. "But I don't speak good English. I can only dance."

Thad's crooked grin relaxed into a sly smile.

"Let me tell ya something, Suzie," he began. "I'm an actor by trade, and this Body Shop gig's only something I do between acting jobs. I got an agent in LA. My contract with The Body Shop is over, and I'm ready to move back. So, this friend of mine goes by the name of Coralie. She books all the big clubs—get you paid top dollar!

"So, ask yourself: Can you make it big? Who knows how far you'll go? Maybe start with dancing, add your looks and natural charm, and I'll bet you can be an actress. Hollywood producers will line up at your door, offering top dollar, babe."

Cautiously stifling my excitement, I smiled back. Honestly, I wasn't concerned about making "top dollar" at this point; I just wanted to support my family. Nonetheless, tagging along with him on a trip to Hollywood sounded like fun. I intended to discuss it with my family before giving him an answer.

***

THAT NIGHT, I talked to Mother about going to Los Angeles. She responded with a quick head tilt, raised eyebrows, and crossed arms, looking quite concerned. "What about your husband?" she asked.

I let out an exasperated breath. "*Eomma*! Gordon is gone."

"But he could come back," she snapped, wagging her finger in my face. "And now you're leaving too? If you leave, he'll never come back. Your children will grow up without a father! Are you even thinking about them? Where are we supposed to go?"

"I'm not abandoning them!" I shouted. "I'm not like you with your alcoholic boyfriend." I paused, feeling a twinge of regret for those words after seeing the ashen look on her face. Mother stared at me for a long, silent minute, then disclosed that she had found my glittered pumps in the closet. She knew I was not working as a waitress.

"*Moodang Honshin*, worship for the evil spirits," she said. "You should get a more respectable job."

When she turned her head in disgust, my nostrils flared.

"Respectable?" I mocked angrily. "Respectable? Where were you when I got accepted to high school, and I couldn't even afford my own tuition?"

Feeling my anger, I paused, closed my eyes, and took a deep breath before continuing.

"Why don't I invite Thad over for dinner?" I told her. "He's my coworker. And you'll see he's also a respectable businessman. He can become my personal manager and look out for me."

Mother shook her head and returned to her room.

***

ONE EVENING, WITH high hopes, I prepared a nice Korean meal for Thad, Mother, and me. Before we sat down to eat, Mother took Dennis, Marylin, and Patrick into the living room and let them watch TV. Thad wasted no time; he immediately became overly friendly and ingratiated himself with Mother, but she was not so easily swayed. The minute she laid eyes on him, she told me in Korean that he was no good.

"This good-for-nothing is dragging you down into a dirty business," she grumbled, then implored, "Okhui, you've already made lots of money. Why don't you quit your job and get a decent one, like tutoring the Korean congregation at church? Most of them are not too good at English, and they need someone like you."

I responded in Korean, cautiously keeping my volume low to not alarm the children, "I need to make enough to move everyone to California. Then we can decide if I want to keep performing or not."

"Are you dating him?" she asked.

I growled under my breath. "No, Mother. Our relationship is strictly business."

Even though Thad didn't understand our conversation, he could tell by the tone of our voices that we were both unhappy. He chewed his food with wide, watchful eyes. "Mrs. Pong, your daughter is a fantastic dancer. *Ichiban!* Number one!" He jovially added a thumbs-up gesture.

I swiftly kicked his leg under the table. "Her last name is Hwang," I corrected him, as most Westerners don't realize Asians introduce themselves with their last names first. He apologized, but Mother waved him off with her napkin.

"He looks like a con man," Mother mumbled in Korean. With that, she finished her meal and joined the three children in the living room. A foreboding silence fell over the house until Thad picked up a piece of *mandu* with his chopsticks.

"These dumplings are really good," he said.

I politely smiled, choosing not to explain what Mother had told me. I knew it was unrealistic to believe that she'd accept my career goals, so I said goodbye to Thad and turned down his offer. He graciously accepted my decision and left the invitation open for me to contact him in California should I ever change my mind. Since his contract with The Body Shop had expired, Thad had no plans to return to Denver.

In all honesty, I didn't resent Mother's disapproval of him, but it would have been nice to have her on my side.

***

LATER THAT SPRING, Sister Oksoon decided to pay us a visit. Now in her late thirties, she appeared much older. Her haggard face was caked with American makeup, and her gray roots were showing.

"I'm staying for a couple of days," she told us. "On my way to Japan—might stop over in Hawaii."

I helped carry her bags into a spare room. "Is it true you're divorced now?" I asked. Oksoon casually shrugged her shoulders. And although it was no shock to me, her "couple of days" turned into a month. We barely talked to one another, nor did she help around the house. Over the years, I had come to accept her faults—until one day, while I was vacuuming, Dennis ran into the living room with a visible cut on his neck.

"Mommy!" he whispered in my ear. "Aunty scratched me!"

Infuriated, I ran into the guest bedroom, where Oksoon sat on her bed, reading. In disgust, I snatched the magazine out of her hand and threw it on the floor. "What do you think you're doing?" I yelled. "I let you stay here, and you abuse my son?"

Oksoon looked up at me and calmly retorted, "The boy needs discipline. You never do anything to punish him."

Enraged by her disrespect, I formed a fist, but she boldly came at me with her right arm—her good arm. I grabbed her by the left wrist, and she yelped in pain. That's when Mother burst into the room.

"Okhui! Stop it!" Mother shouted at the top of her lungs. "Let her go!" I immediately backed off, but Mother continued to take her side.

"She's your daughter," I argued. "Not my sister."

I walked away, and Oksoon slammed her door shut. The next day, she left without saying a word. It was a relief that couldn't have come soon enough, but I was already anticipating future problems with her and Mother and feeling trapped in between.

This was not how I wanted to spend my life. Later that day, I picked up the telephone and made a long-distance call to California.

"Hello, Thad," I said. "My answer is yes. I want to go to Hollywood."

THE ROAD TO HOLLYWOOD

I HAD ALWAYS been curious about Hollywood, but over the next few weeks, Mother constantly rolled her eyes at me every time she saw me planning for the trip. Late one evening, I heard Mother chanting in a soft voice through her bedroom door.

"*Juyo! Juyo!* Save my daughter from that mind-controlling snake trying to drag her into that seedy world."

I reminded her repeatedly that I had accepted Thad's offer, but it wasn't until she saw my costumes and sparkling shoes next to a suitcase that she grasped that there was no turning back. She responded by ignoring me. The weekend before my departure, I hoped to come to an understanding with Mother, but her silence persisted. The tension between us left me breathless with distress.

After a few days, Mother finally spoke, "You lost a good man."

"The only reason you like Gordon is because he signed your immigration papers," I retorted. "Because he helped our family— he helped you and your children. You feel guilty for abandoning us, and now you're relying on him to make peace with your adult children. He's good for *you*."

I paused and explained calmly. "I'm twenty-seven years old. I don't want to get stuck here—I want to keep moving forward. I want more out of life, for myself and for my family." I wasn't sure if she was even listening, but I sincerely hoped she was.

***

IN MAY 1969, I touched ground at Los Angeles International Airport. The weather was much warmer and more pleasant than in Denver. The sun was just setting over the skyline, and I felt a shiver of excitement run through my body.

Thad picked me up in a white Mercedes convertible. Impressed, I told him that he looked "plenty cool," as the American kids said on television. We drove toward Hollywood, and I felt like I was living in a dream world. I even saw the huge Hollywood sign on the mountain, just like in the movies. My heart started to beat wildly.

Heading north on a long stretch of road he called "Sepp-ool-vida Boulevard," we headed toward the famous Beverly Hills. He handed me a map of movie stars' homes he'd gotten from a tourist shop. At a loss for words, I had to pinch myself as we drove by the homes of movie stars like Bing Crosby and Joan Crawford. Then, we headed toward Sunset Boulevard and took the Cahuenga Pass to the top of Mulholland Drive.

"Do you live in one of those houses?" I asked, pointing to the mansions along the hillside. He shook his head and laughed.

"Heck no. I just wanted to show you some of the nicer neighborhoods first. Give ya something to look forward to."

We drove back along the 101 Freeway and took the Hollywood exit, where he showed me the scenic route toward Downtown Los Angeles. In a span of ten minutes, mansions gave way to poorly paved streets and rundown buildings. Leisurely, we drove down Sunset Boulevard, where long-haired, White youths scurried about in loose-fitting clothing or sat on the pavement playing their guitars.

Dozens of psychic shops with signs posted out front offered palm readings; there seemed to be one on every block. But what impressed me most were the sprawling billboards with pictures of the latest movie stars. I desperately hoped that I would see one walking down the street.

Approaching Downtown LA, we stopped in front of a two-story building resembling a warehouse. As he picked up my suitcase from the trunk, Thad said, "This is my studio . . . and I also live here."

My jaw dropped, but I tried to mask my disappointment. Thad told me that he'd prepared his study next door for me to sleep in. He asked for a small deposit to share the place. I appreciated his professionalism, but he was still being stingy.

Letting me out of the car, we walked up a rickety flight of stairs. The termite-eaten floor squeaked beneath our feet, and the smell of old wood permeated the stuffy air. Thad stopped in front of the door with a sign that read, "Coralie Jr. Theatrical Agency." According to Thad, Coralie Jr. Fitzharris-Milburn was one of Hollywood's first great female talent agents. She was also the god-daughter of legendary movie director Cecil B. DeMille.

"The office is closed right now, but I wanted you to see the place," he said. "Coralie will be here tomorrow to sign you up."

Feeling discouraged, I walked the perimeter of the rough tiled floor and sighed. Instantly, I imagined Mother scoffing at me with her arms crossed.

I am a bad daughter, after all. When I peered down the hallway, all I could think was how pathetic this looked, far from the glamorous showbiz lifestyle I had envisioned. I would soon discover that this was how the average showbiz folk lived.

Thad and I walked into the adjacent building and into another much smaller room that he used as an office. The first thing I noticed was a large set of antlers on a mounted deer head hanging on the center of the wall; I swear its eyes followed me around the room.

To distract my thoughts, I decided to ask about the framed eight-by-ten photographs on the wall. In one of the pictures, Thad stood on a stage next to a beautiful curvy brunette holding a baby pig.

"That's me with Jane Russell," Thad explained. "I used to train pigs for television. Pigs are one of the most intelligent animals in the world," he said as though he were giving a lecture. "Did you know that each one has its own unique personality and even different food preferences?"

Thad pointed to the pig held by Miss Russell. "This one liked bacon," he said with a devilish grin. I winced, and he responded with a hearty laugh and pointed to another photo where he held a darker baby pig. "She, on the other hand, liked fried eggs."

From there, he went on and on about how he'd gotten started in the pig-wrangling business. I chuckled; though he was a great emcee on stage, he lacked the same charisma off stage. I smiled, listening to his story.

Then, Thad showed me his family photos on the desk, which included his mother, who was young and wore an extravagant showgirl costume, as well as his ex-wife and his pre-teen son.

After he finished giving me the tour of his apartment, we said our good nights, and I started unpacking.

As soon as I got comfortable on the futon he'd laid out on the floor, I started to miss Mother, my children, and, oddly enough, Gordon. It took me a while to relax enough to fall asleep.

***

EARLY THE NEXT morning, Thad took me across the hall to meet Coralie. A petite blonde version of Shelley Winters welcomed me with a friendly smile and a kiss on the cheek. She appeared to be in her mid-thirties—too young, I thought, to be a big-time agent, but Thad had already explained to me that she was too old and too short to pursue an acting career of her own.

That doesn't seem fair, I thought.

Seating me in front of her desk, Coralie said with a wry grin, "I've been expectin' ya."

I had expected her walls to be filled with glamorous photographs of movie stars like I'd seen in American movies. Instead, she only had a few odd photographs of stage shows. One displayed a man in a top hat emerging from a large black bag, another an Egyptian belly dancer with a massive python. Some performers seemed friendly, others eerie, while a few were on Vegas circus posters.

She handed me three sheets of paper to sign, which I carefully scrutinized.

"Just three pages?" I asked.

Coralie tapped her index finger on the side of her head. "Everything else I need is up here, babe," she said. "I keep my contracts simple. Plus, I trust my clients."

"Coralie's not like any other agent," Thad interjected. "She'll look out for your well-being, and she'll go to town fighting for ya—not only so you land the gig but to make sure they'll take real good care of you, get me?"

She then explained how she had booked Thad for various night-club gigs and movie roles despite her modest office location.

I responded with a polite smile, but I nervously wondered if all the big movie stars started this way.

DANCING FOR THE STARS

CORALIE BOOKED ME my first job at the Pink Pussycat, a legendary burlesque house in the center of Hollywood, located just south of the Sunset Strip. Thad enthusiastically accompanied me to my initial interview. As we pulled up in front of the club on Santa Monica Boulevard, I noticed its exterior looked almost exactly like The Body Shop's—a plain facade with a simple three-line marquee and its headliners in bright neon letters.

Upon closer inspection, I noticed some of the unusual names of their headliners: Peeler Lawford, Deena Martin, and Samya Davis Jr. Puzzled, I told Thad that those names sounded extremely odd.

"It's parody, baby," he explained. "Paying tribute to the original—and hoping they'll visit." I nodded, part of me hoping it was true.

Just before the club opened in the early evening, I met the owners, a Jewish couple known as the Schillers. The husband was on the heavier side and carried himself with an easygoing demeanor.

Clearing his throat, he spoke in a quiet, relaxed voice, "Good to see you again, Thad."

Thad whispered softly in my ear, "Be good to them—doesn't hurt to suck up to the boss."

"Harry Schiller," he introduced himself, extending his hand.

"I am pleased to meet you, Mr. Schiller," I said slowly, enunciating my L's properly while shaking his hand.

"Call me Harry. And you are Suzie Wong?" he asked. I nodded, and his wife introduced herself as Alice.

Harry chuckled and opened the doors to the main showroom, revealing pleasantly surprising, classy décor. Low-hanging light fixtures bathed the room in a red haze, highlighting velvet curtains on either side of the stage. The thick scent of cigarette smoke filled the air, reminiscent of The Body Shop but in a much larger space.

"I'll show you the dressing room later," Alice told me before I followed them down the hallway. Toward the end of their orientation, Harry gave me my schedule and told me, "Anybody can take their clothes off—"

"But not everyone can dance," Alice finished his sentence.

Three waitresses went from table to table, lighting candles and placing squares of paper with a drawing of a pink cat into clear ashtrays.

The evening crowd began to fill up the showroom. At the entrance, a hostess handed each patron two feathers and checked their names off a list. A second hostess then led them to their seats in front of a large thrust stage. Unlike The Body Shop, most customers here were well-dressed married couples, and the wives appeared happy to join in on the fun.

When the audience packed the house, the opening bars from a grand piano blared through the speakers, but there was no band in sight. Noticing my baffled expression, Harry explained that the music was all pre-taped. The atmosphere here certainly felt much more exciting than in Denver.

***

THE NEXT DAY, I prepared my own music and props according to the Schillers' instructions. While Harry led Thad and me behind the stage, a half-dozen dancers hurried in and out of the dressing room. Unlike the girls at The Body Shop, these women looked physically fit, with well-toned arms and legs. I later learned that they were all budding actresses waiting to be discovered, and a few of them had already worked on movie sets.

While Harry helped me put my costumes on the wardrobe rack, the dancers walked right past me as though I were invisible. They certainly weren't as friendly as my former colleagues. Taking a breath, I approached the wings of the stage and peeked out at a nearly full house. A small cluster of waitresses served cocktails while a beautiful, buxom dancer in a transparent silvery gown took the stage.

I waited in the wings for the dancer to finish, then took my place center stage. Admittedly, I felt a little nervous, but once the music kicked into gear, my dance steps became second nature, and I felt ready to take on the Hollywood crowd.

A few days into performing, I noticed a thin-haired, round-faced Asian man in a Hawaiian-printed shirt. Oddly enough, he sat at the same front center table for a third night in a row.

I didn't pay further attention until later when Harry knocked on the dressing room door. "Gentleman in the front row just brought you a dozen roses," he said. "Wanna go out there and thank him?"

I was surprised. From the beginning, I had been advised against accepting gifts, as it conflicted with the club's policy, but since my boss had told me about the flowers, I guessed it wasn't a problem.

My gift-giver was the same Asian man I'd seen sitting at the front center table in the crowd. When I approached him in the hallway, his eyes disappeared as he beamed at me and practically shoved the bouquet of roses into my chest.

Utterly stunned, I stood frozen as he walked away. Just then, I noticed a thick white envelope in the middle of the flowers. Curious and apprehensive, I calmly walked into the restroom, making sure no one was watching. When I opened the envelope, my eyes nearly burst out of their sockets. Inside was a stack of ten crisp one-hundred-dollar bills clipped to a handwritten note from a Tad Matsuoka of Club Hubba Hubba in Honolulu, Hawaii.

Awestruck, I counted the bills again and again. No mistake—one thousand dollars!

Trying my best to remain calm, I returned to the dressing room, noticing Zita suspiciously eyeing me while I pushed the envelope deeper inside the bouquet. I nodded to her with a sheepish grin.

The other girls—including headliner Deena Martin—did not share my nonchalant attitude. Within seconds, the entire dressing room buzzed with whispers about dancers who had married millionaires and never came back to work.

"Wish I had a sugar daddy to take care of me." Zita gave me a sly wink. I got dressed but paid no further attention to the other girls.

When Thad picked me up that evening, the first thing he noticed was the roses. He asked who had given them to me.

"Some gentleman in the front row," I said.

He grunted.

"Something wrong?" I asked.

"Part of the job, I guess," he muttered.

He said nothing else, even when I told him about the generous tip. After all, I figured I could trust him, but the next morning, when I went to retrieve Tad Matsuoka's business card, I could find neither the note nor the money—only an empty envelope. Had the money slipped out? Had one of the girls taken it? Had Thad?

I never found out.

***

OVER THE NEXT few days, I started feeling sad, and not because of the lost money. Mother called me nearly every other day to tell me about what was happening back home. According to her, Marylin and baby Patrick were playing together happily, but Dennis struggled to concentrate in school. Also, her church congregation had started praying for my protection against the tempting clutches of Hollywood.

I didn't respond to the latter, but the sad reality had already hit me. Even though I was earning good money, a growing emptiness gnawed at my gut, and no amount of money could fill that space. It had been six weeks since I'd left for California, and I missed my family terribly. I wished I could be there to see Marylin cuddling little Patrick and to help Dennis with his schoolwork.

One morning, I asked Thad to drive me to Coralie's office and told her I wanted some time off to visit my children. She wasn't pleased and reminded me that I shouldn't "lose momentum." She firmly encouraged me to stay long enough to meet the celebrities at the club.

"Last week, you turned down my invitation to that party at the Cocoanut Grove," she scolded. "Sammy Davis Jr. was at that party!"

"I'm not a party-type girl," I told her.

"If you leave now," she said, "you'll miss every opportunity. Look, Suzie. You need to finish your contract with the Pink Pussycat while you've still got jobs lined up. The Body Shop—a different one, on Sunset—wants to book you. There's also this new comedy club that wants to hire you and Thad."

With slight hesitation, I agreed to take that job, but only as a favor to Thad. Our comedy act was booked at the Tahitian Village near Downtown Los Angeles, where we entertained their dinner patrons. He cast me as a naïve Japanese immigrant, wearing a kimono and asking him for directions. Most of the act involved me standing still as a statue in the middle of a joke while he screamed out punch lines, something about Pearl Harbor, which I didn't understand.

Every night, the audience roared with laughter. At the end of the show, customers approached the lip of the stage and deposited wads of twenty-dollar bills into our tip jar. After the crowds dispersed, Thad and I excitedly sat in the front row of the house, splitting the tips. He set aside a stack of twenty-dollar bills for himself.

"This covers my writer's commission," he told me. He then took out two more twenties. "And this is my manager's fee." Disturbingly, he set aside yet another twenty. "My share of the tips."

Shocked by his tenacious greed, I growled under my breath as I watched him split the remaining eighty dollars between us. Our agreement was that he would work as my personal manager, but in the end, the only thing he accomplished was overcharging me.

JOURNEY TO PARADISE

BY THE END of 1969, I felt a strong urge to return to Denver. We had one final comedy show involving a belly dancer and a live snake. We entertained a large gathering of Japanese American farmers at the Hilton Hotel convention center.

After the show, Thad implored, "You've got a real shot in Hollywood. Baby, you must be the dumbest girl in Hollywood history. You want to be an actress, don't ya?"

I replied, "How can I be an actress if I don't speak fluent English? And how many Asian faces do you see on the movie screen? Even Bruce Lee has to wear that silly mask on his TV show."

"But you're stunning, baby doll," Thad insisted. "And in this town, that's all that matters." His words sounded genuine, but I detected an unsettling undertone.

At my wit's end, I snapped, "You're just trying to use me like everyone else! You follow me everywhere and act like you're my boyfriend. I can't take this anymore!"

Frustrated and gesticulating wildly, I continued, "You never let me work independently! It's always a package deal with you!"

Thad's eyebrows shot up in utter astonishment; he clearly hadn't anticipated such a confrontation. He stood there, mouth agape, unable to respond. I glared at him, shaking my head, resolute in my decision. "I've made my choice," I declared, then left the hotel and, as far as I was concerned, his life.

***

THREE MONTHS LATER, back in Denver, Thad called with a message from Coralie. She wanted to know if I'd consider working with him, but not in Hollywood. He then let out a hearty laugh and practically shouted, "We're going to Hawaii, baby!"

Before I could ask, he continued enthusiastically, "Somebody—a very well-known somebody named Tad Matsuoka—specifically requested for you to come to work at his club!"

I gasped. Tad Matsuoka! How could I forget the man who had left me his business card and an envelope with one thousand dollars in a bouquet of roses? My interest was piqued.

Coralie persisted, "Trust me, by burlesque standards, this place is huge."

Thad slipped back on the call, declaring, "Coralie told me we can work together. And she's going to submit your headshot to *Hawaii Five-O*. In fact, I want you to meet my friend Ted Thorpe, the casting director."

The mere mention of that show intrigued me. "My mom watches that show!" I exclaimed.

"Yeah, it's a big hit right now," Thad said. "Who knows? Show's so popular; it could run for the next fifty years—and you can be in it!"

I laughed at the notion, but deep down inside, I was very excited. Two weeks later, I received paperwork from Coralie, including an AGVA union contract between Coralie, the club owner, and me. To sweeten the deal, the club owner offered me living accommodations until my contract ended.

Despite the generous offer, I told both Thad and Coralie that I needed time to decide. My siblings from Korea were scheduled to arrive, and I had to help them settle in America.

To my surprise, Mother encouraged me to move to Hawaii. Evidently, she knew a woman in her congregation who occasionally lived there and had told her all about the beauty of the islands and the vast availability of Asian cuisine. In fact, the majority of the population in Hawaii was Asian American, primarily Japanese. Since Mother was still fluent in Japanese, she felt she would fit right in.

Plus, she loved *Hawaii Five-O*.

***

JANUARY 1970. SISTER Okyon and my brothers Gyeong and Yong arrived at Denver International Airport. Mother and I dashed toward the arrival gate like Olympic sprinters. We couldn't contain our excitement as we scanned the crowd for a glimpse of my older siblings. Then, without warning or fanfare, they made their grand entrance at the gate—well, maybe not so grand, but definitely older.

At first, I thought they looked like a trio of bankers. Both of my brothers were decked out in light brown blazers and carried matching black attaché cases. My sister wore a dark blue business suit with high heels while I was clad in a flowy maxi dress and bell-bottom pants with flares at the hem, all the rage in 1970s America. I also piled on my mascara to create the illusion of double-length eyelashes, the latest trend, coupled with long hair that extended down to my waist.

"I know it wasn't an easy trip for you," Mother told my siblings.

Yong looked around and asked, "Where are your kids? I can hardly wait to see how much Marylin has sprouted!"

With a slight chuckle, I replied, "Oh, they're having a great time with my neighbors."

While Yong helped pick up their luggage, he leaned in and asked me in confidence, "And what about Gordon?"

I was uncertain about how to answer. I quickly looked for a way to change the subject before Mother chimed in, "He went back to Idaho."

With a breath, I added, "We are separated."

My brothers and Okyon fell into a stunned silence but continued toward the parking lot without bringing it up again.

***

A MONTH AFTER my siblings' arrival, it became clear that our house couldn't accommodate everyone. So, Mother proposed that Okyon, Gyeong, and Yong rent an apartment nearby. After settling in, one of Mother's congregation members referred Brother Gyeong to a job as a sky chef at Denver Airport. Meanwhile, Brother Yong took an incredible job opportunity as a martial arts instructor in Oklahoma. Though we were saddened by Yong's departure, we were thrilled that he had secured employment in America.

Okyon and I began spending more time together, taking leisurely walks through the city park with my children. One sunny morning, as Okyon pushed baby Patrick in a stroller and I held little Marylin's hand, our faithful dog Bobby trotted along at Okyon's heels. She had been persistently pestering me about getting her a job as a cocktail waitress at the nightclub where she believed I worked, thanks to Mother's constant chatter about it. I had always managed to evade her with flimsy excuses.

During this particular walk, she became relentless, endlessly extolling her customer service skills and eagerness to work. Finally, she slowed her pace and pleaded, "Please, Okhui. I could be a big help to you."

The burden of my secret was becoming unbearable, and I could no longer conceal the truth. With a deep exhale and an awkward smile, I leaned closer to her ear, ensuring that Marylin wouldn't overhear. "I'm not really a cocktail waitress," I whispered. "I'm a dancer at that club, and I take my clothes off."

Okyon froze in her tracks, her eyes widening with surprise. I quickly attempted to clarify, "Well, not all my clothes!" I gestured exaggeratedly down my body with a gliding hand motion, concluding in a sassy pose. "I only take off about . . . half my clothes."

"*Aigo*! *Cham*!" Okyon exclaimed, clearly taken aback. "*Giga chanda giga cha*! Oh, my goodness!" She clicked her tongue in frustration and asked angrily, "What have you come to?"

"I have to make a living," I protested. "And the money is great! How do you think I can afford to support all of you every month?

Gordon wasn't making enough, and I needed to pay for paperwork and for my attorney to help bring all of you over here. Attorneys don't work for free, you know?"

Okyon withheld her response, prompting me to spill everything.

"Gordon left me after he found out," I continued. "Mother has some idea of my real job, though. When she saw my shiny shoes and the wardrobe in my closet, I told her I waited tables at one of those fancy American nightclubs. You know, the ones where the girls dress up like bunny rabbits?"

Okyon's face twisted into a mix of guilt and despair. "I guess you're right," she admitted. "We Mun girls stepped into this world on the wrong foot."

I couldn't help but smirk in agreement, reminding her that being a showgirl was tame compared to the jobs she and Oksoon had taken.

"We worked at a taxi dance hall," she countered. Looking downcast, Okyon finally relented. "I had hoped things would be different here." I nodded, and then we watched Marylin playing under the trees.

"Our pride doesn't feed us," I told her. "Sometimes, we have to swallow it."

With that, we embraced our circumstances, finding humor and strength in the absurdity of it all. We understood that as minorities with limited opportunities, we had to face the world as it is, even if it meant taking unconventional paths to survive.

***

LATER THAT DAY, my telephone rang. Thad called to follow up on Coralie's enticing job offer in Hawaii. Admittedly, the idea of working in a ritzier nightclub while soaking up the tropical sun on my days off had me intrigued. But it would be a huge move, so I told him I'd think about it.

That evening, I sat down in front of my shiny new color TV and caught an episode of *Hawaii Five-O*, the same show Coralie was trying to book for me. The electrifying theme song filled the room, injecting me with a surge of energy and hope.

Swept away by the captivating opening montage, from the stunning view of Diamond Head to the swaying hips of a Tahitian dancer in a grass skirt to the bikini-clad beauty running along the sandy beach, I thought, *Why not give Hawaii a try?*

After days of careful consideration, I made the decision to seize the opportunity. With newfound confidence, I dialed Coralie's number and eagerly delivered my answer.

"Hello, Coralie!" I exclaimed. "Count me in!"

***

THE DAY MY sister Okyon and I arrived at Honolulu International Airport, the heavy humidity clung to the air. My blouse stuck to my chest from the moisture, but a sudden, cool tropical breeze provided relief. It felt like a welcoming embrace, a sense of belonging in this unfamiliar place, even though I had never been to Hawaii. It was just Okyon and me on this trip, as she hoped to find work as a cocktail waitress.

As we walked toward the baggage claim, we were greeted by a group of lively young men and women who adorned arriving passengers with vibrant flower necklaces, known as leis, a beautiful Hawaiian tradition.

A short, stout man approached us from the sidewalk door. He appeared to have mixed Asian heritage and introduced himself as Stanley Park. His English had a distinct regional accent, and I struggled to understand him. Eventually, I learned that it was pidgin English, a local dialect influenced by various languages spoken by Asian laborers on the plantations in the early twentieth century.

Stanley explained his diverse heritage, which Hawaiians referred to as "chop suey" or "mixed plate," reflecting the state's multicultural population. Hawaii, he said, was a melting pot.

We loaded our luggage into Stanley's worn Dodge Charger, and as we drove toward Downtown Honolulu, I was captivated by the exotic scenery. Unlike Los Angeles, there were no towering buildings or billboards. Instead, rows of palm trees swayed along the sparkling shoreline.

I asked Stanley if pineapples grew on those trees, to which he humorously replied, "If you say so," leaving me wondering if he was serious.

As we continued along Nimitz Highway, Stanley chatted away in pidgin English, laughing at his own jokes, which I struggled to understand. My attention was drawn to the open windows, allowing the scent of the salty ocean air to fill the car. It reminded me of the Busan coast but with the addition of civilian cargo ships near a majestic clock tower. Stanley referred to it as the Aloha Tower, a welcoming landmark on the pier.

In about half an hour, Stanley dropped us off in front of the Nakamura Hotel on King Street. The neighborhood appeared modest, but the hotel's lobby was inviting, with a small, clean space adorned with earthy brown carpeting.

Appreciating Stanley's assistance, I tried to offer him a generous tip, but he politely declined and left after reminding us he would return later that night. Exhausted, Okyon and I planned to take a quick shower and rest to combat jet lag.

CLUB HUBBA HUBBA

CLUB HUBBA HUBBA beckoned us, located on Hotel Street in Downtown Honolulu's red-light district near Chinatown. Okyon and I sat in Stanley's car, amused by how much nightlife was packed into these two small streets. Passing a strip mall with a Woolworth's department store, I was reminded that I was still in America.

Stanley shared that the club was originally owned by Tad Matsuoka Sr., Tad Jr.'s father, and was known as the Aloha Café before transforming into a jazz and burlesque venue in 1953, eventually becoming Club Hubba Hubba.

As the sun set, the streets began to buzz with activity. Drunken sailors hopped between clubs, and we passed by shops selling "adult" items for them to take home. Stanley circled the block to give us a glimpse of the area. Soon, a group of women emerged from a nightclub called The Glades. Dressed in polyester pants and red crop tops, they flirted with the sailors. However, a closer look revealed that they were actually young men dressed as women, wearing buttons reading "I am a boy," apparently for their protection. At least, I assumed as much.

Our excitement grew as we spotted a bright neon sign hanging on the second floor of a brick building, displaying a caricature of a dancer and the words "Club Hubba Hubba." My nerves kicked in as we approached, but I was thrilled to finally arrive.

"You know," Stanley added as we left his cab. "Dis club's been the grooviest hotspot on Hotel Street since World War II."

As we approached the entrance, my nerves began to race; I tried hard to stay calm. Okyon and I approached an alcove with a glass display case on the outside, prominently sporting a black-and-white picture—of *me*, glamorously clad in a Chinese *cheongsam* and a feathered cape. I assumed it had been the Schillers' favorite photo of me when I danced at the Pink Pussycat, but personally, I thought I looked like a giant chicken.

Still, seeing my photo on bold display made me blush a little. I was flattered and amazed that this nightclub had started promoting me before I'd even set foot in Honolulu. Okyon, on the other hand, stayed quiet even after we opened the front door to enter the club. She did not exhibit an ounce of excitement.

But I certainly did!

Though the cigarette smoke pervading the air smelled the same as every other club I had worked at, I was amused at the sight of the rough-looking, brown-skinned locals huddled by the bar. They turned their heads toward us as we walked inside. Some smiled under their poorly trimmed beards while their eyes communicated a lot more than their wolf whistles could.

A five-piece band played on the side of the stage. Unlike their counterparts on the mainland, they were dressed in aloha shirts and casual slacks. The music built up to a crescendo to introduce a voluptuous blonde dancer dolled up in an extravagant costume.

Eight multicolored lights hung from the ceiling, highlighting a sultry black bodice that looked like it had been painted on the dancer's taut body. Her long, toned legs were sensually wrapped in dark fishnet stockings. I zealously watched as she slinked down a catwalk that extended into the middle of the room, like a *hanamichi* in Japanese *kabuki* theater. When she reached the end, she turned her back and gyrated to the cheers of businessmen and uniformed sailors.

Okyon and I headed toward the back of the room, where a Japanese man with a round Buddha-like belly approached us. He smiled a warm smile, causing his eyes to disappear into his face. Immediately, I recognized him as one of the regulars at the Pink Pussycat—the man who sat at the front table three nights in a row during my act. The same man who had given me the roses with the one-thousand-dollar tip.

"Thank you for bringing me to Hawaii, Mr. Matsuoka," I said, then leaned in close to whisper, "and thank you for the gift." At that point, I decided not to mention it had gone missing.

"My pleasure," he replied with a smile.

I then asked him if he would hire Okyon as a waitress. Mr. Matsuoka grinned at my bold request, then turned to Okyon and gallantly directed her toward a skinny, middle-aged Japanese woman filling the bar's cash register. "Talk to my head waitress, Marsha."

Looking over at Marsha, I noticed a facial resemblance to Mr. Matsuoka. I figured they must be related. Mr. Matsuoka then escorted me up a short flight of stairs leading to his office.

At his desk, he unfolded a newspaper displaying a quarter-page ad featuring photographs of me posing in a bikini.

"We did plenny promotion, yeah?" he said proudly. "We'll even help you get a studio apartment by Holiday Mart. Da shopping center—with one beautiful ocean view!"

I thanked him politely, though I was in complete awe of the level of publicity. Staring long and hard at my photo, I hadn't expected this much attention when I'd taken the job. On my first night, the club was packed with busloads of tourists and locals, resulting in long lines waiting to get in.

During my off hours, I would sit with the band and arrange my own music. According to Coralie's contract, as a headliner, I would not be required to perform more than four shows a night, and the owner could not require me to sit with patrons.

I was definitely pleased about that.

***

AS THE STAR of the show, I enjoyed the small privilege of being able to wander around the lounge area during my break time instead of being stuck in my dressing room. One night, during the show, I took a break and strolled around the bar.

A strikingly handsome gentleman wearing a white blazer approached me at the bar and asked if I'd join him. When he introduced himself as Randy, I couldn't help but be taken aback by his good looks. He appeared to be what locals called *hapa-haole*, someone of mixed Caucasian and another ethnic background, quite often Asian. The term itself came from pidgin Hawaiian slang.

Randy told me he had been born and raised in Hawaii, third generation on his Japanese side from an immigrant family who had worked on the sugarcane plantations. But just as we were about to get to know one another, I saw Thad come out of Tad Matsuoka's office. I caught his surprised expression when he saw me in the company of another man. I hadn't even known he had come in, and I knew he wanted to say hello, but he didn't. With a sad look on his face, he turned away and headed for the exit.

At that moment, the realization hit me. Thad wasn't upset about losing the hosting gig at Club Hubba Hubba. He was upset that he had lost me. As he walked away, he cast one final glance over his shoulder, which left me with a sudden pang of guilt—and a touch of sadness.

In show business, rejection was a constant companion, but knowing this didn't make me feel any better. Six weeks later, I prepared myself for my first audition for *Hawaii Five-O*, which Coralie had arranged.

At the casting office near Diamond Head, I was introduced to local casting director Ted Thorpe, a white-haired gentleman sporting a white beard and horned rim glasses. He reminded me of a middle-aged Santa Claus but wearing a kukui nut lei.

My script only contained three lines of dialogue, but I was so nervous that my words came out as a tangled jumble of nonsense. I tried not to show it on my face, but I was about to have a mental breakdown. I read it once more, a little calmer. Ted then encouraged me to start as a background extra to learn the ropes. He also suggested I take some acting classes, but I knew I had to focus on taking care of my mother and my children. And this meant going back to work and making money.

Still, this experience gave me the encouragement to improve my English. From that point on, I monitored myself to reduce my accent and worked on the different tongue placements when switching from Korean to English.

***

WITHOUT THAD, I was finally working in Hawaii on my own. In fact, dancing became routine for me. Occasional customers soon became regulars, and life settled into a pleasant, uneventful pace. I expected to make a long-term commitment to this job so I could bring my children here.

That is, until one night when an elegantly dressed, middle-aged Korean woman took her seat near the right lip of the stage. While changing, Okyon peered through the dressing room door with unexpected news.

"A lady named Gayo asked to speak with you," she said. "Can you come down?"

Such a request was unusual since women didn't commonly ask for me. I hurriedly made my way downstairs to the showroom floor with Okyon close behind, where she pointed in the direction of the Korean woman seated at a table, surrounded by three men. I recognized Randy, but I'd never seen the other two before.

Gayo chattered away in pidgin English while her companions laughed at her jokes as though they'd been paid to do so. I took a seat, listening attentively but still unsure why I was even present in the first place.

"Domiko's not a real Japanese name," she began, finally acknowledging my presence. I chuckled. When I started a new job in Hawaii, I'd decided to change my stage name, leaving the old persona of Suzie Wong behind.

"My real name is Tomiko," I explained. "I was born in Japan, but when I started working here, I didn't want local Koreans to think I was Japanese. So, I misspelled it on purpose."

"Oh, I see," she said with a subtle laugh, then introduced her companions. "This is George, my club manager. And this is my good friend, Aki. And, of course, you know Randy." Gayo then looked me in the eye. "In fact, Randy raved so much about you that I had to come see your show."

With a sly grin, she added, "I run a bar on Kapiolani, and I could use a good hostess."

"Hostess?" I was taken aback by her offer. Before I could inquire, the band started playing again. Plus, I had no intention of quitting my job so quickly.

"Excuse me," I began. "I need to get ready for my next set. It was nice meeting all of you."

I bowed graciously and left their table, believing that would be the end of it. But in fact, nearly every night after that meeting, Randy showed up regularly to watch my performance. I'd sit with him and listen to his stories about surviving in Honolulu. His dry wit made me laugh, and I learned a lot about how regular folk lived on the islands.

However, not everyone was happy about my newfound friendship. One night, after he left, Okyon took me aside and told me, "Okhui, that man is a drug dealer and a gambler."

"How do you know?"

"One of the customers—Joe Nagata," she said. "He's an electrician, fixes old buildings and stuff. He told me Randy runs a gambling operation in Chinatown. He even deals drugs to those guys."

Not wanting to talk about it further, I shook my head and walked away. Though I had to admit, I'd always wondered about that Joe Nagata. I'd seen him chatting with my sister quite a lot lately, but as far as I could tell, he didn't appear any better than Randy.

***

AFTER NEARLY THREE months of dancing at Club Hubba Hubba, Tad Matsuoka called me into his office with a surprising announcement. He told me burlesque was dead, and audiences strongly desired more revealing performances, like his rival Jack Scione's "All Nude Revues."

My initial thoughts turned to my children and the rumors that would circulate among their classmates about their mother should I continue this career path. When I started this job, I had already established my boundaries, and there were lines I would never cross.

I handed in my resignation. Surprisingly, he understood the weight of my choice and didn't argue. Walking away from his office, surrounded by the lasting scent of his cigar, I grabbed my wardrobe from my dressing room and took one last step onto his empty stage.

I had begun my journey in America on such a stage, engaged in colorful acts, including magic shows, Egyptian snake dance routines, comedy routines, and live jazz band performances. I had been a headliner at this Club Hubba Hubba.

"But now, it's all in the past," I muttered to myself.

Holding my shimmering, sequined dress in my hand, I stepped off the stage and walked out their front door, closing it behind me. I couldn't help but wonder what adventures lay in store for me in this island paradise, away from the bright lights and colorful acts of my past. But I felt ready to start.

HOSTESS BARS IN HONOLULU

AFTER DEPOSITING MY final paycheck, I ate lunch with Randy at Columbia Inn on Kapiolani Boulevard. After my initial meeting with Randy, I continued seeing him for months. Though he was aware that I had just quit dancing, he suspected that something else was troubling me. He handed me a glass of ice water with a straw, but I didn't touch it.

"Something on your mind?" he asked. Gazing into his sympathetic eyes, I exhaled.

"I want to bring my mother and children to Hawaii," I said. "I've been away for nearly three months, and I miss them terribly." Tears welled up as I stared at the straw in my ice water.

Randy patted my hand gently. "I'd love to meet them," he replied.

Shaking my head, I added, "Not only that, I need to prioritize my family. I want to visit Denver. But first, can you tell me more about Mamasan Gayo's bar?"

***

BEFORE I LEFT for Denver, I searched for an apartment in Waikiki, but most places discriminated against single mothers with three kids. Not only was it extremely difficult to find a landlord who'd accommodate me, but those who were willing charged way too much rent. I eventually found a nice apartment near the Honolulu Zoo and let Okyon stay there while I flew to Denver.

My children and Mother were overjoyed to see me—so was our dog, Bobby. It took nearly six weeks to prepare them for the move to Hawaii. When we were just about ready, I called Gordon and asked him to fly to Denver to retrieve the rest of his belongings, including our dog. It was a bittersweet reunion for both of us. To my surprise, he had lost his excess weight and appeared much healthier. He proudly informed me that he had been seeing a therapist and was participating in a support group for veterans suffering from PTSD.

"I'm a different man now, Okhui," he said. "I'm a patroller, and I'm considering running for mayor in Arimo."

"Are you asking me to become a politician's wife? My mind's already made up," I told him, turning down his offer, and then, with a bittersweet sigh, I told him he would always be welcome to visit the kids and me.

Admittedly, I felt a little sad about leaving him and Colorado, the place where I'd first embarked on my journey in America.

***

OUR FIRST FAMILY outing was an adventure to the Honolulu Zoo. Enjoying my time with my children, I soaked up their joy and laughter as much as I could since I knew it would not be long before I would be working long hours again.

The next day, I enrolled Dennis and Marylin at Jefferson Elementary School on the outskirts of Waikiki. Knowing that I couldn't put off work any longer, Randy accompanied me to Gayo's Korea House so I could officially start.

***

SINCE THE END of World War II, hostess bars in Honolulu hired many unemployed Japanese girls, some locals and some expatriates. By the late sixties, a second wave of hostess bars opened—for Korean girls. These types of bars became extremely popular with Hawaii's working class because, like similar bars in Japan and Korea, they offered a pleasant combination of food, drink, conversation, suggestive affection, and romantic encounters that ranged anywhere from passionate short-term affairs to long-term liaisons.

Hawaiian hostess bars were a blend of Eastern and Western cultures. Unlike the average American waitress, a hostess was allowed to sit with patrons and entertain them. Of course, the Honolulu Liquor Commission would approve a hostess bar license, which regulated hostesses not to drink alcohol on the job. But in truth, most of these commissioners looked the other way.

Since most bar patrons were of Asian descent, they were familiar with the *geisha* or *gisaeng* tradition. Their grandfathers had worked on the plantations in the early 1900s, and they brought over this tradition to bring comfort to lonely men who sought companionship. Though the work environment had changed, the market for such bars had not.

BUY ME DRINKEE

THE FIRST THING I noticed about Gayo's Korea House was the revolving neon sign over the front entrance. Stepping inside the smoky lounge, I quickly counted about twenty-two leather-upholstered booths that filled the main floor. It mirrored the atmosphere of a Hollywood burlesque house, only with loud Asian pop songs blaring from the jukebox.

Without pause, a lightly made-up Korean waitress approached us, appearing slightly tipsy.

"Ah, Randy, where you find dis good-looking *wahine*?" She spoke English with a thick Korean accent and beckoned him to sit down at a corner table.

"Domiko, this is Sylvia," Randy introduced us with a confident laugh.

When we took our seats, Randy asked Sylvia to take me to Mamasan Gayo's office to apply for a job and then ordered a beer for himself.

Sylvia giggled. "Buy me drinkee."

Randy replied, "*Bumbai*," in pidgin English, meaning "later."

After a minute of making small talk, Sylvia pointed me toward Mamasan Gayo's office and explained the two types of jobs available: hostess and waitress. Gayo explained that as a hostess, my job would be to sit with customers and look nice. As a waitress, I might get more tips for serving directly. "You choose," she said with a smile. So, I told her I wanted to start as a hostess because I was not familiar with drinks.

Gayo also instructed me to go to a liquor commission, register as a bar employee, and get some licenses.

After she concluded her interview, Randy escorted me through the bar, where he introduced me to a Japanese man wearing an expensive designer suit with his tie at half-mast. He appeared to be in his mid-thirties, good-looking but perhaps trying too hard to look dapper. Three of Gayo's hostesses huddled next to him as he raised a shot glass in a toast. After he downed one shot of whiskey, he kept ordering additional shots, one after the other.

"That's Harold Shintaku," Randy told me. "He is the Chief Attorney for Senate Republicans. He's one of our most frequent customers—loves to roll the dice."

I nodded, not the least surprised. I looked forward to entertaining such prominent clientele.

***

I RETURNED TO the Korea House the next day wearing double eyelashes, thigh-high boots, a low-cut striped blouse, and a leather miniskirt. I thought I'd bring a little Hollywood pizzazz to her hostess bar. With a gracious smile and an upturned lip, Mamasan

Gayo looked me over and replied, "You'll have to wear more tasteful clothes and less makeup. Japanese clients prefer that."

Gayo then took me through the kitchen door, where hostesses were expected to enter. Six hostess girls were already there, sizing me up. At the entrance, Gayo's grinning manager, George, complete with a lit cigar hanging from his mouth, showed me how to use the timecard machine and demonstrated how to punch in.

Having done that, I squeezed between the girls to put my purse on a metal shelf against the wall. Two middle-aged Asian women, referred to as "Kitchen Mamas," were busy preparing a large buffet of Hawaiian and Korean food. The larger of the *ajummas* was a force of nature in the kitchen, multi-tasking with several dishes at once.

"Yeon Ajumma!" a waitress shouted at her with food in her mouth. "What's the house *pupu* tonight?"

I remember laughing the first time I heard the word *pupu*, assuming it referred to something my children shouted when they soiled their diapers. In Hawaiian, however, *pupu* meant hors d'oeuvres.

"*Pipikaula*," Yeon Ajumma answered. "The *pipi pupu* platter."

I stifled the urge to laugh. At that moment, a young hostess rushed past me to make her way into the kitchen.

"Excuse me," I said in English.

The same girl rudely reacted by giving me what locals call "stink eye."

"You Korean?" she asked in Korean, but in a very impolite manner. I was stunned, having never encountered a younger woman speaking so curtly.

Just then, another young hostess entered. I noticed her large double eyelids, likely the result of a surgical procedure; it was becoming fashionable for Asian girls to make their eyes look bigger and more European. Her thick, round lips complemented her reshaped eyes, and her face reminded me of Sophia Loren, as did her ample bosom, revealed by the plunging neckline of her gown. Despite her candor, her voice was soft and gentle.

"My name is June. June Park," she said. "You da showgirl, yeah?"

"How you know?" I asked.

"I can tell by your look, well . . . actually, Gayo told me." She giggled.

As if on cue, Mamasan Gayo returned from the bar, beaming.

"Domiko, there you are!" Gayo exclaimed. June raised her eyebrow at my name, but she didn't ask about the origin of my name. "June is our top champagne girl. She will guide you."

As we entered the main floor, all the customers turned their heads toward me.

The bar was buzzing, and the jukebox blared contemporary tunes, forcing everyone to shout over the music. Every barstool was filled, and waitresses queued up to fill their trays and serve their customers. June led me to her usual table in the center of the lounge. She pointed out a burly man sitting at a corner booth. "That's my friend, Tommy," she said. "Owns a local restaurant in town."

Despite having only lived in Hawaii for three years, June's English was nearly fluent. She beckoned for me to follow her to Tommy's table. When I took a seat across from him, I noticed his eyes were fixed on me, though he never said a word. This was typical behavior for local Asians. They remained quiet to avoid saying anything stupid or to conceal an American accent. Or maybe he was just shy.

Speaking Korean, June asked me to wait with him while she approached the bar to get his drink—a bottle of Primo beer. She returned to the table with a giggling smile, poured the beer into the ice-filled glass, and whispered into Tommy's ear, "I think I'm going to have champagne tonight."

Tommy continued smiling. "On my tab," he said.

Without missing a beat, June returned with an expensive bottle of champagne in a bucket. She confidently advised me that selling champagne was the key to making real money—selling more bottles would result in higher commissions.

I studied her intensely. First, she'd set a white hand towel on the table while she removed the aluminum wrapper on the cap of the champagne bottle. Untwisting the wire, she shook the bottle before pulling the cork, releasing half the champagne onto the towel. Then, she seductively poured it into the champagne glass and stirred the white foam with a wooden chopstick.

"It tastes better when I get rid of all that gas," June chuckled.

I suspected Tommy knew that she'd intentionally wasted most of the champagne on the towel. But he apparently enjoyed the attention so much that he didn't complain. June slid close to Tommy's side, practically sitting in his lap, and asked in a flirtatious voice, "How about another bottle?"

I was surprised by her move, but Tommy gave in faster than expected. June leaned in, whispering that hostesses also earned money through selling "*naekkohana*," Korean for "one for me." *Naekkohana* was a special drink customers bought for the hostess. She gestured to a table where a middle-aged man with silver glasses had his arm around Sylvia, who fed him noodles with chopsticks. Sylvia's drink, she explained, was a mixture of ice water and Coca-

Cola, a common trick to keep the hostess from getting too drunk on the job.

June explained that the wage split for a bar hostess was forty-sixty. The hostess received forty cents on the dollar for each drink she sold, while the house received the remaining sixty. In addition to minimum wage at one dollar and ten cents per hour, a hostess could earn additional money by serving *pupus*, which encouraged generous tips—sometimes up to fifty dollars!

Still, June reminded me that the best source of revenue was made by serving champagne. Each bottle cost the customer twenty dollars, of which the house got fourteen. The hostess who sold the bottle received six dollars per bottle, not as good as the forty-sixty split, but understandable given the cost of champagne.

"Try to sell an average of six champagne bottles per night for me, at a minimum," she said.

While running the figures in my mind, I noticed a dark-skinned gentleman joining his friend at Sylvia's table. He pulled out his wallet and plopped a wad of twenty-dollar bills on the tabletop. Then, another one of his friends did the same, creating a small pile of bills to be spent on food, drink, and "company." Each time the waitress refilled a drink, she would simply reach over and collect from the table's "bank."

Unfortunately, I didn't realize that drinking liquor was part of the job requirements. I rarely drank, and I started getting a bit tipsy, giggling at June's makeshift orientation.

There was absolutely no way to fake champagne since every bottle was opened and poured in front of the customers. Additionally, June had told me she would earn a commission from champagne sales and give me a kickback, making it hard for me to simply refuse a glass.

"June, I feel sick," I whispered to her. That was an understatement; I felt ready to throw up. "Don't tell Mamasan, but I gotta go home."

"I'll cover for you," she said with a nod.

As I staggered into the parking lot, I started to wake up a little. A gentle breeze brushed against my skin, and suddenly, I felt a pang of uncertainty. I realized that all I knew was dance, and I felt as if I were downgrading myself.

I waited for Randy to pick me up. As I groggily climbed into his car, he became very blunt with me. "You sure you want to keep working here? Don't look like ya got much experience."

"I really need the money," I told him. "For my family."

Experiencing dizziness, I opened the window, took a deep breath, and confessed, "Those hostess girls work so much faster. They're more ruthless . . . and their English, except for June, is so thick with local pidgin. I feel like I don't fit in there."

Randy grunted.

I continued, "But my family depends on me. And some still living in Korea. I don't have much choice, yeah?"

"They're not your responsibility," Randy said.

I let out a frustrated growl. "You Americans don't understand. I am responsible for my entire family!"

Randy listened but did not respond. In fact, he kept silent for the rest of the ride home.

CHINATOWN WAGERING

THE NEXT DAY, to get rid of my hangover, I decided I needed some chicken watercress soup. Randy took me to Wo Fat Restaurant in Chinatown for a bowl, then confirmed that Wo Fat's second floor was a secret gambling parlor.

Since I had sobered up, I allowed him to show me around. A burly Hawaiian man sitting in front of an iron door greeted him with an enthusiastic yet gravelly voice. "Howzit!"

The room inside was massive and filled with smoke, reminiscent of a Hong Kong gangster movie I'd recently seen with my kids at the Golden Harvest Theater a few blocks away. Players rolled dice at large tables, surrounded by fifteen to twenty of the most intense-looking islanders I'd ever seen.

The room's few hanging lights cast a dim glow over their pallid, ungroomed faces. Card dealers at the tables greeted us with hollow gazes, all of them dressed in casual aloha shirts and faded jeans. I immediately spotted someone familiar—the customer from the Korea House.

Harold Shintaku took his spot at the dice table. When he saw my face, he winked at me. That's when Randy stepped up, inspected the game, and made sure everything was in order since Shintaku was somewhat of a VIP guest. Part of me felt proud to see Randy calling the shots like that.

I noticed an adjacent room where people were eating and resting. At one empty table, I spotted a plate with lines of white powder on top, unmistakably cocaine, the same substance I had seen Randy use on occasion.

Two middle-aged kitchen ladies tirelessly stirred soup and prepared light meals in an open kitchen. I felt as though I had crossed over into another country, wondering how and why Randy would spend so much of his time here.

***

AFTER A FEW weeks at Gayo's bar, June invited me to her seventh-floor apartment, boasting about its minimalism due to her busy life. With a quirky smile, she showed me a four-foot-tall ceramic Chinese vase in her living room, filled to the top with coins. And to my surprise, she had a shelf filled with books, despite having told me she didn't read at all.

Then, she opened one of the books, showing me that they were each hiding crisp one-hundred-dollar bills between each page. On the top shelf, her bank book revealed a six-figure savings account, but she admitted she didn't know how to read numbers. With a high-pitched laugh, she blamed it on having skipped years of elementary school.

After our conversation, she casually pulled out a bag of white powder from under her mattress. "You like some of this?"

I declined. She appeared surprised but didn't make an issue of it.

***

IN ADDITION TO managing her bar, Mamasan Gayo often featured me as a "celebrity" at various social functions. She marketed me as a foreign movie star and showcased me at events like teahouse parties and campaign fundraisers. One such fundraiser was organized for a local Senator named David C. McClung, who had personally invited her.

Gayo arranged for June, two other girls, and me to attend Senator McClung's event, held at the exhibition hall of the Honolulu International Center. She introduced us respectfully as her "best girls." As soon as we walked in, I could sense a hundred eyes fixed on us, especially on me. My stunning, translucent gown with a high-cut slit that revealed nearly my entire leg certainly didn't go unnoticed. Even women were giving me the once-over.

Feeling a bit uneasy, Mamasan gathered us girls and whispered, "Just ignore the onlookers."

In elegant fashion, we followed Mamasan further into the crowd, where a pair of middle-aged men approached us. Mamasan received a friendly tap on the shoulder, and she casually greeted them with a smile.

"Good to see you, Senator," she said. Then, she turned to the other man and introduced him as "Bobby," otherwise known as Robert Kimura, an attorney and state representative.

While they chatted, my attention was captivated by a striking man approaching me. Devilishly handsome with silver hair and indoor sunglasses, he exuded confidence in a blue business suit. He even had a sturdy Polynesian bodyguard at his side.

He addressed Senator McClung as "David" and inquired about his family. The senator responded with a nod, and they exchanged pleasantries. Mamasan Gayo playfully intervened, introducing the man with a singsong voice as her "favorite liquor commissioner— Mister Hal Lewis."

Senator McClung added, "Don't forget, union leader!" Hal chuckled heartily, leaving me frozen in place, silently admiring him and hoping he wouldn't notice my schoolgirl gaze.

Hal greeted us girls, kissing our hands one by one. When he reached me, he paused, and Mamasan introduced me as the new star attraction, Domiko. In Korean, she emphasized that he was the liquor commissioner and union boss, urging me to remember his face. At one point, Hal turned toward me, but Senator McClung pulled him aside. Hal then said a quick goodbye to Mamasan and me as he followed the senator.

"I'll be sure to visit *bumbai*," Hal called out to us.

Curious about Hal Lewis, I briefly pondered what to say if I ever met him again, though I wasn't entirely sure. Before I could dwell on it, Mr. Kimura interrupted our group, offering each of us a business card. He shared some sage advice, "Girls, there are three things in life we cannot avoid: death, taxes, and the need for legal help. I can't do much about the first two, but my legal services are available to you." He smiled, winked, and then departed with a slight bow.

Mamasan Gayo expressed her satisfaction, saying, "Good job, everyone. We're a big hit out here."

JUNE AND CLUB YOBO

ONE EVENING, I noticed a middle-aged Caucasian man in a silk shirt sitting at a corner booth with a younger, handsome Asian man with a short tuft of hair on his chin. They appeared out of place, not flashy or stylish. Even so, they managed to get June's attention as she sat in between them and beckoned for me to join. She introduced her customers as "Richard Kometani and Haole John," the latter had just been discharged from the United States Navy.

I didn't have the slightest interest, but June persisted. Uneasy and resistant, I bit my lip and approached the Caucasian man. To me, he looked like *janji*, or what hostesses called a "cheap Charlie," a man who mindlessly sat alone in the bar to avoid being bothered by hostess girls.

"Pleased to meet you, Haole!" I exclaimed. He and Richard looked at each other and laughed. Little did I know that *haole* connoted a "foreigner" or "White person" and would never be used as a personal nickname. John told me his last name was Halliday,

which reminded me of Audrey Hepburn's movie *Roman Holiday*—
easy to remember.

"Glad you could join us," he responded in a lighthearted tone.
"So, my good buddy Richard here owns a chain of restaurants,
and one just opened up on Keeaumoku." He paused. "Uh, your
Mamasan's not listening in, is she?"

"Mamasan Gayo no care," June retorted.

Still, Haole John lowered his voice, "Great. I'd like to make a
business proposition."

"Errr—how do you know June?" I asked.

Haole John shrugged his shoulders. "From here," he said. "I'm a
regular. You see, I work as a realtor, and when I get a hot tip, I go
for it. So, I know dis guy—my friend Mario—he's got an Italian
restaurant that's ready to fold. It's a perfect location that you can
convert into a bar just like this one. And best of all, you'll be the
sole owner. No more working for Mamasan Gayo."

"Own a bar?" I whispered to June in Korean, "Sounds like they
want to scam us."

June was so excited about the proposition that her eyes bulged;
she hadn't heard a word I'd said. "I think it's a good idea!" she
exclaimed. "Let's do it. Let's open our own place, just you and me."

Hesitant to boldly object, I kept silent. Inwardly, I was intrigued
by the appeal of owning my own business, especially having seen
how so many of my former employers had unfairly exploited their
workers. I vowed I would treat mine better should the opportunity
ever arise. Haole John then handed his business card to each of us.
We cupped our hands over our ears to block out the loud music
and exchanged phone numbers.

"Call me anytime," John said. "I'll be ready."

June closed our impromptu meeting with several rounds of Scotch and sodas. I felt unsure if June was genuinely serious about their proposition, so after the gentlemen left the table, I confronted her directly.

"June, I don't have that kind of money to open up a bar," I told her. "Besides, I'm sure those guys are only looking to make a commission out of this restaurant sale."

June abruptly put down her Scotch and soda and retorted, "Domiko, a woman like you can—should—run her own business. Look, I never went to school, so you're more qualified than me. I can help you with the money. In fact, I lend you all the money you need. Just pay off loan monthly, with little bit interest, until you own your half." She paused, then looked me directly in the eyes. "Please be reasonable. We're not that young anymore; we're almost in our thirties."

Tightening my brow with a bit of curiosity, I asked her, "You've thought about this a lot, haven't you?"

A mischievous grin lit up her face like the star on a Christmas tree. "Yes," she said. "Yes, I have."

I chuckled. To quote Humphrey Bogart in *Casablanca,* this looked like the beginning of a beautiful friendship.

***

LATER THAT WEEK, Randy and I ate lunch at Coco's Coffee House, enjoying their simple menu of Vienna sausage and chicken noodle soup. They were one of the few eateries that remained open nearly twenty-four hours, which made it a popular local landmark. Though Coco's was part of a national chain, this one catered to people from all walks of life—from *Hawaii Five-O* television stars on break to young people out on the town to shady businessmen holding secret meetings.

After sharing my new business venture with Randy over lunch, it was clear that he was not at all excited, especially since my time spent with him would be more limited.

"This is a small town, you know?" he said. "What will people say when they see you and another *haole* guy eating together?"

"He's a realtor," I enunciated slowly. "And it's just business."

Randy glared at me like I was stupid. I then added, "Plus, June's fronting most of the money."

Randy sighed, "You're new to this kind of business. June's reputation—she'd sell her mother for a bottle of Scotch."

I snapped, "Randy, you don't control my life. And I don't need you making my decisions for me." June may have been eccentric, but at least she was trustworthy. She didn't spend her free time gambling like Randy did, so I felt comfortable ignoring his advice. My focus was set on the potential profit—owning my own hostess bar, just like my Aunty Deoki.

***

FOLLOWING SEVERAL MEETINGS at June's apartment, she presented me with her rebalanced bank book and requested her lawyer draft a promissory note, plus interest, for both of us. I was surprised at how many bases she'd already covered. On the other hand, Randy was right about her reputation. She was not as naïve as I'd originally thought, but since I was already well into the process, I completely ignored my rising uneasiness.

The following week, I scheduled another lunch at Coco's with June and Haole John, but it was Sunday, and with my mother at church, I had to bring my kids since I couldn't find a babysitter. John immediately took a liking to little Marylin and Patrick, occasionally smiling at Dennis. However, June seemed uncomfortable and completely ignored them despite their ruckus.

As the kids finished their lunches, I briefed John on the business proposal June and I had signed. His facial expression indicated he liked our ideas, but when I finished my presentation, he directed his questions at me.

He obviously trusts me more than June, I thought.

"Since the building used to be an Italian restaurant, you'll need to apply for a different type of work agreement," he explained. "And you'll have to negotiate the lease agreement with the landlord, which I can help you with. In fact, I'm sure I can bring the price down to . . . say sixty-thousand dollars."

That's quite a difference from the seventy-five thousand quoted at the start of our meeting, I thought. June and I eagerly agreed, and the next day, we instructed our attorney to begin work on the lease agreement.

***

OUR BUSINESS VENTURE began in the summer of 1971. June and I proudly signed the new lease on Mario's Restaurant on Kapiolani Boulevard and decided to name our hostess bar "Club Yobo," which means "sweetie" in Korean. I sent June to the liquor commission, accompanied by attorney Burt Takarin, to receive the final license because I had to pick up Marilyn from school.

In just under a month, our five thousand square feet of floor space was refurbished, and the letters of Club Yobo glowed in red neon on the marquee. French-style mirrors covered the walls—an idea I'd borrowed from Mamasan Gayo's Korea House—and the ceiling was designed to look like floating purple clouds.

Within a month, Club Yobo became the hottest nightspot among locals, known for having a wide array of hostesses and the most delicious food in town. On our first night, the jukebox blared "How Can You Mend a Broken Heart" by the Bee Gees while scores of customers and hostesses from other bars—including Mamasan Gayo's—waited in long lines to get in.

Later in the season, we had to turn people away as our cash register kept ringing nonstop. Our club attracted a diverse crowd, including local businessmen, politicians, and construction workers.

Business was thriving.

Initially, I appointed sister Okyon as floor manager to oversee the hostesses, and my eldest brother Jeong joined us as a maintenance man. Mother, looking to contribute to her church fund, joined the kitchen staff and proved to be a valuable addition.

At my venue, the kitchen was the main hub of activity, with a large central counter and numerous chairs around it where girls could grab a quick meal before meeting customers in the main lounge. Two kitchen mamas preparing meals and a team of dishwashers scrubbing dirty dishes contributed to the bustling atmosphere. Amid all this activity, Korean chatter sparked into lively conversations while waiting on plates of steaming white rice. A kitchen mama would scoop two scoops of rice and a dish of *kimchi* to each girl. They often gave more food to the girls who tipped them the most at the end of the night.

"It's delicious, Ajumma!" they'd tell the kitchen mama, savoring the taste of *kimchi* among the culinary chaos. Sister Ok Nan, in charge of hygiene, urged the girls to freshen up after indulging in our garlic-laden delights. Customarily, we fed customers plenty of *kimchi* so that the smell would be commonplace.

***

EARLY EACH MORNING, Mother would pick up all the dirty towels, launder them, and then return them in the afternoon before the club opened. One Friday afternoon, right before preparing to cater a large private party for GTE Hawaiian Tel, Mother came by the bar with my kids, each one carrying a set of bar towels in a line like the little dwarfs from Snow White.

I laughed, instructing each child to set them on the table. As soon as Mother entered the kitchen to make lunch, Dennis snuck around the bar while I wasn't looking, grabbed an expensive bottle of Louis XIII whiskey, and ran around the lounge with it.

Chasing after him, I shouted, "Put that back." Finally catching up to him and taking the bottle, Dennis proceeded to chase Patrick and Marylin around the bar, jumping from one barstool to another. Suddenly, Patrick lunged forward and hit his forehead on a corner table. A stream of blood shot from his forehead as he lay on the floor, screaming in pain.

Grabbing a bar towel, I told Mother to apply pressure on the wound.

"*Aigo! Aigo!*" she mumbled loudly. Being a military wife, I could take Patrick to Tripler Hospital, but I needed someone to take over the catering. I considered calling Okyon, but she was recovering from a black eye given to her by her boyfriend, Joe Nagata. She had previously told me she didn't want to be seen in public. I called June to come over and help me with the catering, but she declined.

"I don't waste my energy on private parties," she quipped. "It's like running a marathon for pocket change."

"June," I argued. "You can't rely on champagne customers. Every customer is important." With Patrick crying, I had no choice but to hang up the phone to drive Patrick to the emergency room.

I let Mother take over kitchen duties and hoped Dennis wouldn't get into any more trouble. Letting out a breath, I put little Patrick in the back seat of my car and headed out. Part of me wanted to curse June out, but she wasn't my employee. She had the right to pick and choose her customers.

Still, she had no clue how difficult it was to raise three kids while working in the evenings. Having grown up an orphan and dealing with challenges unique to her own life, she never experienced having a large family to take care of.

June once told me and my mother that, as a little girl, she had been accused of stealing a dress. The arresting officer beat her several times, and when she prayed to God to save her, the policeman snapped, "Little bitch! There is no such thing as God!"

But June never recanted her faith. This is why Mother claimed June was a devout Christian, but in my eyes, she was more of a *cash-tian*—someone who worshipped money. I was quickly learning that we were like oil and water.

We did *not* mix well together.

LIQUOR INSPECTORS, DRUG DEALERS, AND THIEVES

CLUB YOBO WAS jam-packed during the nights leading up to Christmas. One night, while supervising my side of the bar, I heard Okyon calling my name over our new P.A. system. Judging by the tone of voice, I knew right away something was wrong. "June! Domiko! Please come to the kitchen!"

When we arrived, two men in business suits stood waiting for us beside the kitchen door. The shorter one stepped forward to shake our hands.

"Liquor inspectors," he grunted his introduction.

June inconspicuously whispered behind me in Korean, "They're probably searching for the secret envelopes."

Disturbed, I winced as she explained how Mamasan Gayo bribed inspectors with Christmas envelopes filled with cash for "proper" inspections. I suggested, "How about a bottle of liquor?"

June laughed, then paused. "Domiko-chan, they want cold, hard cash."

She slid two envelopes from under the cash register, each holding a crisp hundred-dollar bill. With her usual flair, she sealed the envelopes with her tongue and handed them to the inspectors. They swiftly tucked them into their back pockets and left. Shockingly, every night, more inspectors appeared at our back door, and like clockwork, we kept paying.

The feeling of humility never went away.

***

ONE AFTERNOON, WHILE Mother was peeling garlic in the kitchen and I was taking inventory behind the bar in preparation for Christmas Eve, Randy unexpectedly walked in and declared he was a changed man. Determined to be in my life, he told me he had stopped gambling and gotten a job as a manager at the Wisteria restaurant up the street.

"Why didn't you take my calls?" he asked.

"I'm busy doing inventory for the big night. I don't have time for you."

"Because you're dating that *haole* guy?" he accused me.

"Dating him!" I snapped back at him, but I wasn't going to give him the satisfaction of denying it. "So what if I am? I'm not married to you! And you never worked more than a day in your life! Always hanging around Chinatown. There's no future with you. At least Haole John helps me out at work."

Hearing my reaction, Randy's eyes twitched with rage. He grabbed a tray and slammed it down on the bar counter. In an instant, Mother ran into the main lounge, hearing the commotion.

"What's going on out here!" she shouted, then flailed her arms at Randy. "*Yenomo sekiya*! Damn you! Leave my daughter alone!"

Without looking back at us, Randy stomped out of the bar, and I assumed, out of my life.

Sadly, I was wrong. He returned a few weeks later with his friend, a dark-skinned Portuguese man who resembled a young street hooligan, and they sat together in a corner booth. Even in the low tungsten light of the lounge, I recognized by his bloodshot eyes that Randy must have been high on something.

Randy appeared eager to introduce me to his friend. I took their order without conversing with him until June passed by.

"Walter!" she exclaimed, seeing the dark-skinned man. "Long time no see. Where you been?"

Turning toward June, I asked, "You know this guy?"

June responded, "I know him from Club Korea House." With cheerful dollar signs in her eyes, she slipped into their booth and, in hostess fashion, slid right up to Walter and practically sat on his lap.

Randy grabbed my arm and pulled me close to him. "Domiko," he began. "You thought about what I said?"

"I'm busy with my family," I responded. "And I'm working. Now, if you'll excuse me, I have to attend to my paying customers."

With the jukebox blaring, I was spared from hearing his pleas to take him back. Fortunately, I was able to slip away as soon as Okyon sent another waitress to take their orders.

***

UNFORTUNATELY FOR ME, Walter and Randy began making regular visits to the bar—which turned the situation from bad to worse. Most nights, I would walk in on them snorting cocaine in the back room. I called for June, but she would just join them, laughing it up on Walter's lap.

When it happened a second time, I snapped, "What you *lolos* think you're doing?" June continued laughing. Once playful, June's high-pitched laughter became downright annoying.

Infuriated, I grabbed her by the arm and dragged her through the kitchen, fearing another inspector would soon pop in for his routine visit. I expected Walter to stand up for her, but he did nothing. He cowardly picked up his things and ran outside through the kitchen door. Randy, on the other hand, calmly walked into the parking lot carrying a briefcase.

Turning my place of business into their personal drug den made my blood boil. I followed Randy into to the parking lot to confront him, but as soon as I walked out the kitchen door, he grabbed me by the wrist. In a panic, he pushed his briefcase into my arms and insisted that I take it inside.

"The cops are out here," Randy whispered. "Please, take this into your office."

"What? What's in here?" I asked loudly.

"Just do me this favor," he said. As he ran back into the kitchen, two undercover cops entered through the back door, grabbed him, and shoved him against the wall. Their long overcoats were a clear indication they were undercover cops, just like I had seen on television.

Ignoring the commotion, I went straight into my office with Randy's briefcase in hand—I had forgotten that I was even holding it. Massaging my aching temples, I dropped it to the floor and kicked it away out of frustration.

Suddenly, I heard a hard thud. I had unwittingly opened the briefcase with that kick. Inside was a handgun and a bag of cocaine with several wads of money bound by rubber bands. Teeth clenched, I slammed the briefcase shut, hoping nobody had seen me carrying it. I did not realize it then, but my problems were only beginning.

***

TO MY SURPRISE, Randy returned to pick up the briefcase the very next evening. Still angry, I had expected him to apologize, but he never did. Instead, he arrogantly opened the briefcase and flashed the money in my face.

"You see all this bread!" he exclaimed. "We can go to Vegas right now and start a new life! I can take care of your mama and all your kids. You can shut down your bar. I'll be the one taking care of you!"

"I don't need your money," I told him. "I never want to see you again."

Enraged, he slammed his briefcase shut, turned, and hit the office door hard as he plowed his way out of the bar. I deeply hoped he would never come back.

***

BY THE END of the following year, June and I decided to end our business partnership. Though the trouble began with her boyfriend, she would often point out mine was no better.

"That no good loser Randy is a lousy gambler," she said.

"What about your boyfriend?" I countered in one breath. "He's a con artist, a stalker, a thief, a junkie, a murderer! And who knows what else?"

She never responded to that, but her loser boyfriend was only part of the reason I no longer wanted to work with her. The main reason was that she had no head for business. Every night, she would empty out the cash register and leave me with no money to buy food for the next day. I appreciated her for giving me my start in the business world, but our professional relationship was over.

For an entire week, I secluded myself in my office, wrote checks to pay off June's share of the bar, and transferred the stocks under my name. Since I wanted to make a fresh start, I chose a new name—The Domiko Lounge.

At my request, Haole John accompanied me to my liquor commission hearing since his knowledge and assistance would allow me to save on attorney's fees. We sat in a large room resembling a courtroom and nervously awaited the commissioners. All six of them entered through a side door and took their seats, one at a time, with the steady tempo of a well-oiled machine.

My nerves rattled while I fidgeted in my chair and looked at the long line of applicants seated ahead of me. When a commissioner finally called out, "Domiko Lounge," John and I took out our prepared application forms and approached the desk.

John discreetly tilted his head toward me and whispered, "Guy on the left is the union boss."

I was too busy mentally preparing my answers to make eye contact with any of the seated men, so while the commissioners flipped through my application, I briefly glanced over at the "guy on the left." I immediately did a double-take.

Without making it obvious, I sharpened my sight on his name-plate, which read, "Harold K. Lewis." I noticed his red tie perfectly complemented his royal blue suit. Before I could get his attention, Hal looked up at me with a half-smile, which made me so excited I nearly forgot myself. Thankfully, I was able to force myself to remain calm. He showed no sign of recognizing me.

"What was your purchase price, Ms. Lee?" he asked in a professional tone.

John answered for me, "It's on the application. Fifty thousand for half share."

Hal didn't look at John and instead directed all his questions to me. "It will take about two weeks to get you approved for a temporary license. Is that good with you?"

"Oh!" I stammered. "Oh, yes."

"That's great," John said. "You know, I've been wondering about—"

"Good for me, too," Hal interrupted, then winked at me. Feeling extremely grateful, I breathed a sigh of relief as the other commissioners thanked me one at a time. As soon as we walked out the door, John took me aside, out of earshot of passersby.

"I don't like that guy," he grumbled in a hushed tone. "You saw how he was looking at you? He's not just one liquor commissioner; he's one big-time crooked union leader." John was referring to the International Union of Operating Engineers, and he certainly did not hide his irritation.

"That's not all," he continued. "My brother-in-law owns a small construction company, and one time, this *moke* calls him up and tells him his workers better join the union. He only had five workers at the time, so not worth it, yeah? So, my brother-in-law refused.

And da next day, his bulldozer wouldn't start. Some punk went put sugar in his gas tank. I know it was that old fut that did it. I know it."

"John, you need to relax," I patted his arm and giggled. *Sugar in a gas tank? I've seen much worse back in Korea.*

John shook his head. "Just you wait," he muttered. "He's nothing but trouble."

DOMIKO'S LOUNGE

MY NEW SIGN read, "Domiko's Lounge: Opening Soon." Word got out quickly. I was relieved to finally be rid of the name Club Yobo since many local Koreans considered the term offensive, as it was often used in a derogatory manner. But by this time, my employees were not limited to Koreans. I had hired about fifty hostesses, many of whom were Vietnamese, plus some local girls, and occasionally a few *haoles*.

After closing time, John occasionally helped me carry some of my things to my car before he went home. This mundane routine went on for weeks without incident until one night, as I prepared to leave, I saw Randy's Mustang parked next to my car. Immediately, I noticed that the driver's window was open.

He didn't even bother to get out of his car when I approached him. "Randy? What are you doing out here?" I asked.

"I made some good money tonight," he said. "Wanna go get coffee?"

"You know I don't drink coffee," I said.

I observed the tight grip of his hands on the steering wheel as I silently settled into the passenger seat. I could smell alcohol on his harsh breath. I wanted nothing more than to end this relationship once and for all, and I intended to tell him so.

Heading to Hawaii Kai, he drove in silence. Those thirty minutes dragged on with just his loud breathing. I felt on the edge of a mental cliff, fearing he might push me. His tired, bloodshot eyes turned my way, cranking up the tension.

Where on earth is he taking me?

Randy abruptly hit the brakes near Hunakai Beach, where a few distant cars were visible in the darkness. I was already regretting allowing myself to come along with him.

"Once and for all, you got to choose between me and that damn *haole*!" he growled.

"Take me back to my car!" I urged, frightened.

The windshield fogged up, so he opened the side window a little to let air in. Even in that velvet shroud of darkness, the whispers of the ocean waves caressed my ears, calming me down. But the moment didn't linger.

Swiftly, he reached around my neck with his right hand, aggressively grabbed a handful of my hair, and forcefully jerked my head back. I tried to raise my fist, but he held me down, exposing a handgun tucked into his belt.

In a violent rage, he pulled out the gun and pressed it firmly against the side of my neck. I tightly closed my eyes and managed to let out a quivering whisper, "Please, don't shoot."

"You make me crazy!" He pushed the gun so hard against my neck that I could feel the barrel digging into my skin.

The faces of Mother and my children appeared in front of me. In my gripping terror, I started to pray. *Juyo, help me. If I die here, what will happen to my children?*

Randy pushed the gun deeper into my neck. I screamed. He deliberately pulled my head back, and at that very second, I thought for sure the gun would go off. That's when a jolting sensation came over me, an inexplicable feeling, as though my spirit was telling me, "Your life will not end here." God must have a reason for bringing me this far in my life. He surely wouldn't take it from me like this. And suddenly, an image of my mother's face appeared before me, and I heard her whispering, "I'm praying for you."

Just then, a series of blinding lights swept through the car window, forcing Randy to hide the gun quickly under his seat. The police patrolled that area frequently, and our activities must have attracted their attention.

"Police officer," a deep booming voice called. "Remain calm, and don't make any sudden moves." Startled, I turned toward the voice on my side of the car. A young Hawaiian officer was visible in the window. He looked directly into my eyes with a flashlight. "Let me talk to your friend."

He directed his attention to Randy and commanded, "Come outside with your hands up."

Randy complied. Sweat beaded on his forehead as he bared his teeth toward me like a vicious wolf before exiting the car. As soon as he raised his hands, a row of police cars appeared, their sirens blaring all around us. The officers wrestled Randy to the ground while I collapsed on the car seat. They slapped a pair of handcuffs on his wrists. I recall very little after that. When the officer took me into the police station, I declined to press charges against Randy as he had clearly done enough damage to own his life. Thankfully, after that dreadful night, Randy disappeared from my life once and for all.

***

AT HOME THE next morning, I behaved as though nothing had happened, but Mother noticed the bruises on my neck. Though she chose to remain silent, her eyes said it all. "I told you so."

All things considered, Randy's attack did not dampen my excitement for my official grand opening. I had come much too far to allow some bottom-feeding junkie to stop me from achieving what I had worked very hard to attain. Okyon continued working as my floor manager and maintained an on-again, off-again relationship with Joe Nagata. As long as he stayed away from the bar, I'd told her, I had no problem.

We had made enough to rent a studio apartment near Waikiki that was big enough for Mother and my children. Because I still owed June money, I could not afford a larger room, but the apartment was cozy enough.

Then, finally, the day arrived—our grand opening of the Domiko Lounge. I was fixing my makeup in my apartment when Okyon called me from the lounge's kitchen to tell me to hurry. The food and liquor trucks had just arrived, and she needed me to sign their checks. I drove over right away.

Okyon was right; several trucks had already lined up by my front door. I flagged down the delivery men and instructed them to enter the kitchen through the rear door. Inside, John prepared a rack of prime rib. The aroma was heavenly.

My new kitchen mama, Ajumma Min, known for making the best steamed fish in town, greeted me with a bright smile and announced in a singsong voice, "Look, Domiko! The lounge looks like one flower garden."

With a loud guffaw, she escorted me into the main showroom, where I welcomed a delightful sight. The entire lounge was covered with congratulatory flower baskets. Their sweet fragrance filled my multi-colored showroom.

At the bar, Okyon cleaned up while bossing around our shy, plump bartender we called Ajeossi, or Uncle. Whenever I turned toward Uncle, he would continuously bow. Then, I'd humbly bow in return. I certainly had a unique bar family to begin this new business venture.

QUEEN BEE OF THIS HIVE

WHILE MOST OF the flower baskets covering my lounge held a variety of flowers, one uniquely stood out—a Hawaiian-style basket woven from lauhala leaves and filled with gorgeous roses. Inside was a greeting card with only the name of the donor written on it: Harold K. Lewis.

I chuckled, holding the card to my heart. While I stood happily reading his name, Haole John walked into the lounge and stopped short of hugging me.

"Who sent the flowers?" he asked.

"Hal Lewis," I replied. "You remember? The liquor commissioner?"

"Uh, oh yeah," he muttered. "Well, I got something better."

What an odd reaction, I thought. *Is sending flowers a competition?*

John pulled out a small red box wrapped with a red ribbon. Inside was a bottle of perfume. My eyes gleefully lit up, and I thanked him with a kiss on the cheek. With June out of my professional life, I was lucky to have John help out with kitchen duties at my new lounge.

Excited about the grand opening, I walked over to my brand-new jukebox, put a quarter inside, and selected the latest hit by the Staple Sisters, "I'll Take You There." Just as I had done at Club Yobo, I made sure to play the most current American pop songs. I imagined the cheery laughter of crowds huddling around the bar, soon to be served by beautiful hostesses from around the world.

Surprisingly, it took less than a week for my silver-haired benefactor to make his grand entrance. I was excited that he did so. Clad in a newly pressed blue-gray suit and red tie, Harold K. Lewis marched into my bar accompanied by his bodyguard, a short, square-jawed Hawaiian *moke* with a wide forehead.

In a robust, dramatic tone, Mr. Lewis loudly announced, "I only want to talk to the queen bee of this hive!"

With a sly chuckle, I dashed to the entrance and greeted him with open arms, thanking him profusely for the flowers. "Hello, Mr. Harold!" I exclaimed.

"Please, call me Hal," he insisted with the swagger of Dean Martin. Right away, I called over the perfect hostess for him: Helen, a young girl who spoke fluent English. She was tall with a nice pair of long legs and shoulder-length hair. A true Korean transplant who had adapted quickly to the Western culture, many of my *haole* customers were drawn to her like flies to a honeypot.

Okyon guided Hal and his bodyguard to the best seats in the house. Before sitting down, Hal threw his car keys on the table to mark his territory. His bodyguard, in contrast, remained standing until Hal settled into his seat.

While the other hostesses stood glowingly around Hal, waiting to hear what he would blurt out next, Hal raised his hands and shouted toward Helen, "Give me a bottle of red wine! Any brand.

I no care." Although Hal portrayed himself as a man of refined taste, he drank very little wine, pouring only half a glass for himself.

Just then, I saw the contorted expression on Okyon's face; she clearly didn't like his arrogant attitude, and she certainly showed it.

"And get a drink for my man, Coconut!" Hal playfully patted his bodyguard on the shoulder. I swiftly shifted my focus from Okyon to Hal and his bodyguard. "Why do you call him that?"

Hal laughed. "Cuz it takes one thick head to pick fights da way he does," he said. "Coconut Tim! Thick like one coconut." Hal took a sip of his wine and laughed again. Coconut Tim's face remained stoic, but he managed to nod in acknowledgment. "One time, he picked a fight wit' a *haole* guy from Texas. Guy stood six foot, four inches—more than a head taller than Tim! He got so mad, he shoved the Texan into the ground, pulled off his cowboy boots, and beat him over the head with 'em!"

Once again, he repeated the nickname like a wild wolf, "Right, Coconut?" This made Tim's stony face finally break into a heavy, honking laugh until Hal gestured for him to leave us alone.

Tim headed straight for the bar, where he spent the next hour entertaining customers by demonstrating how to open a can of beer—by smashing it into his nose and sending the contents splattering all over the countertop. He'd then cackle like a maniac who understood a joke no one else did. The hostess girls giggled in delight, tickled by his medieval sense of humor.

"Mamasan," Hal redirected my attention with a gentle hand on my shoulder. "I hate to tell you this, but places like yours—they attract some real low-class types, y'know what I mean? And I'd like you to know, if you ever have one problem with customers who no pay, I'll have Coconut collect for you."

"I'm a problem solver," Hal explained. I assumed he was about to launch into another story, and I was correct. "I just got back from Washington, D.C. Got a call in the middle of the night and had to fly out. And you know who I met with? Governor Ronald Reagan! Now, he was one hell of a smooth politician. But we worked things out real good."

Hal took a sip of his wine and continued.

"I know you're busy, so I should get going." With a mischievous twinkle in his eyes, he added, "But if you're not busy next week, maybe we could have dinner at Chez Michel's?"

I smiled demurely to hide my astonishment. Chez Michel's was one of Waikiki's priciest spots, but I replied professionally, "Can you come back another night and ask me then?"

Hal's eyes sparkled when he grinned. "Great. It's a date." With that, he and his bodyguard exited, leaving me a bit overwhelmed but hopeful.

***

AFTER TWO SILENT years, Gordon unexpectedly called, expressing a desire to visit our children, albeit briefly. In our familiar exchange, I proposed he move to Hawaii to be closer to them and suggested shared custody. However, he declined, citing negative experiences with locals during his time at Fort Shafter decades ago, which had dampened his enthusiasm for living in Hawaii again.

For an entire week, I took Gordon and the children to the most popular family destinations around the island: Paradise Park, Sea Life Park, and the Honolulu Zoo. Gordon never stopped talking about how great Idaho was, but my decision remained firm. Having my own independent career was important to me, even though it had led to our separation. I had chosen this life, and I had no regrets.

Well, maybe a twinge of guilt.

Within a few months, we finalized arrangements to file for divorce. Shortly afterward, I purchased a condo by the Ala Wai Canal on the border of Waikiki, where we lived comfortably for three years while a house that I was looking at in Manoa Valley sat in escrow.

It was perfect timing since more family members were expected to arrive from Korea soon, and I needed the extra rooms once the Manoa house became available. On top of that, I would finally be able to own dogs and have a garden, just like I did in Denver.

BAD TASTE IN MEN

IT STARTED WHEN a small group of young, heavyset locals ordered a dozen champagne bottles. One of them had inherited a fortune from an aunty who had passed away, and he was blowing his money Don Perignon. The scene turned chaotic as I served them bottle after bottle. To make any money with champagne customers, I had to drink with them. Finding myself riding their wave of excitement, I stumbled toward the bathroom, teetering on the edge of throwing up.

Frantically, my sister Okyon summoned John to rescue me. Together, they whisked me away, tossing me into his car like a rag doll. By the time we reached my Ala Wai Manor apartment, I had made a mess of the backseat of John's car. Groggily, I regained some semblance of lucidity and clung to John for support. John pressed the doorbell at my family's apartment.

Mother, visibly displeased to find me in the arms of this *haole* man, stood at the door. To avert a confrontation, John smoothly transferred me into my mother's care and made a hasty exit.

With the alcohol clouding my judgment, I couldn't hold back. I confronted my mother about this unwarranted attitude toward John, defending him passionately.

"John is my manager," I asserted. "He's not a bad guy."

My mother's face remained stoic, and she responded with a chilling, "He's no good for you or Dennis." This simple exchange triggered memories of her own past mistakes, and I didn't hold back. I reminded her of her past boyfriends, including that dirty alcoholic Yim, and questioned her right to judge my choices.

In a crescendo of emotions, I declared, "Thad is no good! Randy is no good, and now John is no good! What kind of Christian are you?" I even mocked her praying stance, reciting her old Korean rituals. But my defiance earned me a sharp slap on the back of my neck.

Undeterred, I pushed back, causing my mother to wobble and lose her balance. She cried out in distress, and during this turmoil, my three children peeked through the bedroom door, wide-eyed and alarmed.

To shield them from the escalating drama, I pushed them away and closed the door, isolating us from their innocent eyes. My own tears welled up, obscuring my vision as memories of abandonment flooded my mind. I couldn't help but wail, "Why did you leave me?"

My mother's response, "I didn't want you to make my mistakes," only fueled my anger.

I retorted fiercely, "I'm not like you! You left us alone! You didn't care about my school or grades. And now you want to act like my mother?"

Tears glistened in my mother's eyes as she turned away to hide her emotions. I retreated to the bathroom to confront my reflection, a disheveled mess covered in orange vomit and smudged mascara. One false eyelash dangled down my cheek.

In the silence of self-reflection, I couldn't help but ask myself, "What have I become?"

EXTORTION, HAWAIIAN STYLE

ONE NIGHT IN an otherwise uneventful year, I spotted a swarthy-looking Asian man with ungroomed hair sitting at the end of the counter. On the thinner side, he looked local but with a pale complexion, as though he'd been avoiding the sun. He appeared tired, judging by the dark circles under his eyes, and reminded me of a scruffy street punk in his faded aloha shirt.

Our eyes met briefly that first night, but I believed he was looking over me. However, he kept coming back every night, ordering no more than two drinks. He always sat in the same corner booth, away from the crowd. On the fourth night, Okyon approached me while I was balancing the books in the office.

"That man asked for the mamasan," she said. "He looks like a bum. Should I call the police?"

I briskly waved her away, too distracted by stress. After she persisted, I agreed to approach him. He stared at me, then gestured for me to sit down. "Are you da owner?" he asked.

Feeling apprehensive, I hesitated to answer.

"You need protection," he said in a hushed tone. His eyes darted to the left and then the right. I tried to play it cool.

"I-I no undahstand wh-what you are talking about. Me no speak Englishee . . ." I faked a thicker accent to sound more "fresh off the boat."

Normally, it deterred people, but not this odd-looking man. His coarse voice sounded louder. "Eh, Mamasan. I know you got family—three kids. And I no like see you—or them—get hurt." Frazzled, I tried to collect my thoughts, but my mouth was too dry to speak.

The would-be gangster continued, "All you gotta do is pay me two grand up front, plus five hundred a week, and I'll give you all the protection you need. You don't play ball; I no can guarantee your safety."

I didn't buy it until he changed his tone. He got up, looked around, repositioned his stubby frame, and sat back down. He then lowered his voice to try to sound tough, "Remember, I know where you live."

The man lifted his shirt, revealing a small handgun tucked into his belt. I knew I had to be careful. He then grabbed my arm under the table. "No mess around," he whispered.

Flustered, I excused myself and hurried into the kitchen. Okyon, worried, followed me and demanded to know what was going on, but I ignored her as I grabbed the phone, cupped the mouthpiece with my hand, and dialed John's number.

Within half an hour, John came to the bar to meet the extortionist, who had been waiting in the same booth the entire time. I casually pretended to busy myself with customers while keeping one ear cocked toward their table. It was difficult to hear from where I stood, but when the extortionist got up to leave, I distinctly overheard him saying, "Tell your old lady I'll be coming down to the club every Friday fo' pick-up."

When he left, I was overwhelmed with panic. "What are we going to do?" I shouted.

"Don't worry. Let me handle this." And with that, John left.

***

THE FOLLOWING FRIDAY evening at the lounge, Okyon pulled me aside near the kitchen.

"The silver-haired gentleman and his Hawaiian bodyguard are asking for you."

I let out a breath of relief and rushed into the bathroom to fix my hair and lipstick.

Hal sat in a booth, scanning the customers while Coconut Tim stood beside him. I sat down across from Hal, calm and collected. A girl tried to take our drink order, but I told her to leave us alone.

Hal leaned forward and whispered in my ear, "I got a call from a friend at the FBI the other day. He asked me if something was going on around here."

I gasped. "The FBI? Why would they call you about my business?"

"Feds told me they've been monitoring everyone coming in and out of this bar. They asked me if I had anything to do with the place."

"Okay," I carefully admitted, "there's this strange skinny man that's been coming around. He's been extorting me."

Hal sat up, taking a more serious posture. "Don't say anything to the police. Leave this to me."

My gut feeling told me not to question him further as Hal got up and left with his bodyguard.

***

THE FOLLOWING WEEK, Hal's word proved to be true. KGMB-TV reporter Leslie Wilcox reported a story on the evening news about a man named Bobby Yaw, who had been arrested for extorting businesses in the Kapiolani and Keeaumoku area. In her report, she stated that Bobby was dying of cancer, found guilty by the courts, and indicted. I didn't know if it was Hal's efforts or Haole John's that led to the man's arrest, though Hal informed me the FBI could trace the cash.

Tragically, Bobby wasn't stealing for himself; he had just wanted to leave money for his family after he died. Despite his threats, I soon learned that I had been one of the lucky ones. Extortion was commonplace in the hostess bar industry. Recently, a *mamasan* at a nearby bar had been assaulted after work. She'd suffered a blow to her head and was robbed of three thousand dollars cash and some jewelry. At another nightclub near Waikiki, two extortionists were caught in an FBI sting operation that led to one arrest and the other killed during an exchange of gunfire.

Fortunately, business returned to normal within a few weeks. Although I was never privy to the details of what had unfolded, I did have some lingering questions. Did Hal use his "connections" to tell the guy to lay off? Or did John tip off the FBI?

I didn't care. Either way, it was a huge relief for me.

GRANDMA'S SECRET RECIPE

MOTHER OFTEN LOOKED after the children while I was at work. But when I was at home with them, I had to stay on my toes. One morning, I ran into the kitchen just as Mother poured some cornflakes into a bowl for Marylin. Mother then poured some milk and three tablespoons of sugar on top. With the first mouthful, Marylin's eyes widened in horror, and she spat everything out on the table. Mother slapped her on the side of the head and admonished her. "Just eat it!"

Marylin took another spoonful hesitantly and spat it up again, this time crying. Her face turned red as a tomato.

"What's the matter?" I wiped off her mouth and tasted the cereal. The three tablespoons full of sugar had been *ajinomoto*, or monosodium glutamate—MSG. Mother didn't know how to read, so she never labeled her jars and had gotten the two mixed up.

Clicking her tongue, Mother mumbled in Korean while I labeled the jars with a felt pen and showed her the Korean words.

Continually correcting labels for my mother while raising three children was certainly no easy feat.

I fondly recall moments when Mother Pong would prepare lunches for the children. She had a knack for making seaweed-wrapped rice balls called *musubis*. Their appearance was peculiar; they looked like baseballs with a long strand of kimchi protruding from the center. Sometimes, the seaweed wasn't wrapped tightly, and the ball would burst open like a flower.

On numerous occasions, Dennis felt so embarrassed by these unconventional culinary creations that he decided to either give away his *musubi* or sell it to a hungry passerby for a dollar. There were instances when Dennis came home visibly upset because of these lunchtime predicaments.

Upon witnessing this, Mother Pong took it upon herself to remedy the situation. Dennis frequently mentioned how other kids had cool lunchboxes that their parents had bought for them, featuring characters like Spider-Man, Superman, or even Barbie. Determined to make Dennis happy, Mother Pong headed to the renowned Holiday Mart to buy a trendy lunchbox for him.

However, her choice left something to be desired. The lunchbox she selected was actually designed for construction workers, made of stainless steel and complete with a man-sized thermal bottle, which she filled with Korean cold barley tea. Dennis was taken aback, commenting that it resembled a lunchbox belonging to someone's father. Despite his protests, Mother Pong insisted that he take it to school. Unfortunately, this led to teasing from other kids, who joked that he had accidentally grabbed his father's lunchbox instead of his own. It was just one of the many memorable experiences Dennis had.

But in all of these cases, I wasn't there to witness them. Hearing my children tell these stories after the fact made me feel guilty, and it became clear I should spend more time with them to be a part of their growth.

THE DON HO SHOW

ON A BALMY August evening, Hal decided to cash in on my offer for a dinner date. In my quest to maintain some professionalism, I suggested we bring Helen along, only to have my proposal swatted away like a mosquito. So, I put my foot down and told Hal that any dinner we had would be about business and business alone.

"Sure thing," he replied with his familiar, sly grin.

Hal stuck to his word, behaving like a gentleman. Little did I expect we'd end up at the Polynesian Palace for an extravagant dinner featuring a live performance by Hawaii's beloved international entertainer, Don Ho.

During his set, Don Ho locked eyes with our table after his first song and waved directly at Hal, who confidently waved back.

"Don and I go way back," he said. After the performance, we took a leisurely stroll down Duke's Lane, a block away from Lewers Street. I couldn't help but smile at Hal.

"Tonight was incredible!" Hal exclaimed before I could say anything. "I'd love to repeat it and get to know you better. Have you ever been to Vegas?"

I hesitated. "Hal, I'm not ready for that kind of commitment. Not yet."

He chuckled, undeterred. "I understand. So, this week, I have some union business to attend to in Reno. I'll be away for a while, but once I'm back, I'll give you a call."

"Take all the time you need," I said, not expecting to go any further than a business friendship. With everything I'd been through, I was neither stupid nor naïve. I had no doubt that any relationship would end as badly as all the others.

***

BACK AT WORK the next evening, Helen informed me that she, too, had gone on several dates with Hal, and we both laughed about it. Yet, while he was away in Las Vegas, I actually enjoyed getting long-distance calls from him. Even though I knew he was a playboy, I liked hearing his voice and listening to his labor union stories. Hal was delightfully nostalgic about his past, which I found quite endearing.

In the evenings, John willingly babysat when I worked late. He cherished time with the kids, and his commitment to my family was a refreshing priority. Finally, I had a dependable presence in my life.

Unfortunately, Mother remained unimpressed and constantly complained, "That no-good *haole* only cares for your two youngest because they're *hapa*. He doesn't treat Dennis good at all."

"Dennis is a big boy," I argued. "He doesn't need to be pampered."

Irritably, Mother shook her head at my rationale and rambled on and on about how I was dating yet another loser. "Last night," she reminded me, "he took Marylin and Patrick to eat pizza and left Dennis at home for me to watch."

I ignored her, refusing to argue in circles.

On the bright side, my business was flourishing, and that enabled me to bring home bags full of cash, which I would leave on the floor to count the next morning. More than happy to help, Mother stacked the coins in organized piles while she counted them, setting aside funds to help my brothers immigrate to America. This had the bonus effect of stopping her from complaining about John.

Shortly thereafter, I played the role of the family's immigration agent, bringing more brothers from Korea to Hawaii. Brother Yeong arrived in February 1973, followed by Father and Jeong a year later. A few months afterward, Jeong's wife, Jeongja, and their four daughters joined us. I helped them find a nearby apartment while we waited for the escrow to close on the Manoa Valley home.

Before we even set foot in that house, there was an abundance of family drama. John always joked that my home reminded him of a Greyhound bus station because all my siblings were constantly moving in and out.

One day, after a heated argument with her boyfriend, Joe Nagata, Okyon moved into our already cramped apartment and started picking on Brother Yeong.

"I can smell alcohol on your breath even in broad daylight!" she screamed at him. "You're always at the bar, wasting your money."

"It's my money," he argued. "Why is it any of your business?"

"I was the one who got you that painting job," she said. "Through one of my customers. And you squander it on those bar girls, you loser!"

"You're only mad at me because your Japanese boyfriend left you again!"

"At least I've never had three of them leave me every other year!"

When she mentioned his three ex-wives, that was the last straw. Yeong was so exasperated that he scooped up Okyon's whole body and was about to throw her out of our seventh-floor window. Mother and I frantically rushed to intervene, and in the ensuing argument, we all fell into one chaotic heap on the floor.

It looked like a scene from a slapstick comedy, but trust me, no one was laughing.

The following week, my sister kept telling me that if her boyfriend called, I should ignore it. "I don't want anything to do with that bastard," she repeated.

One day, the phone rang, and it was Joe Nagata. My sister mouthed to me, "Tell him I'm not home."

"She's not home," I told him and hung up promptly. Less than twenty minutes later, I noticed the phone was missing. Following the cord, I realized Okyon had dragged it into the children's room and, to no one's surprise, was chatting away with Joe Nagata as though everything was normal. Unfortunately, she made me look like a liar.

***

BROTHER YONG CONTINUED to live with his new wife, Carolyn, on the mainland, though he regularly visited Hawaii during the holidays. Brother Chang, however, wanted to stay in Korea and expressed to our family that he was happy and had no desire to come to America.

I transferred the apartment deed to Okyon so she could take over the remaining mortgage. With that settled, we moved into our new Manoa home just before Christmas. From there, we welcomed two more family members into our home: Princess, a poodle given to us by a loyal bar customer, and Duffy, a Yorkshire terrier John gifted me. With a higher income, I was able to enroll my children in private schools.

With a new spacious front yard, Mother wasted no time in designing her new garden with chili peppers and lettuce. Bursting with enthusiasm, she fashioned an array of vibrant hibiscus and plumeria into a rainbow pattern, a cheerful sight under Manoa Valley's blue skies. Procuring stones, Mother constructed an eleven-koi fishpond, enhancing our garden with colorful Japanese carp.

She then planted a bottlebrush willow tree just off-center of her garden, and over time, it grew to an impressive height, adorned with birds of paradise growing in strategic positions around the koi pond.

Navigating the role of a stage mom, I found myself managing my talented children and providing them with opportunities I never had growing up in Korea. Dennis and Marylin enrolled in music classes, honing operatic vocal techniques with the renowned Eunice DeMello. Meanwhile, Patrick received piano lessons from Mrs. Hashimoto at Punahou. Our home echoed with music, bringing immense joy to my spirit. It was undeniably one of the most delightful phases of my life.

During Eunice's annual recitals at Farrington High School Auditorium, Dennis's higher vocal range left the audience stunned, earning me compliments from fellow parents. "He inherited it from his biological father," I proudly declared.

Eunice recognized Dennis's special gift, urging me to encourage him further. Flattered, I eagerly kept my eyes open for future opportunities.

***

AMIDST ALL THE chaos of the hostess bar business, one undeniable truth became clear: Mother was right. I needed to spend more time with my children, no matter how challenging that might be. However, altering my demanding work routine proved to be a formidable task, and taking evenings off seemed like an impossible luxury.

After every last call, I'd count my earnings from the cash register before heading home. Driving along the same desolate road from Kapiolani to University Avenue, I found myself engulfed in deep contemplation about my life. Raindrops splattered against my windshield, mirroring the tears that welled in my eyes, and I started to question why I couldn't have a more conventional life.

Maybe, just maybe, Mother was on to something. Perhaps I needed to get to know God the way she did.

ENTERTAINING KILLERS

JACKSON INABA STOOD about five feet tall and had a loud, hearty laugh that could fill the entire lounge. He was certainly one of our most interesting regulars. His huge personality made up for what he lacked in height, and every night he came in, he'd make a big entrance sporting a most unique outfit: a funny ten-gallon hat, black jeans, and a tight brown leather coat.

Jackson exuded a cool swagger as if he had studied the movie *Shaft* too often. On one memorable occasion, he dramatically unzipped a large leather bag that was brimming with money for all to see, fueling the persistent rumor that he might be connected to the *yakuza*, the Japanese mafia. Undoubtedly, the rumor must've been true.

One night, he came in with one of my hostess girls, Sophia. I ran to the door to greet him when he caught sight of a burly Hawaiian Chinese man sitting at the bar, glued to the TV news. Jackson suddenly stopped in his tracks and whispered in my ear, "Does that fat man come in here often?"

"I barely know him," I said. "But he's been in here a few times."

A look of fear crossed his face, and Jackson ran out of the bar, leaving Sophia completely baffled. After that odd interaction, I noticed that same three-hundred-pound Hawaiian Chinese man visiting more often.

I started noticing his oversized aloha shirts and poorly bleached jeans, as though he'd attempted to remove unwanted stains too many times. Whenever he shifted in his seat, I cringed, expecting the barstool to break. And his eating habits were atrocious. I once caught him picking up a handful of boiled peanuts and shoving them into his mouth, whole—shells and all.

Recognizing these questionable characteristics, one can imagine my surprise when one of my hostesses, Jade, greeted him with a great big hug. Her affection toward this man was unusual, as she was never this friendly with other customers. Curious, I huddled closer to them.

"Oh, Mamasan!" she exclaimed, taken by surprise. "This is my friend, Ronnie. He's, ah—a schoolteacher."

I stared at her incredulously. "Schoolteacher?" I asked in Korean. "He looks like he just ate his students."

Not getting my joke, Jade looked at me blankly. Even though Ronnie hadn't understood a word I had said, he laughed like a happy hyena—our Korean language must have struck him as funny. In either case, Ronnie pulled out a hundred-dollar bill and loudly slapped it on the bar.

Like bees attracted to a flower's nectar, a gaggle of hostesses swarmed around him, cunningly asking him to buy them drinks. The spontaneous response from the hostesses caused Ronnie to shy away until only one or two girls remained.

Years later, we shockingly discovered this same quiet man had confessed to burying a DEA informant alive on Maili Beach. The victim's name was Arthur K. Baker, and his body washed up on the Waianae shore on Oahu's west coast.

Not long after that, Ronnie confessed to murdering Charles "Chuckers" Marsland III, the son of the city prosecutor, whose body was found in Waimanalo on the east side of the island. I was absolutely stunned. For years, we had been entertaining a professional hitman!

And it didn't stop with him. Over those same years, a series of news stories caused me to wonder if some of the men drinking at my bar—the ones my hostesses associated with—had just committed a murder.

I shuddered at the thought.

But truthfully, before I learned of Ronnie's gruesome crimes, I had always thought of him as an overgrown child: simple-minded and used to getting his way. When I saw him sitting in the courtroom on television, he behaved like a teenage delinquent, angry at himself for getting caught. He was criticized for not showing any remorse, but I believe, if he had any, he was too emotionally immature to show it.

I chose to conceal this part of my life from my children. However, I would share a more glossed-over account of these stories with customers who asked me if I'd known about any of these criminals they recalled seeing in my bar. I would share these stories with my mother as well, and she would pray for my safety and the safety of my children.

***

IT TOOK NEARLY two years for Jackson to reappear. Suddenly, he showed up one evening with hostess Sophia and another younger girl. The girls walked by his side, clinging onto his arms as though they were both dating him.

"Mamasan, this is my little sister, Sue," Sophia began. "She needs a job." Her little sister was a thin waif of a girl with long, light brown hair, innocent eyes, and freckles on her nose, bearing very little resemblance to her sister. I assumed they weren't actually related and happily welcomed a new hostess to bring in more revenue.

Although I was happy to see Jackson again, throughout the night, something felt odd about his manner, as though he'd undergone a complete change in personality. His usual boisterous manner was more subdued, his tone softer, and he'd always leave after only a few drinks.

The following week, I learned that Sophia and Sue had rented two separate units in the same apartment building that I used to live in, and over the next month, the "sisters" continued to arrive to work together. Sophia would serve Jackson drinks in a corner booth, but he became increasingly agitated and temperamental as the nights wore on.

About a month later, Jackson nervously pulled me aside for a private conversation. "Mamasan, I want to thank you for your hospitality," he began, "but I won't be coming back for a while." He spoke in his usual combination of broken English and native Japanese. He told me that he'd been indicted by a federal grand jury and would have to testify soon.

Then, he hurried out the door. Though I didn't know exactly why he'd been indicted, somehow, I knew I wouldn't see him again.

The following week, Sophia came to work alone. The worried look on her normally placid face made me feel uneasy. I felt a sharp, inexplicable pang in my chest.

"Is everything okay?" I asked. Sophia turned toward me but didn't appear to hear the question.

"*Eonni*," she addressed me respectfully as though I were her older sister, "I am sorry, but I need to go to Sue's apartment." She took a deep breath, then continued, "Sue always calls in the morning, but I haven't heard a word from her all day. I can't get hold of her."

Sophia stuttered when she spoke, "This evening, when I pulled into the apartment complex, my sister's blue Dodge was sitting undisturbed in the lot. I didn't think about it just then, but I have this strange feeling . . ."

She lapsed into an incomprehensible combination of her regional Korean dialect and pidgin English. The more she spoke, the more frantic her voice became, and I could tell that she feared the worst. I felt the same fear, so I encouraged her to go home.

After a few hours, Sophia came back and told me the rest of the story, utterly horrified. She had gotten hold of the resident manager and the police. The apartment was chained from the inside, but the police broke the chain. As soon as they cracked open the door, a strong odor wafted over them. They found the naked bodies of Sue and Jackson lying side by side.

She stuttered as she spoke. I stopped her right there; I didn't want to hear any more. That was the last time I saw Sophia at my bar. She never came back to work.

The next evening, a Hawaiian detective came over to ask what I knew about my hostess, Sue. He looked around the bar and then whispered in my ear, "The way that dead man Jackson held the gun, it looked like a murder-suicide, but—"

I let out a breath. What he said next chilled me to the bone. "But I have my doubts. This is an ongoing investigation, so if you hear anything, let me know." The detective gave me his number, and I promised to keep my ears open.

Several weeks later, a May 1976 edition of the *Honolulu Advertiser* reported that Jackson and an unidentified lover were found shot to death in a Waikiki apartment. Jackson had a prior arrest for attempting to sell heroin to an undercover officer, and he had agreed to testify against his suppliers in exchange for a lighter sentence. His murder has remained unsolved, but rumors circulated in my bar that both he and Sue had been hit by a local mobster.

I lay awake the night after I read that article, fixated on the image of Jackson and Sue lying dead in bed. I could hear my children stirring in their sleep in the other room, and in those moonlit hours, I realized I now lived in this underground world in which my bar had become tightly woven. My thoughts turned to Hal Lewis, and I pondered whether even he could shield us from the dark underbelly of paradise.

PART THREE

UNDER NEW MANAGEMENT

GORDON AND I had been divorced for nearly three years, and over the last year, he began regularly sending birthday and Christmas cards to the children. He wrote letters, telling them how much he missed them. Mother suggested that I send the kids to the mainland to visit him. I agreed it was a good idea.

During summer vacation, I allowed Dennis to travel to Arimo, Idaho. It was the first time I had sent any of my children away, and admittedly, I was worried about letting him travel alone. Traveling as a minor was not uncommon in those days, and I made arrangements with the airlines to have a chaperone accompany him.

When I told Mother about my fear of Dennis getting lost and being unable to find his father at the airport, Mother laughed and asked, "How many Korean boys land in Idaho?"

Nevertheless, Mother insisted on packing a Bible and a tiny cross necklace in his suitcase, while I entrusted Dennis with two hundred dollars to pass on to Gordon for food. I later discovered that Dennis used the money to buy snacks and left Gordon hungry.

The next summer, I sent Marylin, who had turned twelve, and Patrick, who was ten, to visit their father. It felt very rewarding to provide the kids with some extra time with their father, and Gordon appreciated it as well.

***

BY THE LATE 1970s, loyalty among hostesses was becoming non-existent, and it was now commonplace for girls to work in multiple bars in one night. My bar was still making money, but the constant stress and worry about my business became overwhelming, outweighing the benefits. At this point, I considered hiring a new manager to run the bar.

One afternoon, as I was buried under a pile of paperwork at the bar, a petite Asian woman strolled in and expressed interest in a job. She sported a dragon-themed T-shirt and worn corduroy pants, and her face lit up with the cutest dimples when she greeted me with a local-style hug. I couldn't help but notice her arm was in a sling, and she explained that she'd strained her muscles while trying to lift beer cases at her previous bartending gig.

She introduced herself as Cynthia Ho. "But everybody calls me Aunty Hobo," she declared, followed by an infectious burst of laughter. Her round body settled on a barstool, and her feet dangled above the ground. She had an undoubtedly pleasant demeanor and an impressive resume, complete with managerial experience.

On her first day, she showed up at the kitchen door, lugging a towering stack of pots and pans. I was genuinely impressed by her enthusiastic approach to her new job.

Aunty Hobo's charm worked like magic on our customers. In no time, she was drawing in more patrons than I ever had, and she transformed my lounge into a local-style bar featuring authentic Hawaiian and Asian cuisine. The bar became very profitable in a short amount of time. Unlike the hustle and bustle of hostess bars, our new place felt like a big, welcoming family, creating a cozy hometown atmosphere. I was proud to tell customers that Aunty Hobo was our head chef, as her *pupu* platters became legendary in town.

Every morning, she sourced the freshest seafood from the renowned Tamashiro Seafood Market or the fish auction by the waterfront. Her ahi poke, a popular Hawaiian dish made with fresh ahi tuna, was the best on the island. But that's not all—she served perfectly steamed fish with a delicious soy sauce and cooking oil mixture, topped with Chinese parsley, green onion, and diced ginger. No wonder she was voted Best Bartender in the "Dining Out" section of the Sunday paper.

***

IN 1977, AFTER the release of the movie *Saturday Night Fever*, disco became a huge dance craze. This inspired me to get back into dancing professionally. I worked hard and started teaching dance, determined to rebuild my dream career. Within six months, I became a dance instructor at the Fred Astaire Dance Studio on Kapiolani Boulevard, where I met the famous Korean songwriter Gil Ok-yun. When he saw me dance, he was so impressed that he offered me a job in Japan.

Ecstatic about the opportunity to become a professional dancer, I prepared for my big break. Mother Pong scolded me about my sudden career change, but I was determined to make this my new career. I asked Haole John to watch the children while I performed as an adagio dancer in Japanese nightclubs over the next two months. I figured since it was a short tour, I'd be back home rather quickly.

While in Tokyo, I discovered an invention called the *karaoke* machine, which allowed random bar patrons to sing in front of a crowd. *Kara-oke* was a compound word in Japanese—*kara* meaning "empty" and *okestura*, a Japanese cognate for orchestra. Could this become the next popular trend in the United States?

Maybe I can cash in on this, I thought. But at the time, I had no means of doing so. It was just a flippant idea.

MY DAUGHTER, THE MODEL

TIME PASSED BY quickly while I was dancing in Japan. Though I loved my brief stint, I was overjoyed to return home to my children and my mother.

When Marylin turned thirteen, I thought it would be the perfect time to introduce her to the world of ballet. Since I held a deep passion for dance, I was convinced she would share the same joy. Little did I know that dance lessons would come with more than just mastering pirouettes and pliés.

One day, while shopping for her practice outfit at the mall, Marylin unexpectedly plopped herself down on the stairway and pouted. She didn't hesitate to express her feelings.

"Mom," she blurted out, her voice mixed with frustration and exasperation, "whenever I'm with you and your Korean friends, they call me 'fatso!'"

My heart sank. I knew that Korean women could be very blunt and insensitive, but she'd never let on that she'd understood them or cared.

"What are you talking about?" I asked. Reacting with denial may not have been my best choice, but Marylin didn't respond. She stared forlornly across the mall, and when I approached, she got up and walked toward the next store on our list without saying another word.

After returning home, Marylin eagerly watched as Mother sat in the kitchen preparing her favorite potato dish. After boiling half a dozen potatoes, she peeled off the skins, poured a cup of sugar into the pot, and tossed in a couple blocks of butter. When she prepared to add another cup of sugar, I couldn't hold back.

"No! Not again, *Eomma!* You cannot keep feeding the kids mashed potatoes like that."

Mother retorted calmly, "As long as their tummy is happy, it's okay."

I lowered my voice to a stern whisper, "Haven't you noticed Marylin's chubby cheeks? I just signed her up for a ballet class. She has to watch her diet."

I wasn't very quiet, and Marylin turned around and stomped off to her room. I let out an exasperated breath. She had never behaved like that before, but I supposed I should have expected it. I then decided to enroll her in Gipsy Norton's Modeling Agency to teach her to better express herself.

Fortunately, this turned out to be a sound decision. Gipsy's classes were a turning point for Marylin's self-esteem. She had her braces removed, her glasses replaced by contacts, and she soon lost a lot of her childhood baby fat. I even encouraged her to compete in a local teen beauty pageant. But even with her newfound confidence, Marylin confided in me that she couldn't see herself walking down a runway, let alone competing with all those beautiful girls.

But I didn't let up on my encouragement. She applied to the Miss Hawaii Teen pageant and ended up proving herself wrong by placing as first runner-up. Shortly afterward, Marylin landed a modeling contract with a major Japanese cosmetics company.

We figured she could work in Japan during spring and winter breaks while attending high school in Hawaii. Within the year, she quickly became one of their top models, and I was very proud of her growth.

I also had the advantage of Haole John planning to temporarily move to Japan and help his friend set up a restaurant franchise. The timing couldn't have been more perfect. Since Marylin was underage, I hired him as her chaperone and allowed her to live with him. Through modeling, Marylin gained the self-confidence she never had before. She even gained a stronger sense of self-respect at a younger age than I ever had.

SOMETHING'S WRONG WITH DENNIS

MY OLDEST SON, Dennis, was Mother's favorite, and she protected him the most. Dennis was attending a private school at Hawaii Baptist Academy when his academic performance started to decline. I had to transfer him to public school at McKinley High during his junior year, and soon after, I received a note from the school stating that he had been absent for weeks.

It made me want to scream. Mother had often reminded me that I needed to pay more attention to Dennis. Once again, she was right. Reflecting on Dennis's childhood, I remembered how challenging it had been for him to simply sit still. Strangely, when he was little, he went through a period of chewing on furniture. Other times, he'd run straight into a wall without looking to see where he was going.

During his elementary school years at Hawaii Baptist, I'd have to pick him up from the principal's office after complaints that he had been daydreaming. His poor academic performance was the reason he had to be taken out of that school, but he didn't improve in public school either. His odd behavior led to one of his teachers finding a dead marijuana plant in his locker. Dennis didn't realize that the plant needed sunlight to grow.

In later years, children with Dennis's type of behavior were diagnosed with attention deficit hyperactivity disorder, or ADHD. But in the late seventies, this was not a recognized condition. At the time, I had assumed that the cause of his behavior was pure neglect on my part. I asked myself, "What happened to my child? Where's the prodigy who stunned the audience at his voice recital?"

Admittedly, he did lack the one important thing that every child needs: time spent with a parent. I would experience the fruits of that neglect soon enough.

In Dennis's senior year, he put in the effort and saw a slight improvement in his grades. But one April morning, all his hard work simply vanished. Mother barged into my room, screaming, "Something's terribly wrong with Dennis!"

I rushed after her into Dennis's room in a panic. The overpowering smell of marijuana hit us like a brick wall. There he was, sitting on his bed, eyes bloodshot, staring out the window. My heart raced, and it felt like I was being sucked into a teenage drama.

In a frenzy, I stormed through his bedroom, nearly tripping over an empty guitar case. I paused for a moment; this case housed the guitar I'd bought him just after he'd graduated from his voice lessons—the same guitar he wowed his uncles with at every Thanksgiving dinner. I screamed in frustration and then dug through a mountain of smelly socks, underwear, and stained shirts. I unearthed a plastic bag of that oh-so-familiar white powder. The kind I used to find hidden in the back room of my hostess bar.

Mother, equally baffled and horrified, pulled a tiny bottle of Scotch from his book bag. By this point, I was beyond mad that my teenage son had decided to use alcohol and drugs.

Then, something inside me just snapped.

"Get up!" I screamed, yanking the covers off him. "Get out of this house! I don't even want to think about having a son like you around!"

Dennis's response left me stupefied. An hour later, he quietly packed a suitcase, leaving it open as he walked out the front door, dropping a T-shirt and a couple of school textbooks on the way. Heartbroken, I stood there, biting my lip, fighting the urge to chase after him. Deep down, I knew he needed this solo adventure to straighten himself out, even if it caused me to shed a river of tears.

In the days that followed, we didn't know where Dennis was. Mother noticed the dark circles under my eyes and kept questioning if I'd made the right call. In my constant state of worry, I simply tuned her out.

As the days dragged on, the house seemed shrouded in perpetual darkness. My energy drained, and I couldn't even focus on my business. Mother, on the other hand, remained an unwavering pillar of faith, praying to heaven night after night.

Then, one Sunday morning, about a week later, it felt like our prayers had been answered. While I was in the kitchen making sandwiches for Patrick and Marylin's lunches, I heard a knock at the door, a distinct Dennis-style knock. I almost couldn't contain my excitement and relief, but I had to play it cool. I gently placed the sandwiches in front of my youngest children.

There he stood on the porch, Dennis, a scruffy, disheveled version of his former self, clutching the same suitcase he'd left with.

His face was as blank as a freshly printed sheet of paper, and though my maternal instincts screamed for a hug, I resisted.

Opening the door wide, I welcomed him back into our lives.

"I'm hungry," Dennis mumbled.

Without missing a beat, he slid into a seat between Patrick and Marylin. Patrick, in an act of genuine compassion, slid his older brother his own sandwich.

After a meal that could only be described as uncomfortable and too quiet, Mother, with her knack for finding life lessons in everything, compared Dennis's return to something she read in the Bible. I wasn't familiar with the story, so she later sat me down and told me the story of the Prodigal Son.

MY SISTER'S FUNERAL

ON THE AFTERNOON of June 18, 1981, I arrived home and noticed Mother solemnly seated in the middle of the living room, praying. Okyon sat next to her with a sorrowful face. When Mother turned toward me, she opened her eyes, which were pink and puffy from crying. Puzzled, I approached them, but they both sat stiff and quiet with an occasional sniffle.

"What's going on?" I asked as I closed the front door behind me.

Mother struggled with her words. "The police came to Okyon's apartment earlier. There's been a suicide."

Suicide? Who?

"It was sister Oksoon," Okyon interrupted. "She jumped off the overpass."

A million thoughts rushed through my head, and I was suddenly reminded of something horrific I had heard earlier. That morning, I had heard a news story on the radio about someone throwing themself off the School Street overpass. I shuddered with the sudden realization that it had been my eldest sister.

"I didn't even know she was living here," I began.

Okyon responded by bursting into tears. She wasn't one to get emotional, particularly over Oksoon, but now her feelings could no longer be bottled up.

"*Aigo!*" she sobbed. "Poor Oksoon had many demons. It is our family curse."

Mother cleared her throat. "Oksoon was always defiant and vengeful toward me," she said. "I'm sure that's why she never told us she was here."

***

THE FUNERAL OCCURRED later that month. We decided to scatter Oksoon's ashes off Waikiki Beach, so with Cynthia's help, we rented a fishing boat. This is an island tradition. We then picked up her ashes from Mililani Memorial Park. Mother carried the urn wrapped in a white cloth and set in a box. Father, who lived nearby, joined us. It was a bittersweet reunion, as it was our first almost complete family gathering in America, but sadly, for their eldest child's burial.

During the ride from the mortuary to the pier at Fishermen's Wharf, Mother and Father mostly stayed quiet, exchanging short sentences. At the pier, Cynthia's friend Naka, our skipper, greeted us. He pulled out a big cigar from his pocket and lit it up. The strong, exotic smell irritated my throat; Naka raised his brow at me, saying, "Cuban cigar."

It added a funny twist to the somber occasion. Mother boarded the boat first, with Father, Okyon, my brothers, their wives, and me following behind. She introduced us to Reverend Park, a slender, youthful man wearing dark-rimmed glasses, who informed us that he would be giving the eulogy.

Brother Yong and Carolyn flew to Hawaii from the mainland. Brothers Yeong and Jeong had known Oksoon best, though Yeong remained stoic while Jeong mouthed a silent prayer and wiped away a tear. No one talked much during the funeral.

Reverend Park gripped his Bible firmly and steadied himself, trying to adjust to the undulating water. Our family gathered around him, each of us trying to maintain our balance, though I started to feel a little seasick.

After Reverend Park gave his final blessings to Oksoon's wandering soul, he sang "Amazing Grace" in his gentle baritone voice. I sang along with him, having learned the English lyrics in my childhood. My brothers and sister joined in, and then we held hands in prayer.

Jeong then handed me a pair of white gloves to put on. I picked up the box from Mother's lap and took out the urn. After I sprinkled a handful of Oksoon's ashes into the water, I looked over at Mother. When she nodded, I leaned over the side of the boat and poured the rest into the ocean. The wind blew some of the ashes back toward my face, and I coughed. The taste of my sister's ashes irritated my lips. As I wiped my mouth, I watched the ocean swallow her up.

This was just like her, I thought. *Even in death, Oksoon found a way to get in the last word.*

DENNIS'S GRADUATION

IT WAS 1982, and in Hawaii, the excitement over a high school graduation rivaled the crowds at the Super Bowl. For my family, my eldest son's graduation ceremony from McKinley High was no exception. When the principal announced, "Dennis James Lee," it was music to my ears.

Dennis walked up to the podium to receive his diploma, raised both arms high in the air, and joyfully waved to us seated on the open football field. With enthusiastic applause, I waved back with a big *shaka* to wish him *aloha* and future success. I felt genuine hope that his future would be bright.

Cheerfully, the graduating class walked across the lawn in their black robes and caps with golden tassels. Most of their faces were barely visible beneath the stacks of colorful flower leis piled up to the top of their heads. Giving flower leis has always been a Hawaiian tradition for graduation. While the fragrance of ginger and carnations wafted through the air, throngs of parents, aunties, uncles, cousins, and friends gathered by a cluster of trees, waiting to give congratulatory hugs; each tree bore the first letter of the graduates' last name, arranged in alphabetical order from one end of the lawn to the other.

During Dennis's tumultuous high school years, I'd felt as though I was teetering over the edge of a cliff every time he wound up in trouble. But now, he was marching with his diploma firmly in hand. He had accomplished something that I never had.

After graduation, however, Dennis decided he did not want to continue his education for the time being, though I hoped he would eventually change his mind. I also knew it wouldn't be long before I needed to find a college for both Marylin and Patrick. Even though I had saved money from Marylin's modeling jobs in Japan, college tuition was still very expensive. Many long nights sitting at the kitchen table, calculating and recalculating my budget, brought me to the realization that now would be the best time to get back into the bar business.

***

THE OPPORTUNITY PRESENTED itself when I received a call from my attorney, Bob Kimura, who asked if I would be interested in taking ownership of the Osaka Yakiniku House on the corner of Keeaumoku and Young Street. Apparently, the owners were ready to close shop, so the timing was perfect.

Bob immediately applied for a new liquor license on my behalf while I contacted all my original hostesses to find anyone available to work. Half of my regular girls were ready to come back, and the other half recommended new hostesses.

Without a second thought, I named my business The New Domiko Lounge. Bob wisely suggested that I work with a partner to ensure there would be enough capital for expansion. Eager to show off my new girls, I emulated Mamasan Gayo's marketing technique and promoted my restaurant by inviting the girls to work at a campaign fundraiser for Bob, who was planning to run for a seat in the state House of Representatives.

Bob held his fundraiser at the La Mancha nightclub, down the street from my new lounge, the perfect opportunity to find a potential business partner. To my surprise, as I was just about to introduce my girls to the guests, a familiar silver-haired gentleman appeared at the door—a ghost from the past.

Concealing my amazement, I greeted him with a hug. "Hal Lewis! Long time no see!"

"Been busy with business. Union business," he said with a smile.

"You still looking good," I commented. Other than having lost some weight, he hadn't changed a bit since he went off to Reno. He still wore his trademark dark sunglasses and blue tweed suit. He even kissed my hand in the same boisterous and overly affectionate way.

"Domiko," he began. I chuckled at how he still called me by my business name. "I've been living out of a suitcase for the past year, flying back and forth to DC. I was hoping we—"

Before he could continue, Bob joined us. "Hey, Hal," he began. "You know, Domiko's looking for a business partner." He winked, then pointed his finger playfully at Hal as though he were flicking a pistol. I gasped under my breath. I honestly hadn't considered it, but Hal's connections as a liquor commissioner made him the perfect candidate.

Hal looked at me—intrigued—and agreed to meet with us the next day at Fisherman's Wharf for lunch. Bob and I prepared our proposal and presented it to him, though it was clear Hal was interested in more than just a new business venture.

As a savvy businessman, I knew his support and financial backing were the right cards to play, so he showed me an impressive venture capital portfolio and a counterproposal to buy half of my company. The fact that he could process our liquor license quickly was what Bob called "icing on the cake."

There was, however, a conflict of interest since Hal could not legally hold half ownership of a bar until he retired. Fortunately, he was ready to do so. Later in the week, Hal and I met for dinner in Waikiki to finalize the deal. Before we began our discussion, he casually extended an intriguing invitation.

"I got a meeting with a friend of mine in Waianae this weekend," he said with a wink. "Why don't you come with me? We go get lunch after."

Waianae? I thought. Waianae was pure country, located way on the other side of the island, so I naturally assumed that nothing much ever happened out there.

But a long drive with Hal sounded like fun.

THE WAIANAE COAST

I THOUGHT IT oddly humorous how locals prepared for a forty-five-minute drive to Waianae the same way mainland folks prepared for a cross-country road trip. Early in the morning, Hal came by to pick me up in his brand-new Lincoln Continental to go to "Henry's party" on the west side. Like the Waltons on television, Mother, Dennis, Marylin, and Patrick lined up and waited with me on the front porch. When Hal arrived, I introduced him to my family.

"He looks like a gangster," Dennis said.

Mother giggled, not understanding Dennis's remark, but she cared enough to speak English so Hal could understand, "Wow! He is very handsome." Delighted, she walked right up to Hal and proceeded to feel the muscles on his arms. Jokingly, Hal started to flex his muscles, making us all laugh.

"Is he Christian?" Mother asked.

"Catholic," Hal replied.

"Good choice!" Mother shouted jovially.

"No wonder your daughter's so beautiful," he told Mother, giving her a big bear hug. Hal added, "Tell you what, next weekend, I'll take you all to lunch."

"So, where's your bodyguard, Coconut?" I asked.

He winked and pointed at me. "You're my bodyguard for the day."

I chuckled. The long drive was very relaxing and went without incident until we came across road construction along Kamehameha Highway and got stuck in traffic for fifteen minutes. As we sat patiently, Hal asked a question I had long been dreading.

"Domiko," he began, "that Haole John you got working for you—is he still your boyfriend?"

I let out a breath, recalling how John never wanted me to do business with Hal. Now, I knew the hostility went both ways.

"John's not really my boyfriend," I told him. "He takes care of the kids, and he treats them good. Plus, he's a good cook. I need him in the kitchen. At the bar, I mean."

I stopped my argument, feeling I'd already made my point. But I had my own questions for Hal, questions I'd been putting off for a long time. Since we were already airing our grievances, I figured I shouldn't wait any longer.

"Honolulu's a small town, you know?" I said. "I hear things."

"I don't know what you're talking about," he retorted without looking me in the eye.

"I heard you're still married," I told him. "And I heard you still live together."

"Wife and I are separated. Sorry, I should've told you sooner," Hal admitted, taking a deep breath. "We never finalized our divorce. Our daughter, she's six and wants to live with her daddy.

My wife and I agreed on the living situation so I could spend time with my daughter. You understand, yeah?"

With one hand on the steering wheel, he reached for my hand and kissed it—a quick kiss, which made it obvious he wasn't comfortable discussing his family matters with me.

I let out a breath. As I looked out the passenger side window, I smiled at the gorgeous scenery. It was a beautiful day. When we passed several acres of pineapple fields, I knew we were halfway to our destination.

"When I first came to Hawaii," I told him, "I thought pineapples grew on trees."

Hal laughed. "That used to be my nickname wit' da teamsters," he said. "I never told you dat story?"

I shook my head, indicating that he had not.

"Oh, I was having breakfast at the Fairmont Hotel in San Francisco—used to work the San Francisco waterfront as a rep for the Merchant Seaman Union. And the union boss for the warehouse workers was none other than Jimmy Hoffa. He called out to me, 'Hey, Pineapple.' He always called me 'Pineapple'—his little joke.

"'As long as you stay out of my warehouses, Pineapple, I stay out of your business. We got a deal?' And den we shook hands and sealed da deal."

Hal burst into a loud, boisterous laugh, leaving me utterly puzzled. There had to be more to the story, but he clearly wasn't sharing. Come to think of it, I remembered Jimmy Hoffa's name from a newspaper headline. Hoffa was the president of the International Brotherhood of Teamsters and had been missing since 1975. Apparently, no one ever found him, but there were many rumors.

"I don't know what really happened to him," Hal explained. "In the old days, they'd just plant a bomb in your car. Like they tried to do with me."

"Bomb?" I exclaimed. "Somebody put a bomb in your car?"

He took an embarrassed pause. "It was on the front page of the papers," he said. "Don't you get the *Star-Bulletin*? April 17."

Inwardly panicking, I was ready to chew him out, but I remained calm. "I may have heard something," I said. "I don't pay much attention to the news."

This, of course, was not true. I always kept the daily newspapers at home, even though I hadn't caught up on reading them. I promised myself I'd check on the story of how someone tried to murder Hal with a car bomb.

"I was attending the union's thirty-first Annual Convention at the Hilton Hawaiian Village," he explained. "And some *lolo* put a bomb near the windshield wipers of my Lincoln Continental. But the bomb went off when I was approaching the car—I was only a few feet away. When I called the cops, they surrounded the parking lot." Then, he chuckled in his nonchalant manner. "Takes more than that to rattle me. Anyway, I'm pretty sure my friend Henry knows who did it."

He kept his eyes ahead on the road. Keeping one hand on the steering wheel, his free hand reached for mine, and he kissed it. I smiled at him and softened a little.

When we arrived at the Waianae party, I found out that Hal's friend "Henry" was none other than Henry Huihui, an alleged member of the Waianae crime family. This dowdy, unassuming, middle-aged man was a big name in Hawaii, with his fingers dipped in nearly every industry in the state, including the island's drug trade, gambling, and prostitution rings. His name had been whispered in my old bar for years.

Hal assured me that Henry's reputation was based upon "unsubstantiated rumors" and that his "family" was comprised of ordinary local folks. Even so, any affiliation with the notorious Waianae family was enough for me to be leery.

The party had already begun, held in a grandiose front yard of a large plantation manor. Pikake leis, plumeria, and *ti* leaves decorated a central buffet table. Along the border of the property, amidst a cluster of banyan trees, I watched as little Hawaiian children played chase, laughing and giggling. In the center of the yard, three rotund Hawaiian cooks tended a huge roast pig on a rotating spit. Most of the crowd was made of local Hawaiians, but I could tell by their fairer skin and almond-shaped eyes that many had mixed Chinese, Japanese, or Portuguese blood.

Hal's nephew, Benji, was the first to greet us with a hug. A well-built, college-aged man with a sporty tan, he thanked Hal for pulling some strings to get him a job. A small crowd soon followed, greeting us with hugs and handshakes. In fact, everyone at the party was very polite and welcoming. I questioned if this family was truly an infamous crime family.

Hal spotted the guest of honor amidst the crowd, but I felt hesitant to meet Henry Huihui. However, Hal insisted that he personally introduce me to him. After a quick hug, Henry and Hal moved toward the banyan trees for a private meeting. From the distance, I overheard Henry telling Hal he'd make some calls, but I couldn't hear any specific details.

Hal then beckoned me to sit near Henry's table and requested two glasses of red wine when I sat next to him. I'd barely taken a sip when Hal began to speak to Henry's defense.

"Guys like Henry, Larry Mehau, and me," he said. "We tryin' fo' keep the peace. But if we get targeted, we need muscle. And Henry provides that muscle. In fact, Henry knows how to play both sides of the fence. To keep the peace. You catch?"

I sat there with my glass frozen before my lips. He stared at me intently, watching for my answer, but I only nodded, feigning a quiet understanding. Looking over at the Huihui family cooking roast pig over a grill under the banyan tree, passing another round of Primo Beer, I believed everything about them appeared normal.

Hal leaned back and smiled, satisfied with my reaction.

THE LAST DOMIKO'S LOUNGE

THERE WERE MORE than a dozen bars in the Keeaumoku area. Mine was popular mainly because of my girls. However, John repeatedly advised me not to rely on pretty hostesses. "Pretty girls come and go," he said, "and there's bound to be dry spells if that's how you're hiring. We're gonna need some new ideas."

"What about satellite TV?" I asked.

He looked at me as though I were crazy. "You think people will hang out at a bar all day and do what? Watch sports?" he asked.

"Why not?" I insisted. "I watch MTV all the time. In fact, one of my best customers suggested it to me. Watching sports is a popular pastime in Hawaii."

This same customer, I explained, also informed me that concert promoter Tom Moffatt owned a business that marketed these satellite dishes. That was enough to win John over.

One week later, Tom Moffatt Productions delivered a large satellite dish mounted atop a truck that nearly took a spill onto the pavement. Once the dish was set up and connected to the central television in my lounge, I was sure it would be a huge hit.

Sure enough, word spread around town quickly. Every week when Monday Night Football was on, my bar was standing room only. As soon as my bar demonstrated steady growth, I decided it was the best time to introduce the fad I had experienced as an adagio dancer in Japan—*karaoke* machines!

Soon, I built six private rooms, each equipped with its own *karaoke* machine, and every night, these rooms were packed with enthusiastic patrons.

On one particular night, a stocky elderly customer named Mr. Watanabe, owner of a local food chain, brought along three of his employees and two *haole* business clients from the mainland. They made a grand entrance, decked out in Aloha shirts while the *haole* gentlemen wore business suits.

Mr. Watanabe pulled me aside and whispered in my ear, "I want only young, pretty girls for my clients." I immediately called over half a dozen of my girls to escort them into the karaoke room.

One of my hostesses was an older lady named Maja, who was in her mid-forties but had aged pretty well. When she expressed her desire to join the girls, Mr. Watanabe shook his head at me. Unfortunately, Maja paid no attention and insisted on sitting between the two *haole* clients, one of whom turned beet red, holding back a disgusted grimace. I gestured for Maja to leave, but this made her grab onto the gentleman's arm tighter.

I continually gestured for her to come with me, but she ignored me. At that point, I had no choice but to scream at her in Korean, "Maja! They want only young girls!"

Maja froze in place and then reluctantly left the karaoke room. The six girls I'd selected settled in with the customers, creating a lively atmosphere, having paid no attention to Maja leaving. Soon, the table was filled with *pupu* platters while each girl held their own champagne bucket and encouraged the gentlemen to get up and sing. The *haoles* gladly indulged themselves in performing American standards, which delighted me as they were songs from my childhood.

The highlight of the night was hostess Yumi, our best singer, with her long wavy hair and leather mini skirt. Everyone was happy, and the festive mood lasted throughout the long night. Each of Mr. Watanabe's employees gripped the microphone, reluctant to release it, firmly convinced that they were the greatest singers ever to grace the world.

Shortly after that night, Maja started working at another bar. She took three of my girls with her.

***

UNSURPRISINGLY, THIS BOOMING business started to affect my social life. While having lunch with Hal in Waikiki, he asked me again about my relationship with John. I winced, then reminded him that John was instrumental in helping me manage the bar. Plus, he tended to my children. Though Hal made no further comment, the cross expression on his face told me that he wasn't very pleased.

Hal appeared upset throughout our lunch, picking apart his steak with his fork, but he didn't bring up the subject again. In fact, he allowed me to run my business without any interference.

I continued dating Hal while Haole John helped me out at the bar. John was also a great babysitter to Marylin and Patrick. One night, I invited John out for his birthday dinner at the Old Spaghetti Factory in Ward Warehouse. Little did I know that this non-date would have repercussions.

After we ordered our food, John started complaining that Dennis had ordered the most expensive dish, which we knew he couldn't finish. Still, I assured John that I would cover the cost, but I couldn't shake the feeling that he didn't feel enthusiastic about me indulging my firstborn.

The next morning, while John prepared slices of meatloaf for a *pupu* platter, I stopped at the bank to deposit money. As I pulled back into my parking lot, Hal and his bodyguard, Coconut Tim, burst through the lounge's front door. I chased after them, mentally pleading that Hal wouldn't hurt John.

Hal ran ahead of his bodyguard and into the kitchen. I heard him scream in a loud and angry tone, "You damn *haole*! Get out of my kitchen!"

As soon as I reached them, I caught sight of Tim's bloodshot eyes as he grabbed John in a headlock.

I screamed at Hal, "What the hell are you doing? Are you crazy!"

I'd find out later that he'd called Dennis the previous night, who'd told him I'd gone out to dinner with John and the kids. But that was no excuse for his behavior.

"Freaking *haole*!" Tim growled at him. "You come into our territory and mess around with my man's lady." As soon as he made his point, Tim gave one last squeeze as John screamed in pain. When Tim relaxed his grip, John slipped out of the headlock and, with his arms raised, took a step back toward the door.

"Hey, braddah, I don't want no trouble." With that, he walked out the door, shutting it behind him.

I lunged at Hal. "What's the matter with you?" I snapped, pounding him on his chest. "I told you John works for us!"

Hal brushed me away in disgust as if I were nothing more than an annoying cockroach. He gave me a long, hard look before he suddenly pushed me out the kitchen door and backed me butt-first into a booth.

"I don't care!" he roared. "This is *my* investment. If he comes around again, I'll throw his ugly *haole* ass into the Ala Wai Canal!"

I growled under my breath. "So typical. Acting like a rooster ruffling his feathers before the big cockfight!" I retorted.

He stared at me with anger while I got up and walked away. Unfortunately, he was correct. The bar was his investment, and he had every right to fire any personnel he wanted. And worst of all, the damage had been done. Sad and confused, I made one last plea to Hal not to let it all end like this.

The next day, when I called John, he hung up on me.

***

IRONICALLY, HAL CALMED down a lot after that incident. Within months, he became a strong father figure to my children, and they all took to him immediately. They never even asked why Uncle John stopped coming around, and soon, I grew accustomed to his absence.

Later that summer, Hal took Dennis and me to the University of Hawaii Rainbow Warriors football game at Aloha Stadium, where they played against San Diego State. During halftime, Hal mentioned a prior conversation he'd had with Dennis.

"I told him I lost my father when I was about eleven. My father meant everything to me. When he passed, it was devastating. He used to take me hunting when I was small. Then, one day, he got the flu, and that turned into pneumonia. Before I knew it, he was gone."

I felt flabbergasted. In all these years, I had never seen this vulnerable side of him. I knew all too well how a parent's absence in your formative years could affect you.

Hal continued his story, "My mom married some rat bastard who treated her like trash. I was a big guy, you know. I ended up beating the crap out of him. But instead of thanking me, my mom hit me with a frying pan and kicked me out of the house. I got passed between my aunties and my grandmas. Eventually, my grandma paid my tuition."

I listened as tears began to well up in Hal's eyes. "So back in high school—St. Louis High—I used to play football—running back. After practice, I'd sit on the bench and watch all my friends' dads picking them up. And after the games, the dads would go sit by their kids. But I never had dat.

"Dat's when I learned to never depend on anybody, and it wasn't easy. You see? A braddah's gotta know when to take what God's given him, no matter how bad or how good, and make up your mind about what to do about it. To do the best with what you got."

I sat there in complete awe. Something clicked in my mind, and I knew why I had been attracted to Hal time and again. In a way, we were kindred spirits.

Hal straightened his posture and cleared his throat. His tone lightened up. "Well, I think I got through to your son," he said. "I mean, he listened good. Sometimes, a boy just needs a man to spend time with him."

After that, Dennis got a full-time job working at the Safeway supermarket after briefly working as a singing waiter in a Waikiki restaurant. Marylin began studying at the Art Institute of Seattle, which eased my schedule quite a bit, but my hectic life would pick up again when my youngest boy, Patrick, graduated from Iolani High School.

While looking for a business college, Hal suggested his alma mater, the University of San Francisco. Finally, Patrick got accepted to Rensselaer Polytechnic Institute in New York and transferred to the University of San Francisco after one year. He made his home in California from that point on.

***

BY THE LATE 1980s, hostess bars across the island fell into a rapid decline. New drunk driving laws were a contributing factor, in addition to the fall of the housing market, which caused the construction industry to slow down and stifle the economy. People were watching their pocketbooks and reigning in their discretionary spending. Sadly, this resulted in people having less money and less leisure time to spend at bars.

To make a profit, I had to offer better and more creative deals to attract prospective hostesses. Since *karaoke* and sports bars were now commonplace, I had more competition.

Another aspect of the bar business's decline was how single men were no longer content with spending their evenings in one bar, preferring to go "barhopping" in search of better deals and more appealing women. Repeat customers and customer loyalty became a thing of the past.

But the worst part of all was that most competing karaoke rooms had devolved into a hive of illicit activities, allowing gambling, strip shows, and even prostitution. Worst of all was the backroom drug deals that appeared to happen more and more often.

Dope dealers would enter a private room, dim the lights, and spread a line of white powder on the table, then invite the girls willing to partake. The high-class, well-respected *mamasans* of bygone days had disappeared, and substance abuse had become rampant.

This was the beginning of the end.

THE FATE OF JUDGE SHINTAKU

JUNE 1987. WITH the kids busy in college, I knew I would need money to keep paying their tuition. So, despite the struggling bar industry, I decided to start a new bar called the Burgundy Lounge in Makaloa. This time, I had a different idea to compete with other bars. I held karaoke contests with the musical duo Paul and Terry as host, a tradition we continued every weekend.

Our grand opening involved a truckload of buffalo wings as *pupus,* inspired by appetizers I'd eaten at the Tropicana Las Vegas, where I'd just vacationed with Hal.

As always, this new bar came with interesting patrons and unexpected experiences. One evening, when repeat customer Judge Harold Shintaku dropped by my bar, I observed his typically reserved demeanor taking an unusual twist. He would fixate on me for extended periods, occasionally pointing his wrinkled finger across his booth as if indicating an invisible presence. In a slurred, drunken voice, he muttered, "I would like to have another drink."

I firmly informed him he'd reached his limit, and that marked the final encounter I had with him.

Hal later told me Shintaku had quit as a judge partially because of his gambling problem. Although he was a big supporter of Hal's union, Shintaku was no longer the respected judge he once was.

According to a newspaper article, it all began when a reputed mobster calling himself "Uncle Charlie" confessed that his brother had bribed Judge Shintaku over his double murder trial. Judge Shintaku overturned Charlie's conviction and, in a letter to the editor, made public a written article defending the acquittal. In it, he claimed that there had been discrepancies between the victim's wounds and the method the prosecution postulated had taken place. Reading the article, his argument sounded so scatterbrained that I thought one of my girls had written it for him.

Hal explained that Judge Shintaku's current mental state was a result of the stress he'd suffered after being assaulted by rival mobsters. He'd been taking bribes to put their associates behind bars.

His story came to a tragic end less than a year after his last bar visit. The local evening news reported that Judge Harold Shintaku had been found dead in Las Vegas after jumping from the third floor of the Stardust Hotel. His wrists had been slashed, and the Vegas police reported it as a suicide.

A few years later, the law finally caught up to "Uncle Charlie," who was sentenced to twenty years for murder, and shortly after that, the same happened to Henry Huihui, which ended the empire that had been the "Waianae family." Their arrests and subsequent trials caused the crime circuits to come to a stumbling halt. And with that, the undercurrent of organized crime, which had been the lifeblood of many bars, soon dried up.

***

JUST WHEN I thought business couldn't get worse, my bar stood in the way of a new commercial development, and I was forced to sell as soon as my lease was up. It was time to rethink my future. On our final day, while preparing to close early, three middle-aged men showed up at the front door.

"Don't close up!" Hal shouted from behind me while I was holding the "closed" sign in my hand. He had recognized one of the men approaching the door.

"Why not?" I asked.

Hal let them all in as one of them exclaimed, "Howzit, Hal! My good buddy here, Roy Akaki, hit a hole-in-one today!"

He put his hand on the shoulder of his celebrated friend, Roy, a friendly, handsome fellow. Tall and a bit on the thin side, he seemed to be the type of guy I would get along with nicely. I chuckled. I assumed they must be rather high-profile golfers to pal around with Hal.

"They told me you serve da best *pupus* in town," Roy said, flashing a friendly smile with a twinkle in his eye. Hal let out his boisterous laugh and patted Roy on the back, praising his accomplishment as he seated his friends at the front table. Reluctantly, I put away the sign and opened the kitchen. The golf celebration lasted another three hours, and at the end of the night, before leaving with Hal, I looked around the bar one last time.

Walking through the lounge, my heart felt heavy as I ran my fingers over my leather seats and wooden tables, achingly holding back my tears. I never learned how to run any other kind of business.

"Don't worry, Domiko," Hal broke my reverie. "I'm going to take you on a cruise. From now on, we'll live a life of luxury."

FAMILY PASSAGES

WHILE HAL AND I eagerly planned our vacation cruise, unforeseen issues with my siblings came up once again. My youngest brother Chang had chosen to remain in Korea. With his health declining, Mother continued to pray for him, and I felt more responsible for him, as I had for all my siblings as they got older.

Ever since Chang was a child, he was the most fragile of my brothers and sisters. One day, he wrote a letter to inform me that his eyesight had deteriorated and, therefore, he needed medical attention.

Without hesitation, I contacted a travel agency to fly Brother Chang to Honolulu, where I rented him an apartment near Mother. I also enrolled him in the Ho'opono Services for the Blind, a state-run agency that would provide the services he required.

Brother Gyeong lived in his own place on the outskirts of Waikiki and frequently visited, but his behavior became increasingly erratic as time went on. Concerned, I took him to a doctor who diagnosed him with schizophrenia, and he informed us that my brother was suffering from paranoid delusions. When his condition worsened, his doctor temporarily admitted him to The Queen's Medical Center, where he was placed in the psychiatric ward.

I felt a little guilty since I had planned my vacation in the middle of his suffering.

After a few weeks of visiting Gyeong in the hospital, Mother and I were forced to accept that he was beyond our help. One day, he broke my window, entered the house, made saimin, and didn't turn off the stove before leaving. The house almost caught fire.

We had no choice but to let him go wherever his mind would take him. He became homeless, and it agonized me to see him wandering the streets, carrying a large duffel bag with one Japanese flag and one American flag sticking out. From that day on, Mother spent every night in her bedroom earnestly praying for his recovery.

On the night before my cruise, I asked my mom about Gyeong. "How can we be sure God exists when bad things happen to us?" I wondered.

Mother remained calm, took a deep breath, and tried her best to explain. "We can't always understand why God allows difficult times," she began. "In a world with a lot of wrongdoing, we're bound to face disappointments and tough situations. But I believe that if you pray for the wisdom to tell right from wrong, you can start to see the reasons behind these challenges in life. Through the tough times, you can discover how God can make things better and positively change your life."

She gave me her Korean Bible and said, "Read Romans 8:28," helping me find the chapter and verse.

The scripture read, "All things work together for good, to those who love God and are called according to His purpose."

Mother continued, "Learning to see 'bad things' as 'hidden blessings' is something God wants His children to practice for their spiritual growth. If you accept God's help in dealing with hard times, you won't become bitter. Choosing to trust that God has a plan through your struggles can help you avoid bitterness and grow in His love."

Intellectually, I could not grasp such an understanding of God. To be honest, everything Mother said sounded beautiful—lyrical even—but for whatever reason, a gnawing pain inside made me leave the room. Perhaps it was her manner of speaking that brought tears to my eyes. In my heart, I believe I may have understood some of it.

***

SINCE MOTHER NOW lived in a middle-income housing community near Chinatown, my Manoa home was suddenly empty; all my children had already moved away. And judging by the way she regularly pawed my front door, my dog Princess wanted to run, too.

A few months after Mother moved out, Princess suddenly died, as did Duffy several months after that. For the first time in a long while, I truly felt alone. I missed seeing Mother carrying the laundry basket up and down the stairway and the way she'd often stop partway up and shout, "*Aigo*! My knees so sore! I have to rest!"

Every time, I would rush to help her up while she laughed about the cracking noise we heard coming from her knees.

"We can't escape getting old," she'd often say. "Someday, you're going to understand what I mean."

She was correct. Even though she was absent for most of my childhood, I now realize just how much my mother contributed to my life and to my children's lives. As I stood looking around the living room, memories continuously flooded my mind.

I dusted off the top of the piano and the bookshelves, then headed toward my children's former bedrooms, and while fumbling through their old clothes, I thought of Patrick and how much I missed picking up his smelly socks and cleaning out the closets.

As I returned to the piano, I recalled how deeply I missed hearing my children play music in the living room, pretending that they were performing as a band.

It had been fifteen years, I reminded myself, but it felt like only yesterday when I had moved in with three little children. They had all grown up far too quickly.

***

ON AUGUST 9, 1990, shortly after my forty-eighth birthday, my ex-husband, Gordon Lee, passed away at the young age of fifty-six. Marylin and Patrick flew to Idaho to attend his funeral, but I remained behind. The last time I saw Gordon, he was visiting my children, but unfortunately, I was too busy tending my new bar to spend any time with him.

Around that time, Patrick informed me that his father had suffered his first heart attack while staying in a local motel. Apparently, the police had been searching for a drug dealer, and they'd mistakenly raided Gordon's motel room, which tragically brought on the heart attack. Paramedics were called, and Gordon was revived. He recovered quickly, but I suspected this incident may have hastened his early demise.

In all the years since Gordon and I'd first met, I had only visited Idaho once. My children and I spent many years apart from him, and I wasn't sure if any of them knew how great a man he was. In contrast, the older members of my family recognized him as an unsung hero, having been instrumental in bringing my mother and siblings over from Korea.

Now, his tombstone stands among the graves in Arimo, Idaho, and I wonder if my descendants will remember him the way I do. I will never forget how special he was. As a Staff Sergeant, Gordon should have received a medal of honor for his dedication to the Mun clan.

***

SINCE BEING DIAGNOSED as legally blind, Brother Chang had been living in Hawaii for six years when he was diagnosed with lung cancer, and he would fight the disease for two more years. Chang was confined to hospice care in his home in Kakaako, where Mother and I took turns taking care of him.

During one of my days with him, I got a call from a casting director, Margaret Doversola. I had known Margaret for years, and she had occasionally sent me out to work as a background extra on *Hawaii Five-O* and on auditions for other small parts throughout the years. I'd only worked as a background extra once in a blue moon to supplement my income whenever business slowed down, so I never gave it much thought. Acting roles for local actors, especially Asian American actors, were rare, so I never expected much.

But when I heard the news, I jumped up and down with excitement: I had booked my first speaking role for an ABC family drama called *Byrds of Paradise*!

Coincidentally, I had been cast to play the *mamasan* of a Korean bar, and filming would take place at the former Club Hubba Hubba. Hearing me jump for joy, Chang turned toward me, barely able to hold his head up but just enough to give me a confused stare.

"What's the matter?" he asked.

"I got the part!" I cheerfully exclaimed.

His face lit up. "*Nuna* (sister), I knew someday you would become a movie star," he said.

As I looked at his proud expression, I didn't have the heart to tell him that a small part on a television show didn't make me a movie star. Still, I stayed awake most of the night, trying to perfect my three lines of dialogue, ecstatic with the thought that I had finally booked a real acting job.

***

1994. ON THE morning of filming, Mother called me at 4 a.m.; I only had a mere three hours of sleep. Mother relayed the sad news that Brother Chang had passed away in his sleep. My heart shattered. Holding back my tears, I immediately drove to his apartment, where I found Mother reciting Bible verses while she lovingly cradled his body in her arms.

Though I felt disheartened, the words of Mother's prayer were those of celebration to welcome my brother to heaven. Although I wasn't quite sure if I believed in an afterlife, I did recall my childhood friend Mina telling me about it.

Mother and I patiently waited for an hour for the coroner to arrive, and it took another hour to complete the paperwork. Fortunately, I still had half an hour left before my call time. Mother grumbled as I dashed out of the apartment. Though I felt some guilt over leaving her alone, I had to get to the set, and I did not have time to cry.

***

THE EXTERIOR OF Club Hubba Hubba looked the same as when I'd left twenty years ago. The production company had left the building intact and untouched, as did the city and county since no one had been interested in renovating the building.

The neon sign with a caricature of a dancer that once glowed bright red and yellow still hung over the second floor, but now the paint had faded. I parked in a nearby lot as instructed and walked around the building to the entrance. The display case that had once featured my headshot was broken and splattered with specks of black paint.

When I approached the alcove by the front door, my eyes lit up at the sight of a familiar Japanese man with a round face who stepped out to greet me. Older now with thinning gray hair, Tad Matsuoka Jr. was elated to see me.

"Domiko!" He embraced me gently with a giant grin, resembling a proud father at his daughter's graduation. Even in his joy, his voice was so gentle that I could barely make out his words, "So happy to see you." Evidently, I had forgotten how soft-spoken he was, and I had to lean in closer just to hear him whisper, "After today, I'm selling the property and retiring."

I smiled uneasily. I shouldn't have been surprised as most of the buildings on Hotel Street had been around since the early 1900s. This club had been the liveliest club in Downtown Honolulu for decades. After the Second World War, sailors on shore leave would arrive by busloads to enjoy a show or drinks at one of the bars. But as military patronage dwindled over the years, so did businesses.

As a result, the streets were eventually overrun by prostitutes, drug dealers, and junkies. Before I could wallow in more nostalgia, a female production assistant escorted us inside, where I was struck by a wave of familiar nightclub scents: the thick, musty aroma of dust and remnants of leftover cigarette smoke.

While the film crew tirelessly worked on the lighting equipment they'd set up in the old showroom, I could still hear the opening drumroll in my mind, the horns blaring my burlesque music where I'd once sashayed onto the now-empty stage.

The assistant director then approached me and introduced himself by his first name, Chris. He promptly walked me out the back door toward an adjacent parking lot where three trailers had been parked for makeup, wardrobe, and hair. Delighted, I chuckled when I saw my proper stage name posted on my dressing room door: "Tomiko Lee."

As I set out on my acting journey, I made the deliberate choice to separate my professional name from the name I'd used for burlesque and my bar business. This move allowed me to shape a fresh, professional identity, drawing from my childhood name, Tomiko. The Japanese name I'd been given when living as a child in Japan was now my official screen name.

Yet, at that moment, a sudden wave of melancholy washed over me. I couldn't help but feel a pang of sadness, longing for my little brother Chang to be here and witness this transformation.

After donning a sequined dress at the wardrobe truck, I went to the makeup trailer, where I took a quick peek at the script. When the makeup artist finished working on me, Chris returned to escort me back to the club, where I heard the familiar phrase, "Quiet on the set!"

I took another long look at the empty catwalk where I'd once strutted in my faux *cheongsam* before an audience of captivated male customers—until a man's voice snapped me back to the present.

On the set, lead actor Timothy Busfield, who played a high school teacher, was confronting one of his students, Kim Lee, who was illegally working at my character's bar. The beautiful young actress who played Kim was a college undergrad at the state university.

During the rehearsal, I dove into character and fired off my first line at Timothy.

"If you want to talk to a girl, you gotta pay!" I played it up, inspired by the many over-the-top Asian actors I'd seen in films. The director took me aside and whispered for me to tone it down for the real take. On his cue, "Action!" I delivered my lines, then added a grumbling "*Babo ya!*" as I walked away. This meant "jerk." The director shouted cut, and the crew erupted in laughter and applause. Many among them still recalled my presence from multiple occasions on the original *Hawaii Five-O* set, where I had served as an extra.

After I completed a series of close-up takes, which they called coverage, I was told to relax. I sat mildly in the corner while Kim spent her downtime reading her lines.

Timothy Busfield turned on the charm as I observed the on-set hustle. I was almost convinced he was about to pop the question—

to go grab lunch. Though flattered, I wasn't in the mood to date anyone.

Tim parted company with me, and while the actors and crew were joking around and having a good time, I barely paid attention. Thoughts of Brother Chang lying lifeless in Mother's arms consumed me, as well as the image of total strangers carrying his body away on a stretcher. I wandered toward a barstool beside an empty shell of a bar and sat in silence.

Childhood memories flooded back. When we were very young, we used to sneak into theaters, hiding under the chairs for the next show. My little brother always believed that someday, his sister would become a movie star.

By mid-afternoon, the production crew was wrapping up and leaving. Tad Matsuoka approached me to say one last goodbye, and I gave him a hug. I couldn't help but wonder, *If Tad had never seen me dancing in Hollywood, I probably wouldn't have come to Hawaii.*

In fact, I may have stayed in Hollywood, seeking work as an actress in the movie industry, knowing full well that the competition would be ten times as fierce as it was here.

As I walked out the rear door toward my car, I looked up at the sky; it was only three o'clock in the afternoon, and the sky was gloomily overcast with near-black clouds. A splash of light rain drizzled down on my face, but I could not distinguish between the raindrops and my tears. The devastation of my brother's death had finally dawned on me.

MARYLIN'S PAGEANT CAREER

MY DAUGHTER MARYLIN returned to Hawaii after an adventurous two-year stint at a mainland college, determined to finish her bachelor's degree at the University of Hawaii.

While working for a local advertising firm, she caught the eye of a beauty pageant coordinator. He had gotten a gig working for an international pageant and wanted to recommend Marylin for Miss Korea! I was thrilled beyond belief. In her youth, I'd enrolled Marylin in many teen pageants, and she'd gotten as far as first runner-up. Since I'd retired from the bar business, I now had the free time to manage her career.

Months flew by, filled with training, practice interviews, and workouts sandwiched between work and school. Our lives revolved around the pageant, and I became more obsessed than a squirrel gathering acorns.

Marylin was meticulous, maintaining an appointment book with her pageant events neatly written. She never missed a meeting.

Before the Miss Korea pageant, I dragged her to an old Korean fortune teller on Liholiho Street. The ancient man knelt on a woven mat, placed a tattered, dog-eared brown book filled with cryptic drawings on a tiny table, and asked, "What brings you here?"

"I want to inquire about my daughter's pageant," I replied, keeping it brief.

He asked her name and time of birth, leafing through the brown book with a wet finger. He jotted down numbers and Chinese characters, then declared, "A tiger trapped in a dark dungeon. You'll have difficulty finding the way out. You might be rewarded, but I doubt you'll become a queen."

"What? How do you know?" I protested, to which my daughter whispered, "Mom, calm down."

I snapped, "Shut up! This guy doesn't know what he's talking about! Let's go!" I left money on the table and stormed out.

On the way home, Marylin remained flustered. She confessed, "Honestly, I can't picture myself as a beauty queen like those other girls. I'm only doing this for you!" Tears welled up in her eyes.

Her final pageant loomed that night. Marylin had racked up titles but never quite clinched the top spot. When the host began the fateful announcement, "First runner-up goes to . . ." my heart pounded louder than a rock concert drumbeat.

There was my daughter, standing at the center of a massive stage in a pink evening gown bedazzled with sequins. I imagined she couldn't see us from the blinding spotlights. "Marylin Lee!" The words hit me like a ton of bricks, and I practically melted into my seat.

This was her third time placing as first runner-up, and although I'd braced myself for disappointment, I'd at least clung to a sliver of hope.

As we exited the theater, we passed throngs of photographers surrounding the winner. For a moment, I watched with a heavy heart, then immediately walked out of the auditorium with my daughter in tow.

Returning home, Marylin slammed the door, dropped everything, and stomped upstairs. We lay on her bed, side by side, silently staring at the ceiling. Two years of preparation had gone down the drain in an instant, leaving a void.

I glanced at Marylin and felt a lump in my throat. "Maybe we should consider another pageant?" I suggested.

She replied firmly, "Mom, I've had it with these pageants. Don't push me anymore."

That's when I realized that the dream of her becoming a beauty queen was perhaps more mine than hers.

Reflecting on her own dreams, Marylin expressed a desire to move beyond pageantry and ultimately decided to focus on her future while working on the mainland. With Dennis out of the house and Patrick in San Francisco, Marylin's departure left me sitting alone in an empty living room.

Memories of my children's laughter echoed through the hallways, prompting me to ponder the swift changes life had brought.

MY STINT AS A FILM
AND MUSIC PRODUCER

MOTHER OFTEN TOLD me that I consistently steered my children in the wrong direction. She told me I wasn't guiding them sufficiently in their spiritual growth.

I chose to ignore her, but I would soon learn she was correct.

In 1998, Dennis moved to LA to build his acting and music career. Having spent years in Hawaii honing his craft at Wayne Ward's acting workshop, he began landing supporting roles in local theater.

I helped him and his friends secure an apartment on La Brea Boulevard so they could get on their feet. One of his roommates was a writer named Tony Young, who was also from Honolulu. Eventually, Dennis met a Korean American director, Youngman Kang, at a Hollywood audition, and they worked on several independent films together.

***

MEANWHILE, I CONTINUED my relationship with Hal Lewis, and we often had lunch at the Pineapple Room at the Ala Moana Shopping Center. One consequential afternoon, we encountered record producer George Chun, known for his collaboration with Tom Muffin, the concert promoter and an old friend of Hal's.

Our conversation that afternoon inspired me to produce a music album for Dennis, which I suggested to him right away. Hal excitedly agreed to help me in this endeavor, having been a professional musician in his younger days.

This project had me shuttling between LA and various music studios. I immersed myself in music, understanding its nuances. After each recording session, George snatched the tape and dashed off to his trusty car to blast our tunes. The intended audience, he said, grooved to our music on the radio, not confined within the walls of a grandiose studio. George opined that the album would benefit from the "mainland sound." Taking his advice, I partnered with Frank Day from Oceanside Studio in Hollywood. Over the next couple of years, local musicians at Audio Resource and I worked diligently, finally producing Dennis's debut CD, *Smile*.

Promoting the album was an uphill battle. The local Honolulu radio stations weren't welcoming, the general sentiment being, "He's not Hawaiian." Frustrated, one day, I decided to take matters into my own hands. Armed with six Hawaiian chocolate candies, I strode up to the intercoms at the local Hawaiian radio station and pressed the button. I confidently requested to meet the music director, but they hung up on me, leaving me listening to a long and awkward dial tone. I returned home with only a box of melting chocolate and a bruised ego.

To our dismay, only a handful of stations were kind enough to inform us that Dennis's style was neither "hip" nor "trendy" enough for their oh-so-modern format. It seemed like every door was firmly shut.

Then, a glimmer of hope appeared on the horizon. One day, while flying back home on Hawaiian Airlines, I spotted a magazine that featured two songs by local artists: "Mambo Number #5" and "Hula Girl." I couldn't contain my excitement and yelled out, "That's my son!"

Unfortunately, while "Hula Girl" made it to the charts, Dennis was still struggling to gain recognition. That's when my mother's wise words echoed in my head, "Show business is risky business."

Just when it seemed like all hope was lost, George Chun came to the rescue. He suggested we set up a showcase on the Ala Moana center stage. George hired the best musicians on the island to make Dennis look as cool as possible and created a signature wardrobe look, complete with a stylish black turtleneck sweater.

A few nights before the big showcase, I attempted to choreograph some dance steps for Dennis, but it quickly became evident that he was as graceful as a bull in a china shop. He even knocked down a lamp from a nightstand with a loud, thunderous crash. When I looked at his disheartened face, I felt only sympathy.

My mother wasn't slow to make judgments; she told me I had inadvertently made his career revolve around me. Perhaps my son felt the same way. Later that summer, he walked away from it all. He told me that his heart was simply not in it. Thus, Dennis promptly returned to Los Angeles to resume his film career.

***

BEING A NOVICE music producer was financially draining. One day, en route to mortgage my house, Mother and sister Okyon chided me for my relentless business pursuits. Mother astutely observed the pattern of my obsessive tendencies to indulge in wild ventures in the entertainment industry.

"If you loved God as much you love your show business," Mother said, "you would get a flood of blessings from heaven." I shook my head, oblivious to her point. But at the very least, I understood that Mother desired that I settle down and probably get married. Most likely to Hal Lewis. However, I never shared with Mother that my relationship with Hal was quickly coming to a bitter end.

After returning from a business trip on Christmas Eve, Hal took me to the Catholic church that he occasionally attended. As I walked behind him, a foul, musty odor swept past my nostrils. I certainly knew it was not the incense used during liturgies, but it felt strange that no one else seemed to notice it. Looking over at Hal, it felt as though he were wrapped with a long scarf of mildew—a filthy spirit, perhaps.

In my heart, I knew this would be the last Christmas that I would spend with Hal. As the following year dragged on, he stopped taking my calls. And I never called him back.

THE PASSING OF MOTHER
AND FATHER

THE BITTERNESS FROM the neglect I had endured in my childhood faded as I grew older. I learned to forgive my parents and even took it upon myself to tend to my father's health in his old age.

During our family gatherings, Sister Okyon continually brought up how our father never contributed to my education. She'd point out, "You never supported Okhui's schooling, but she helped you come to America." Father would simply scratch his head and remain silent. Sister Okyon was determined to make sure he never forgot his shortcomings. However, I felt that this matter was in the past, and our father was now a frail old man. I didn't want to cause him any distress.

When Father immigrated to America, I was determined to give him a better life in Hawaii. He happily lived in paradise for twenty-eight years before he passed away in February 2002 at the age of ninety-seven. Due to the poor documentation of birth records in Korea, he may have been closer to one hundred.

Mother's passing hit me a lot harder. In May of the following year, after my father's death, Mother went on her final journey. Lying in her casket, she was beautifully made up—her lips were tinted red, and she wore her favorite diamond earrings with the four-color Minnie Mouse watch we had bought her at the Disney Store. Her white *hanbok,* which she had requested to be laid to rest in, was surrounded by bright red and white roses. Since white symbolized purity, the white roses had been added, which she particularly loved planting in her garden.

This beautiful *hanbok* had been tucked away in her closet for many years until that morning. Dressing her in it was our final farewell. As I studied her beautiful face, her prominently high cheekbones, and her thick dark eyebrows, I could not hold back the tears.

The morning before she died, before her spirit left her body, she was somehow aware her time had come. I still recall our last conversation. We stood together underneath the blooming bottlebrush tree she'd planted in my garden.

"*Yesunim,* Jesus is real," she whispered under her breath. "He has been paying me visits recently."

Mother's eyes peered right through me, and then she turned her gaze up toward the sky. A lump formed in my throat. Memories flooded through my mind—the many years she had been absent from my life and every battle we had fought over my career choices disappeared in that moment.

"I apologize for not being a good mother, but I have long recognized that you have been an exceptional mother," she praised. "God knows your heart. Your care for your children and all of us is remarkable." Mother's lips tightened. "Okhui, even in your struggles, there's hope that one day, your hardships will turn into blessings."

The next day, she was gone.

Mother's funeral was held at Hosoi Mortuary in Chinatown. Dennis sang "Amazing Grace" in her honor. All our friends and family—including my extended family from my bars—attended and graciously offered their condolences, as did the members of her church congregation. Surprisingly, Roy, the golfer I'd met on the day I was about to shut down my last bar, was in attendance.

Roy nervously shook my hand, and at that moment, I imagined Mother sitting up in her coffin and nagging at me, "I don't like him. He reminds me of your father." Though that sounded silly, it's exactly what she would have said. I would have loved to have heard her say that one last time.

***

LUNCH WAS SERVED in an adjacent room after the service. I sat at the main table beside Reverend Seonghil Chang of the Hawaii Korean Central Church. "Your son Dennis has an amazing voice," he said earnestly. "He could earn a decent living as a singer."

I nodded politely, not wanting to admit that Dennis had tried to do just that many years ago. Before I could thank him, a familiar voice behind me caught my ear.

"Domiko," an older woman whispered. To my surprise, I turned to see a middle-aged June Park, my former business partner from the Domiko Lounge, standing in front of me in modest mourning attire.

"Sorry for interrupting," she said. "Can we talk?"

Still stunned, I nodded as she led me to the other side of the chapel, out of earshot of everyone. Letting out a breath, she looked around the room with a hint of sadness in her eyes as though she were a lost child.

"You're very fortunate to have all of your family here," June began, "but I think there's something you should know about your sister Oksoon." She hesitated, and her lips quivered. "I was responsible for her death. I killed her."

I winced, then stared at her blankly. My sister had committed suicide. "What do you mean you killed her?"

"Oksoon showed up at my bar shortly before she passed away," she said. "She wanted to apply for a job—I didn't know who she was. She told me her name was Gikuko."

"We thought she was living in Japan," I said, letting out a breath of relief. Whatever June was trying to confess, I knew she couldn't be responsible. "My sister never even told us she came to Hawaii."

June continued, "I realize that now. She never talked about her family either, but I knew she was an addict the moment I saw her. Lord, help me. I supplied her with heroin, coke, ice—anything I could get my hands on. Last time I saw her, she couldn't even find a vein to shoot up, so she shot it under her tongue. I was horrified, but I couldn't do anything. Then, that night—the night she didn't show up for work—that's when I saw her on the news."

June choked; she could barely form her next words, but I sat anxiously listening without even blinking. I understood where her guilt was coming from.

"The police came to my b-bar," she continued, "they told me that she had relatives and mentioned you by name. I was too afraid to come see you. I couldn't tell you all these years, but I can't hold it in any longer. I had to tell you the truth."

Tears streamed down her face. "Domiko," she wept. "Your sister's death made me realize how much I'd messed up my own life. So, I entered rehab, and there I met a local boy—a Christian. He changed my way of thinking. And he told me I must first forgive myself for the sins of my past."

Those words triggered my frustration. "For your sins?" I echoed with my fists clenched. "What about the money that kept disappearing from our lounge? Have you forgiven yourself for those sins as well?"

June paused, caught off guard by my comment, then briefly burst into her characteristic high-pitched laugh. "I am sorry, Domiko," she said. "I feel really stupid for having done that. But having all that cash in bed with me—even for one night—felt so good."

"Do you know how much trouble you made for me?" I kept my voice low despite my anger. June came to her senses quickly and laid her hand on my shoulder.

Letting out an exasperated breath, I recognized that she was being sincere and vulnerable, but now that we were bringing up the past, I couldn't help but let out a stifled bit of laughter. Somehow, her confession made me feel better, even if it would never replace our lost revenue. Mother used to say forgiveness was a basic lesson that *Yesunim* taught his followers, especially when you are unaware of the challenges or the abuse your tormentor has gone through. At that moment, I found it in my heart to forgive her.

"June," I began. "You didn't kill Oksoon. She lived a hard life and made her own choices, good or bad. There was nothing you could've done."

"It-it's difficult for me to accept," she said, "but I understand now that it's all in God's hands. All we can do is learn our lessons and keep living." She raised her eyes to meet mine and told me with confidence, "Domiko, I attend church every Sunday—Korean Christian Church in Liliha. I would love for you to join me."

My face squirmed, feeling a little uncomfortable about the invitation. "I don't think I have the time."

June nodded. "I understand," she said. "But remember, the door is always open for you." Then she went on her way.

***

AFTER THE SERVICE, we drove in a procession to the burial at the Hawaiian Memorial Park in Kaneohe. The weather was beautiful; Mother would have liked it. With the gentle sound of leaves dancing in the trees nearby, the reverend picked up a handful of soil and sprinkled it on Mother's coffin.

"Ashes to ashes, dust to dust," he began. That was the last day I saw my mother on this earth. Her flesh would become part of the soil. Thinking back, I remember her telling me about the many gardens she had planted since moving to America. She planted seeds and uprooted dead plants, then she planted even more. Each year, in the middle of summer, the vegetables and colorful flowers greeted us outside her window.

At the end of the planting season, Mother rejuvenated the soil, and the life cycle would begin anew. Mother desired to create a perfect garden, but I have learned that there is no such thing as perfection. Like the serpent in Eden, Mother always believed that the family curse of drug addiction began with a similar serpent that her great-grandmother had killed long ago in her kitchen.

Mother had lived a hard life, but her attitude never wavered. Though she once abandoned me as a child, she came back to help raise my children. Through the various twists and turns of her own life, she went about living in a simple, subdued manner. With sincere wisdom, she would often tell me, "Cherish today. You should always cherish this moment because this is the moment that God has provided you. Pray to Him and let Him guide you."

Lately, those words made me wonder if my life would have been easier if I were not so ambitious. But such speculation was pointless. Mother had known in her heart that I would never have settled for less.

MY BROWN BOOK

ONE MORNING, WHILE I was watering my flower garden, the mail carrier came toward me and handed me an envelope. Turning off the hose, I wiped my hands and opened the letter. Inside was a soft green leather-bound certificate with the words "Kaimuki Community School for Adults" written clearly on my high school diploma. I couldn't contain my joy. I leaped in the air, crying tears of happiness under the bottlebrush tree my mother had planted. At the age of fifty-eight, I had finally earned my high school diploma. I felt grateful for Hawaii's state program, which provided education regardless of one's age.

I had always wanted to continue my education, and I eagerly looked forward to entering Kapiolani Community College, where I planned to take a course in ESOL, English for Speakers of Other Languages. I have learned that life is a continuous learning process, and for me, the journey of learning is a lifelong endeavor without a conclusion. Now, I was ready to formally embrace my educational goals by attending college.

***

KAPIOLANI COMMUNITY COLLEGE was situated near Diamond Head, surrounded by beautiful mountains and wild cacti. Before entering the registration office, I felt a tightness in my chest, wondering which class would be suitable for me. Explaining my situation to the front clerk, I explained my discussions with my counselor and the requirements for an English placement test.

She pointed me toward the test room, where a local student assisted me with the computer. The resulting test placed me in ESOL 94, a class mostly for foreign students new to the United States. After almost four decades in the United States, I finally found myself in an English as a Second Language class, learning to read and write proper English. Sitting in front of their computer, I felt like this small window was introducing me to a new world.

To be fair, the ESOL 94 classroom at Iliahi, room number 204, appeared a little rundown, with dust-covered blinds and a rattling air-conditioning system. Despite being the oldest person in the group of young foreign students, I happily sat with them. Age was not an obstacle for me because I believed that learning knew no bounds. My heart remained forever youthful when it came to acquiring knowledge.

Our English teacher, Mr. Noji, a Japanese American man in his mid-fifties, entered with an enthusiastic greeting in both English and Japanese. The subject for the semester was "The Environment."

When given an assignment to write about our reasons for joining the class, I admitted I felt a little out of place among this mixture of Japanese, Chinese, and Filipino students who were "fresh off the boat." Some spoke with thick accents, making it hard to understand them, but I presumed their writing skills were more advanced considering the prerequisite of this class.

After class, I walked down the steps of the ESOL building. The exterior lawn was lined with trees and shrubbery, which made me reminisce about myself as a young girl walking through my Korean school campus carrying a brown paper-covered book. Tears welled up in my eyes, and as a leaf fell on my head, I wiped away the tears and hurried to my car. I had no time to dwell on the past.

***

AT THE END of the semester, I experienced a significant milestone when my article discussing environmental issues was published in the *Kapio Newspaper*. This filled me with immense joy. I remembered having to borrow a pencil to complete my homework as a young girl, but now, I had a published article that held more value for me than any music album or independent film I'd ever made.

One morning, just after finishing my registration for the next four years as a full-time student, I received a phone call. With a somber voice, Dennis shared the news that he was in trouble. My heart raced with concern. Without delay, I dropped everything, rushed to refund my tuition at the KCC administration office, and caught a flight to LA.

RETURN TO HOLLYWOOD

FOR NEARLY A decade, Dennis had been working hard in Hollywood to find steady acting work aside from playing Asian bad guys. Meanwhile, Marylin beautified the stars behind the scenes at E! Entertainment, and Patrick crunched numbers as a vice president at a movie-financing bank. But Dennis, tired of waiting in the wings, had discovered a new calling—producing independent movies.

In the late '90s, Korea was making waves in the global film industry, heavily investing in its cinematic potential and forging new partnerships with Hollywood. Dennis, with his unique foot in both cultures, was riding the crest of this wave, positioning himself as one of the leading young Korean American filmmakers in Hollywood.

Fate intervened when Dennis networked his way to Shim Hyung-rae, Korea's comedic genius who had grand visions of creating a sci-fi blockbuster as a director but lacked the Hollywood know-how. Dennis immediately partnered with Younggu Art Entertainment to co-produce Shim's film *Dragon Wars*, an epic tale of a giant, ancient serpent's rampage across LA in a quest to evolve into an all-powerful dragon.

Over the years, both Dennis and Shim faced rejection after rejection while hunting for funding and distribution for their respective film projects. Even though Shim had built a powerhouse CGI team with talent from Seoul's top universities, his financial dilemma remained unsolved, so their production team, I presumed, would be hard at work securing financing.

That's why I was befuddled when, during the most intense phase of pre-production, I'd get calls from Dennis—not from a studio, but from a Las Vegas casino. He had been chauffeuring Shim and potential investors there every weekend.

With a laugh, I teased, "I hope you're not spending all your cash on slot machines!"

Dennis let out his usual chuckle before he changed his tone, nervous and more somber.

"This isn't the Hollywood dream I signed up for," he said. "I feel more like a bodyguard for the *yakuza*."

Over the course of the next few weeks, Dennis told me how working with Shim reminded him of a scene straight out of a gangster movie. One time, he'd found himself at a Mandalay Bay penthouse suite surrounded by suits and a bevy of starry-eyed actresses who had accompanied an investor named Choi.

According to Dennis, this smarmy-looking Korean gentleman took out his checkbook and casually wrote a seven-million-dollar check to Mr. Shim.

"Can you believe that?" he asked me. "At that moment, the game changed. This is just the beginning. And the cameras are ready to roll."

I smiled, getting the sense that things were looking up, but some-how, deep inside, I could feel an unclean spirit around my son, and a familiar one at that.

D-WAR

ON THE FIRST day of filming, the movie set occupied a huge section of Downtown Los Angeles, complete with army tanks and machine guns surrounded by enormous lights and other heavy equipment. I would zealously visit the set from time to time, watching assistant directors escort stars like Robert Forster and Jason Behr to and from their trailers. I became an uncredited assistant to Dennis on the set of Shim's film.

When Shim needed more working space, the production office moved into a larger facility at the Los Angeles Center Studios. Shim was a very confident man who was well-recognized by everyone in Koreatown. He was known to play village idiots in episodic Korean sitcoms, and he was a household name.

Meanwhile, Dennis met with studio executives from Warner Brothers who wanted to partner with him, especially in the field of CGI. Since they knew this was a growing, in-demand technology, they knew they could save money by outsourcing visual effects to Korea.

At its inception, *Dragon Wars* was set to be the priciest movie in Korean cinematic history. Upon perusing the script, it struck me that the narrative didn't align with modern Hollywood's style of contemporary fantasy. It had been written with an old-fashioned Korean male perspective, and it was downright sexist. Nevertheless, Mr. Shim was resolute in his decision not to seek advice from anyone, including Dennis and his American writer friends.

***

AFTER THREE LONG years of developing and producing *Dragon Wars*, I received fewer and fewer calls from Dennis. I was about to renew my tuition for four more years at Kapiolani Community College when I finally received a strange phone call from him. He sounded distant and distracted. This behavior did not sit right with me, so I booked a flight to Los Angeles to talk to him in person. Because I couldn't reach Dennis when I landed, I stayed with Marylin at her house in Marina Del Rey, LA.

Later that day, I dropped by Dennis's Koreatown apartment, only to find myself stuck at the front door. He briskly led us into the hallway, insisting we dine out. Throughout, he avoided my gaze, his voice devoid of emotion. His bloodshot eyes and nonchalant demeanor gave the impression he couldn't care less about my visit.

Over the next two days, our dinner outings continued. During our second meal, Dennis candidly announced he was broke. I was taken aback. Despite Shim's measly payments, I regularly supplemented his income. Puzzled, I asked him for clarification, but he quickly grew annoyed.

The following morning, Dennis called to tell me that he'd gone to a meeting and would not be home until late, so I decided to visit his apartment again. The apartment manager, an elderly Korean gentleman, appeared troubled and invited me to talk in his office.

"I'm glad you came," he said as I walked inside. "I need to talk to you. Do you know your son is always late with his rent?"

I gasped. This made no sense. "But I've been giving Dennis money this whole time," I said. "Why isn't he keeping up with the rent?"

He clicked his tongue in a frustrated manner. "I think he's in trouble."

Letting out a trepidatious sigh, I asked, "Can I take a look inside his apartment?"

If I hadn't known better, I would have assumed that no one had lived there for months. Mail was piled up on the corner of the kitchen counter, and the garbage disposal smelled like it had been clogged for weeks. In the bathroom, the toilet bowl was covered with stains of dried urine, and the bathtub contained a build-up of black soap scum. There was no toothpaste or soap near the sink, and the rug was filthy. Underneath the bathroom sink, empty whiskey bottles, spoons, and syringes lay scattered about.

I was absolutely floored by what I saw. When I opened the bedroom door to allow the air to circulate, I noticed that the drapes were torn and stained. His closet contained both women's and men's clothing, the latter being too small to fit him. I felt as though an iron vise gripped my heart.

I took a deep breath and spent the entire day cleaning the apartment. As the undeniable truth sank in, I nearly broke down in tears, lamenting over and over: *For over a century, our family has been destroyed by drugs, and still, this curse will not release us! Can we never be free?*

When Dennis returned late that night, I grabbed the spoons from under the bathroom sink and confronted him at the door.

"What the hell are these things?" I shouted.

His eyes were wide with confusion as he stammered, "They're—they're props for the film!"

"Do you think I'm stupid?" I screamed, then took a moment to calm down. "Take the second room. I am staying here tonight."

He ducked into his bedroom. I chased after him, but he shut the door in my face. All through the night, his violent coughing kept me awake. Feeling helpless, I decided to lie down on a futon in the middle of the living room, but I couldn't sleep.

I felt the room closing in on me and saw long, dark shadows creeping across the apartment walls. To deter my fears, I convinced myself that these shadows were simply nearby traffic moving under the streetlights.

I closed my eyes to get some sleep, but for some reason, a song kept repeating in my head, the result of a K-pop music video Dennis, Youngman, and I had just worked on months ago. This memory stood out because it was the first Korean music video to be shot in LA with the K-pop sensations Ivy and J.Y. Park.

Images of these sexy young girls wiggling their hips on camera flashed through my mind. Ivy's dance moves reminded me of my burlesque days. Then, the images shifted, and I saw her body change into a giant snake, like the computer-generated monsters from the film *Dragon Wars*. An image of my great-grandmother popped out and slashed the snake across its head, as she did many decades ago, and then faded away.

I shook myself awake, realizing it was just my runaway imagination. But as the night dragged on, I felt my misery increase. I barely slept after that.

I returned to Honolulu the next day since there was nothing I could do to help.

All I could do was wait. Every night, I searched the internet for information about common narcotic drugs and their effects. Dennis wouldn't return any of my calls, so I decided my top priority was to find places in Los Angeles that could help him.

***

IT HAD BEEN two years since Mother passed away, and I hadn't once looked at her memorial portrait. Then, one day in early November 2005, I dusted off the top of the frame.

"Mother," I whispered, "If you are with God, tell him I need help."

At that moment, the phone rang; I quickly answered.

"Mom?" It was Marylin. I could immediately tell she was upset by the way she spoke that one word.

"Is something wrong?"

There was a pause. "Dennis just visited me at work. He looked awful. And he asked me if he could borrow three hundred dollars."

"I just wired him one thousand last week," I retorted, then fell silent. It hurt more now that my daughter was involved.

Marylin's voice sank to a whisper, "I think it's drugs, Mom. He lost a lot of weight. His face is all wrinkled, and his fingernails and clothes are filthy like he's been living on the streets."

My heart skipped a beat. I took a deep breath, trying to remain calm. "He must have gotten kicked out of his apartment," I said. "Do you know where he's staying?"

"He told me the Days Inn, near Koreatown."

Agitated, I quickly devised a plan. "Can you go over there after work and pay for his hotel till Saturday?" I asked. "I'll make a reservation to fly to LA right now. Oh, and make sure you only pay with cash. Please tell Dennis that I'm coming to take care of his expenses so he doesn't run off."

As soon as I hung up the phone, I booked the next flight to Los Angeles. Later in the afternoon, Marylin called me again. "Mom, he looks better today. I just paid for four days at the hotel with cash."

Suddenly, a disturbing thought struck me. "He might try to get a cash refund from the hotel," I said. "I hadn't thought of that."

Marylin was stunned. "Neither did I! I'll go back and check right now." Sure enough, Dennis had tried to withdraw the entire sum, but he was only able to get reimbursed for the last day, so he had no choice but to spend the night there.

According to my research, most rehab centers were prohibitively expensive, though we managed to find a few that fit within our budget. I had saved some money for Marylin's wedding, so I dipped into those funds.

Marylin and I eventually chose The Comeback Treatment Center in Anaheim. Kent, the center's counselor, informed us it would cost nineteen thousand dollars. Desperate to get help for Dennis, I agreed.

As soon as I landed in Los Angeles in the late evening, I hurried into Marylin's car at the curbside pick-up area. Wiping each other's faces dry, we headed toward Dennis's hotel in Koreatown. Marylin had just gotten engaged a short six months ago, and she shared a little about her wedding plans with me.

I sighed. This should have been the happiest time of her life, but it was now tainted by the gravity of her brother's addiction. Feeling uneasy, Marylin asked what we should do if Dennis didn't cooperate, as neither of us had a backup plan.

Before I could entertain that thought, Marylin's cell phone rang.

"It's Dennis," she remarked, then addressed him, "Yeah, I'm with Mom now. We'll be there shortly. Okay, good." She ended the call and told me, "He's anxious to see us."

By the time we arrived in Koreatown, it had gotten very dark, with streetlights few and far between. Approaching the Days Inn, we prepared ourselves to face Dennis. I warned Marylin, "Watch your keys and your purse, in case he tries to take the car and drive away."

"I think you've watched too many movies, Mom," she replied with her eyebrows raised. I laughed, and so did she; that was the first time we had laughed together in a long time. For the moment, it felt good, but that feeling disappeared when we spotted Dennis sitting on the brightly lit front porch. The first thing I noticed was his weight, or lack of it. His once-chunky frame was now thin and lanky. When he saw our car approach, he ran toward us.

When Marylin pulled over, I noticed Dennis didn't have any luggage. And most distressing, there was no life in his eyes, no emotion, and his putrid body odor was nauseating.

"I'm hungry," he said, then lapsed into local pidgin. "When are we going eat?"

Immediately, I grabbed his arm and shoved him inside. "We'll talk in the car!"

He looked at me, alarmed. "What are you doing?"

I pushed him into the back seat and sat next to him. Then I leaned forward and whispered into Marylin's ear, "Lock the doors."

Quickly, I grabbed Dennis's sweaty hands, held them firmly, and looked into his eyes. "Listen carefully," I said. "We're here to help you!"

I tried to speak calmly, but my words elevated to a high-pitched shriek, which made Dennis laugh uncomfortably. Then, for only the second time in his life, I smacked him on the side of his head. "I've had enough of your garbage! Right now, once and for all, you must be honest with your family! Everybody knows you're on drugs."

Dennis's leg began to shake, and he anxiously bit his fingernails. He snapped, "Where are you taking me?" From the look in his eyes, I knew Dennis realized that there would be no escape, no excuses.

Marylin turned to face him. "You need professional help," she said.

"You're overreacting," he retorted.

"*Imusekkiya*! (Blast you!)," I barked.

I took a moment to calm down. After studying the road map, Marylin started the car while I kept my eye on Dennis. He remained quiet as traffic became more congested on the I-5 freeway going south. After a long pause, Dennis looked out the window and grumbled, "I have no money, no girlfriend, no family of my own."

"Whose fault is that?" I snapped. "Look at us. Look at what we're doing now. Chasing after you in the middle of the night."

Getting off the freeway, Marylin drove through an industrial area of Anaheim and pulled into the parking lot in front of the rehab center—toward what appeared to be an old house. It felt unsettling to see the exterior in such poor condition, and on the inside, it looked even worse.

The house had a large living room, four adjoining bedrooms, and a small office near the entrance. It was totally not worth the price I was paying, but I had gone too far to turn back. Three young Caucasian men—two of them heavily tattooed—sat in the living room watching television. My assumption was that they were recovering addicts, too.

Just then, a Caucasian man of medium build in his mid-forties approached us. With graying sideburns, he wore an LA Lakers basketball cap, typical of Angelenos.

"Hi, Mrs. Lee," he said. "My name is Kent, and I'll be your son's counselor."

After we exchanged greetings, he welcomed us into his corner office and handed us a ten-page contract to review. Admittedly, I knew nothing about the program, and when I saw the same worried look on Marylin's face, I sensed she had the same reservations.

I put my purse on the table and reiterated, "Like I said over the phone, I don't travel with too much cash. I'll give you five thousand dollars up front, and I'll wire the rest when I get home."

When I put the money on Kent's desk in rolled-up wads of hundred-dollar bills, his eyes lit up like sparklers on the Fourth of July. He then apologized for not accepting credit cards because patients often used stolen ones.

I was unsatisfied with that explanation, but my mind was so focused on Dennis that I was willing to accept it if this program provided the help he needed. Marylin and I filled out the forms while Dennis went to his assigned room, threw himself on the bed, and immediately passed out.

REHAB THERAPY

AFTER THREE MONTHS, the rehab program was nearing its end, but Tony, Dennis's ex-roommate, contacted me, claiming that Dennis had been seen wandering aimlessly around Koreatown, holding a Bible in his hand. He had also lost a lot of weight and was spotted talking to a shady man, most likely a drug dealer.

At this point, I only felt one emotion—anger.

Can he really beat this addiction? I asked myself, but I had no answers. Flabbergasted, my heart leaped into my throat. Once again, I flew back to Los Angeles and had lunch with Marylin and Dennis.

He appeared even thinner than before, and his face was gaunt. I felt a dark energy surround him. A rank scent of wet mold spewed from him, and from the look of things, I knew he wasn't completely off drugs.

I felt so heartbroken that even lunch tasted bitter. Later that evening, I decided it would be a good idea to have dinner with the rest of the family. With a pang of guilt, Dennis declined to join us, so I made a reservation at Fred Segal's in Melrose, inviting

Marylin and her now-husband, Simeon Spiegel, along with Patrick and his wife, Cindy. Patrick brought along his little children—my grandchildren—Koa and Kaipo.

Every time I met with my youngest children, I felt guilty because I had spent so much more time and money helping Dennis, but I was happy that they both had made successful lives with very little help from me.

***

DUE TO HIS erratic behavior, Dennis was fired just before *Dragon Wars* wrapped production. Realizing there had been discrepancies in his paycheck, I pursued legal action against Shim Hyung-Rae for unpaid wages. Because of these legal hang-ups, Shim was unable to release the movie on schedule, and I eventually forced his hand to offer Dennis a settlement, demanding a producer credit and one million dollars.

When I returned to Hawaii, I received an email from the attorney informing me that Dennis had signed an agreement for a meager seven thousand dollars and a "Los Angeles Producer's credit." Absolutely dumbfounded, I struggled to listen to the attorney's incoherent ramblings over the phone and his excuses for this bone-headed settlement.

"I spent weeks arguing with that pig-faced director, trying to get him to pay my son!" I shouted, enunciating every syllable of every word. The attorney didn't respond, and I felt as though I were screaming into an empty room.

Enraged, I flew to LA the next day and rented Dennis a room in a two-story apartment complex in Hollywood. I bought new furniture and a state-of-the-art computer, feeling hopeful that he would pull himself together, find a decent job, and make a fresh start.

The day after I returned to Hawaii, Dennis called me, asking for money. Calmly, I complied, but the very next day, he called again to tell me he was depressed.

"You're depressed?" I shouted. "Who makes you depressed? I just paid for your apartment, bought you furniture and a brand-new computer so that you can start all over. Now you're 'depressed'? You must be out of your mind. Go find a job like everybody else!"

"You don't even try to understand me!" he shouted back.

At that point, everything seemed hopeless; getting through to him seemed impossible. I screamed in blind fury, "I must have been crazy to give birth to a son like you! How could your damn father leave me with such a miserable son?"

Dennis's absurd tales of needing money for car problems—towing one day, the same car getting stolen the next—got on my last nerve. My patience evaporated. I couldn't bear it anymore.

"I've had enough of you!" I snapped over the phone, frustration oozing from my voice. "This is the end! I'm done!" The rush of blood coursing through my head made me lose my balance, and I crumpled onto the floor, my gaze fixed on the ceiling. Out of stress, disjointed words came out of my mouth, echoing my mother's words in times of anguish. Only now did I understand their meaning.

"Oh, Father! What have we done to deserve this? *Juyo! Juyo!* Help me! Help my son!" My body trembled and convulsed uncontrollably. An odd impulse drove me to open a neglected, dusty Bible Mother had left on my dresser, marked by a plucked palm leaf.

The marked page led me to Philippians 4:6, "Do not be anxious about anything, but in every situation, by prayer and petition, with thanksgiving, present your requests to God."

I closed the Bible, then opened it again to a random page. The verse from 1 John 5:14 stood out to me, "And this is the confidence that we have toward Him, that if we ask anything according to His will, He hears us."

"His will," I repeated out loud. I let that idea resonate within me for a while. Perhaps prayer isn't about asking God for favors. Perhaps it is about aligning with what God has in mind for your life's path. If you ask for something that God doesn't give to you, maybe it's a sign that there's a different route ahead of you. A path according to God's plan, not your own.

Through my tears, I pleaded, "Oh God, help me! How long? God, how long?"

Closing my eyes, I saw a vivid image of my mother praying. She was invoking the Holy Spirit. In my mind, I knelt and prayed beside her. It was at that moment I realized the movie's seven-thousand-dollar settlement had been a blessing in disguise. Had he won a larger settlement, Dennis would have wasted the money on drugs and jeopardized his health. He would have continued down a destructive path, consorting with criminals and vagrants.

Like his father, Dennis possessed not only passion but also self-destructive compulsions. At that moment, I released it all into God's hands to allow my son to find his own path to healing and redemption. With renewed resolve, I embraced the uncertain but trusted divine guidance to unfold—one step at a time.

***

AFTER MY LAST outburst, Dennis didn't call me for months. Though I was worried, I could not allow him to interfere with my daily life. Appropriately enough, while Okyon and I were shopping at Kahala Mall one afternoon, I ran into June Park again.

"Sister, you don't look so good," she said, looking me directly in the eyes. "What happened?"

"I have more wrinkles, don't I?" I asked.

June clucked her tongue and caressed my face. "You look tired—like something has sucked the spirit out of you." She paused, then reached for my hand. "Why don't you come to our morning prayer group?"

I shook my head, but just as I was about to turn her down, June interrupted me. "God can bring you miracles," she said. "If you ask, you shall receive."

I sighed and looked at Okyon, who nodded in encouragement.

"We've tried everything else," my sister pointed out.

I conceded. "Okay," I said. "I'll come."

***

I ARRANGED TO meet June at my mother's former church, Korean Christian Church, before sunrise on September 11, 2002. June had invited me to a morning service commemorating the first anniversary of the World Trade Center attack. Prior to the service, June's prayer group had already assembled in the front pews.

Stepping inside the church, I greeted June and nervously took my seat. I noticed the brand-new carpet, and as we conversed, I sensed a change in June. Her voice had matured since we last worked together, and she appeared more focused and down to earth.

Nine elderly women sat with us in front of the pews. The pianist played "Rock of Ages" over the PA system. Overwhelmed with emotion, I burst into tears after the first verse. A voice in my head urged me to kneel on the red carpet in the aisle, and in my desperation, I complied.

I could hear the elderly women softly chanting, *"Juyo! Juyo!"* At that point, Pastor Samuel Kim approached the pulpit and addressed our circle. I returned to my seat, feeling emotionally unraveled, while June handed me a box of Kleenex. Pastor Kim gathered everyone in a circle in the middle of the sanctuary to share their stories.

Listening to their tales, I recognized similarities to my own struggle—family problems and burdens too heavy to bear. But unlike me, they spoke of the trust they had in Jesus Christ and how it guided them. Although I didn't fully grasp that trust, when it was my turn to speak, I felt ready to share my own challenges.

Pastor Kim showed genuine sympathy while listening to me, bowing his head and raising his hands toward my head. He asked everyone to pray for my son, Dennis Lee. Feeling a glimmer of hope, I focused on my lost son. Six of the elderly ladies formed a circle around me, held hands, and chanted harmoniously, calling on the name of Jesus.

As they prayed with such fervor and intensity, I was overcome with both sadness and joy. After our prayer circle ended, I wasn't sure I understood what had happened. Was I doing it right?

When I asked June, she explained that prayer isn't about following a formula but an open invitation to communicate with our Heavenly Father. At the very least, I felt an inner peace.

I faithfully attended their morning service at dawn every day for six weeks.

***

ONE MONTH LATER, at about 2:00 a.m., my phone rang. Staggering out of bed, my heart started beating faster.

"Who would call at this hour?" I asked out loud, anxious about answering the phone—frightened even. It was very likely to be Dennis.

"Hello, Okhui," a woman said. "My name is Susan Han. I was one of the makeup artists on *D-War*. Do you remember me?"

"Oh, yes," I said. "Of course, I remember you." I paused, knowing full well why she was calling. And I knew it would not be good news. Susan was a Korean crew member from *D-War* with whom I had once shared my dismay over never knowing the fate of Dennis's father.

Susan cleared her throat. "During the filming of *D-War*, you asked if I could find out what happened to Dennis's biological father, Kim Gwangyeong, the actor, right?"

A chill ran down my spine. "I remember," I said. "Yes, that was his name."

Susan continued, "I'm sitting with the co-director of the movie Kim acted in. He knew him very well. Would you want to speak to him?"

I agreed.

"Excuse me, Mrs. Lee," he said. The voice belonged to an old man with a thick Busan accent. "I'm sorry to bring you some unpleasant news."

I did not have to guess. "I assume he has passed away?"

"Ah, yes," the old voice answered. "He died right after he made his second film."

"Do you know how he died?" I asked.

There was an awkward silence. "Er . . . well, Kim was a true artist," the man began, then he stopped and sighed.

"May I speak to Susan?" I blurted out.

"Kim Gwangyeong died a madman," Susan said after getting back on the phone. "His body was found in the middle of Myeongdong, naked in the snow."

Grief-stricken, I put the phone down and closed my eyes. Susan had confirmed what I had long suspected—that my former lover, Dennis's father, had been dead all this time.

The image of the last time I saw him alive lingered in my mind— he was waving at me from the street corner as the cab driver slowly took me away. I looked in the rear-view mirror as his image shrank into the distance.

Though it was now confirmed that Kim was no longer with us, I took solace in the fact that Dennis would carry on his legacy. I lamented the fact that he had died without dignity, but I also felt consolation in receiving closure over a significant part of my life.

CEDAR SINAI

SEPTEMBER 2007. AMIDST a gloomy, rain-soaked night, my phone suddenly chimed, and some unexplainable voice in my gut whispered to me, "It has to be Dennis."

"Mom?" His weak, raspy voice reached me through the phone, and his next words sounded muddled. Despite the frailty in his tone, a surge of relief washed over me. I was happy he was alive.

"Are you alright?" I immediately asked. "Where are you?"

His response held a blend of certainty and uncertainty. "I'm fine," he told me. "But I need some money to retrieve my cell phone and find a place to stay."

My heart sank. I transferred the money the next morning, but days passed with no word from him. One week later, another sudden phone call brought a heavy, sinking feeling upon me.

"Mom," he said in a strained, gravelly tone. "I'm in the hospital." He paused; I prepared for the worst. "My hands got infected."

Inside, I panicked but managed to prevent myself from blurting out anything that might scare him away. He gave me the name of the hospital—Cedar Sinai—and his room number: 315. Although worried, I still needed to make sure he wasn't lying to me again. I called the hospital to verify the information and then immediately booked a flight to Los Angeles.

Upon my arrival, Marylin picked me up and drove me to Cedar Sinai. She had visited Dennis earlier that week, and the doctor had told her that his infection was from the overuse of hypodermic needles. Painful as this was to hear, it confirmed my worst fears, and I needed to focus on solutions.

As soon as we entered Dennis's room, he turned his head away and grumbled incoherently under his breath. His hands were covered with bandages the size of boxing gloves, rendering any movement of his arms impossible. Lying in bed with medical paraphernalia attached to his entire body, he reminded me of the Vietnam combat troops I had seen aboard the military cargo plane many years ago.

"When I was driving up here," I began, "I saw rows of *Dragon War* posters all over the public billboards."

Dennis only responded with a grunt. I noticed he had lost even more weight, and his skin had turned a darker shade of yellow. When he turned to look at me, his eyes were red and sunken, and I could see veins bulging on both sides of his forehead. It was as if his entire body had been taken over by an evil spirit.

Emotionally torn, a part of me wanted to slap him for being so foolish, while the other part longed to embrace him. He averted his gaze. I knew he wasn't interested in conversation, so I sat silently in a chair beside his bed and prayed to God for help, but I didn't know what to say. Still, I kept repeating phrases like *"Juyo Juyo,"* borrowing from my mother's words.

To lighten the mood, Marylin turned on the television, but our thoughts were focused on Dennis, who was nervously shaking his legs and biting his fingernails.

An hour later, a middle-aged doctor came in to examine him. When he finished, I followed him outside. "Can you tell me about his symptoms?" I asked.

"Mrs. Lee," the doctor began with a sympathetic smile. "I believe your son is one of the luckiest men alive. If he hadn't come in when he did, he might have lost both of his hands, and the infection could have reached his heart, which would have been fatal. For now, I think it's safe to say he'll be all right, but I'll need him to come in for physical therapy next week."

"What's going to happen to his hands?" I asked.

The doctor paused. "Well, there's a lot of muscle damage, so we're not sure if he'll regain full use of them." Lowering his voice, he continued, "He also has hepatitis C. For that, he's going to need to see another doctor. I can give him a referral."

I let out a long breath. After our discussion, I returned to the room and told Marylin that I couldn't afford to stay in Los Angeles for a prolonged time.

"Mom, you should take him back to Hawaii," Marylin said. "I think there's something about the islands that would give him a sense of peace."

I nodded, hurrying back to Dennis's bedside. I saw sweat trickling down his forehead. I thought he'd protest against the idea, but instead, he spoke calmly.

"I met a Catholic priest yesterday. I didn't know what to say to him. He told me to repent my wrongdoings. Then, he prayed over me. After that, I felt this intense burning sensation," he said, sounding amazed. "It was like I was on fire, all over. Strange, huh?" He fell silent, his gaze fixed on the ceiling, lost in thought.

***

UPON RECEIVING THE doctor's diagnosis for my son, I understood that Dennis would need to stimulate the muscles in his hands for his recovery. With that in mind, Marylin and I decided that once he was discharged, we would purchase a guitar for Dennis. This would serve a dual purpose—aiding in his physical rehabilitation while also potentially paving the way for professional opportunities in the future.

As we made our way north toward the Guitar Center on the Sunset Strip, my eyes scanned the surroundings. The moment we reached Sunset Boulevard, a wave of nostalgia washed over me. There, in place of the once-iconic Pink Pussycat Nightclub, stood a new venue called Club 7969. Memories from years past flooded my mind as I vividly recalled the day Coralie had booked me to perform at that same club.

The building's physical appearance remained unchanged, but the original neon burlesque sign, a symbol of a bygone era, had vanished, leaving only echoes of the vibrant past that had once thrived within those walls.

I took a moment to let it sink in but didn't voice my thoughts out loud. As we drove past the Blessed Sacrament Church, located further west, Dennis shared with me its noble mission of feeding the homeless. During his time on the streets, he told us, he had relied on the church's charity for sustenance, and it was through a nun's intervention that he'd ended up at Cedar Sinai. As he rambled on, recounting his survival and the harsh realities of life on the streets, my mind drifted back to my own tumultuous memories.

The image of the former Pink Pussycat nightclub remained seared in my mind, serving as a painful reminder of all the struggles I had endured. Memories of my days as a burlesque dancer, performing in Denver, Los Angeles, and Honolulu, and working as a hostess flooded my thoughts. This journey led me to run a hostess bar, sacrificing everything to provide for my three children.

In the depths of my heart, all that remained was an overwhelming mixture of sadness and anger. These emotions, forged by my hardships, burned inside me, fueling a deep-rooted determination to overcome the challenges that had defined my life thus far.

It gave me a little spark of hope.

THE ROAD TO RECOVERY

RETURNING TO THE islands, it didn't take long for the situation to take a turn for the worse. Dennis abandoned rehab and expressed his desire to give Los Angeles another chance. He revealed this to me late one night, arriving home after midnight and flopping down on the couch. All I could do was throw pillows at him in my anger.

After a few nights, I simply left him alone. I spent many sleepless nights letting the frustration consume me, and all I could hear was the ghost of my mother's voice warning me, nagging me. She'd tell me that I must keep praying. She would stress the importance of prayer, but deep down, I questioned whether my prayers were truly making a difference.

Sometimes, I wondered if I could actually hear God through prayer, but because I was filled with so much self-doubt and uncertainty, I couldn't see any clear signs of Him. I kept thinking I might encounter a dramatic signal, like a loud booming voice from the sky screaming, "Hey, over here! I am the Lord, your God!"

I realized that those extraordinary events only happened in movies, like that scene in *The Ten Commandments* when God spoke to Moses through a burning bush. In truth, it took years for me to understand how to hear God's voice. It was a gradual process.

The Bible has touched my heart many times, inspiring me and moving me forward. The scriptures speak directly to my innermost thoughts and worries. In these Biblical verses, I've discovered divine guidance that lights up my path and connects to me spiritually. These sacred pages hold timeless wisdom and have brought me peace through divine motivation.

As the years went by, I learned that God had been communicating with me in subtle, often multifaceted ways. Sometimes, He speaks to me through a gentle whisper of my conscience, guiding me toward righteousness and wisdom. Other times, He graces me with dreams and visions, granting me glimpses of His divine plan. In these encounters, I recognize the presence of the Holy Spirit, a guiding force that I have learned to rely upon.

I realize now that God's voice resonates not only within my being but also through the people who have crossed my path. He speaks through them, using them as vessels to deliver messages of hope, encouragement, and guidance. It is through these diverse channels that I am reminded of His unwavering love and the profound ways in which He is actively involved in my life. In cultivating a relationship with Him, I find solace, inspiration, and strength.

Upon Dennis's return home, exhausted and burdened, his weary eyes betrayed a profound sense of loss. Despite his incessant grievances about the transformations that had taken place in Los Angeles and his desire to go back, I couldn't help but feel a wave of relief, knowing that he was now safe and sheltered within the confines of my home. I offered a suggestion, hoping to lighten his burden. "Have you thought about reaching out to Director Youngman? Maybe he could hire you for his upcoming projects."

Dennis nodded, though his response lacked clarity.

Filled with hope, I silently prayed that this opportunity would mark the inception of a new and promising chapter in my son's life. A few weeks later, I heard the strumming of guitar strings coming from my son's room. Deep down, I knew that it signaled the beginning of his new journey.

***

I REMEMBER MANY strange dreams I've had since I was very little, dreams that fascinated me, some so vivid and inspiring that I accepted them as inspiration, perhaps meant to guide me toward a direction I needed to take.

Later that night, I had a unique dream. I found myself suspended in the air, embraced by a vast dome-like firmament as a gentle breeze encircled me, carrying me toward a billowy cloud. Suddenly, Jesus appeared above me, clothed in a flowing robe adorned with golden tassels. A wintry gust guided us both as we glided together, side by side, above an endless expanse of crystal-clear, unending river stretching into eternity.

The sun shone its bright light on the river, transforming its surface into a dazzling spectacle of glistening diamonds. Each facet of this divine jewel broke away, forming luminous streaks of light that delicately entered my eyes. With each ray of light, its brilliance grew, gradually overwhelming my senses until it enveloped me in a blinding radiance.

And then, my Lord and Savior bade me farewell, and my spirit effortlessly traversed to the opposite bank of the river. I became weightless, as light as a feather, while the ethereal strains of a harp reached my ears, soothing me into a state of profound tranquility. It was then that a celestial voice resonated within me, unmistakably that of an angel.

As I descended back to the earth, I found myself humbly kneeling before an altar beneath a resplendent crystal dome. The melodious echoes of the river continued to reverberate like a gentle lullaby soothing my soul. Upon awakening, tears welled in my eyes, and I recognized the same chimes I'd heard at the temple on the night my son had been conceived. With that realization, I felt a newfound sense of peace.

***

THE DREAM LEFT me with a strong conviction to promptly visit a Catholic Church. Over the next several months, Dennis and I participated in a Bible study class with some parishioners at the Sacred Heart Church Punahou on Wilder Avenue. After some struggle, he stayed committed until the class ended just before Lent.

On Ash Wednesday 2008, Dennis and I stood in line at this same church, waiting to be anointed. I could feel his nervousness as he took small steps toward the priest and raised his head toward him. The priest looked at my son, and then he dipped his right thumb in a bowl of ash and made the sign of the cross on Dennis's forehead.

"Remember, son, that thou art dust, and unto dust thou shalt return," the priest spoke softly. When it was my turn, I silently asked God once again to forgive me—to forgive me for living my life contrary to His will. All the years I'd spent entertaining and pleasuring hordes of men flashed in my mind. It was no wonder I'd never felt fulfilled.

Tears streamed from my eyelids. I looked toward the roof and told myself to release the weight of the memories of my past. I blinked away warm tears, and my vision cleared just enough to see a stained-glass window depicting Jesus's suffering on the cross with his mother at his feet. I had always thought of myself as a strong, tough woman, yet I was easily brought to tears in the presence of the Lord!

I recalled when I'd told Dennis about his father's passing last year shortly after receiving Susan's call. He'd sat quietly and expressionless, but I could see the pain deep in his eyes. I'd often wondered if the challenges in Dennis's life had manifested from some internal spiritual warfare.

Later that evening, I got down on my knees, and I prayed for my son to be released from our family curse. With a deep breath, a cascade of memories came crashing down, all intertwined. Dennis's journey, steeped in shadows, mirrored his father's. Kim Gwangyeong's journey had tragically ended while Dennis's was still unfolding.

There was a divine intervention that spared Dennis—a tug of war between the angels and demons, played out in dreams, visions, and real-life choices. I firmly believed that the ominous, haunting specter of drugs was a puppet, with the devil himself pulling the strings from the shadows. But I couldn't let that discourage me. I knew I needed to follow what God had in store for my future.

THE MAKING OF A DOCUMENTARY

IN NOVEMBER 2008, Dennis's colleague, director Youngman Kang, sought an investor for a segment in his second documentary, *Haiti Street Kids*. I thought this could be a valuable opportunity for Dennis. At the very least, it would allow him to stay active in production work.

Having experienced poverty during wartime, I had long been an admirer of the philanthropy of many celebrities, and having followed the career of my favorite actress, Audrey Hepburn, I found her altruism inspiring. Motivated by the desire to make a positive impact like her, I felt it was important for Dennis to understand the challenging lives that children on the other side of the world had to endure. That felt crucial to me, so I took a risk and supported Youngman's project in Haiti.

For the first trip, Dennis jetted off to Haiti by himself in late December and tracked down the former street kid Wilner St. Fort, who had appeared in Youngman's previous documentary, *Haitian*

Slave Children. Word spread like wildfire among Haitian street children when Americans arrived, and before they knew it, Youngman and Dennis booked interviews with dozens of children raised in an orphanage run by an American named Michael.

When Michael was interviewed, he claimed he'd been running his Port-au-Prince orphanage for almost two decades. Youngman's documentary crew was certainly excited to meet someone who had devoted his life to helping impoverished children.

Youngman portrayed Michael as a hero and a mentor to Wilner, who had grown up under his care. Now in Belle Fontaine, Wilner ran his own orphanage. But in July 2009, when Youngman invited Dennis and me to conduct more interviews in Haiti, the situation changed.

After many hours of flying, we finally arrived at the Port-au-Prince airport. We picked up our luggage from the carousel, and as we stepped outside the terminal and approached the airport entrance, a small crowd of locals tried to hustle us over just about everything.

Outside, the sky was a clear, warm blue, the gentle breeze reminiscent of Hawaii. We met Wilner outside the airport and instantly connected like family. I gave him a warm hug, happily surprised by his height compared to the older footage of him as a young teenager.

Now in his early twenties, Wilner flashed a big, toothy grin and introduced us to his friends. "Hello, Mom," he greeted me. "This my sponsor, Stephen Garrett. He is Scotsman."

I loved that he called me "mom." He then introduced us to two young adults, Jimmy and Emmanuel, who were also former street kids under Michael. I was impressed by how well-dressed they were. I even caught a whiff of their fragrant European perfume, a remnant of their French colonial days. Though Jimmy was very talkative, Emmanuel was shy, silently standing to the side.

After swiftly gathering our belongings, we hired a driver to take us to the Holiday Inn in the city center. Just after leaving the airport, I noticed large piles of garbage everywhere. Despite this, everything else was vibrant and colorful. The streets were bustling with people, along with colorful *Tap Tap* buses. Women carried items on top of their heads as they navigated the busy street, reminiscent of old Korea. My heart felt heavy seeing skinny dogs roaming around while chickens ran amok everywhere.

Fighting off the jet lag, I recommended we take a break before embarking on our journey. Despite the humid hotel room swarmed with mosquitoes, we managed to grab some sleep.

The next day, we woke up, unpacked our film gear, and started shooting interviews at the breakfast table.

"Where did you learn English?" I asked Wilner.

With his toothy grin, he replied, "You see, my home in Belle Fontaine is twenty-six miles from Port-au-Prince. During the journey, I talk to trees, rocks, or birds—anything I come across—to practice conversations in English."

I was impressed.

***

WE PREPARED FOR our trip to Belle Fontaine and made a pit stop at a nearby grocery market to buy food for the children. After negotiating with a local driver, we set out on our journey, unaware that it would evolve into a twenty-six-mile rollercoaster ride. The twisty, steep roads through rocky mountains had us gripping our seats. Even with a seasoned local driver behind the wheel, Dennis, Youngman, Wilner, Stephen Garrett, and I held on, crossing our fingers that driving off a cliff wasn't on our itinerary.

Arriving at Belle Fontaine, I noticed the road had been patched up by locals with uneven rocks and paved with their bare hands—it made for a bumpy ride. The village itself, however, radiated peace. Women gracefully balanced baskets on their heads as donkeys carried supplies and goats wandered freely. This corner of Haiti brought back beautiful memories of my childhood in Busan.

Meeting the orphans was a moving experience that fueled my desire to extend my mission work beyond filming. Wilner was remarkably dedicated to these seven orphans, ranging in age from five to sixteen—all were thrilled to see us. Their eyes lit up when we delivered boxes of food—chicken, rice, and spices—along with Hawaiian cookies and candies from home.

The following day, our film crew visited Michael in Port-au-Prince. The joint interview with Michael and Wilner was successful, and I donated some funds to the orphanage, as well as provided food and clothing for the children.

Our next stop was Jimmy's orphanage in Cité Soleil, where I witnessed the harsh living conditions of the impoverished locals amid mountains of garbage. Despite lacking basic amenities like toilets and running water, these dust-covered children gathered happily to sing for us, showcasing their resilience.

On our last day, Wilner snuck Dennis a handwritten note with his email, telling him not to look at it until he returned home. My son agreed, and when we later reached out to Wilner, we got hit with a bombshell. Michael, the gentleman we'd painted in such a positive light, turned out to be a child molester, and Wilner was one of his victims. This revelation forced us to pull all of Michael's footage and switch the focus of the documentary in the middle of post-production.

***

IN NOVEMBER 2009, our crew returned to Haiti to complete the documentary while addressing the allegations Wilner had made against Michael. Upon landing, we immediately checked into a hotel near a popular city park. That night, as I tried to sleep, a stabbing pain in my skin jolted me awake. Frightened, I tried to pray, but an inexplicable language barrier interrupted my thoughts—I was unable to express myself in either Korean or English. My words sounded like pure gibberish.

The next morning at breakfast, Youngman showed up late.

"I had a scary dream of being chased by a man in a creepy Haitian mask. He kept saying he was a Vodou man."

Strangely enough, I'd had a similar dream. I confessed this to him.

Overhearing our conversation, Wilner told us to take our dreams seriously. The indigenous religion of Vodou was a blend of African traditions and Roman Catholic beliefs involving spirits.

"In Christianity, you can be forgiven," Wilner explained. "But in Vodou, crossing a priest is bad fortune."

With that in mind, we took these dreams as a warning and made seeking justice for Michael's crimes our top priority. Despite hurdles involving FBI jurisdiction, we were eager to share the inspiring stories of Wilner, Jimmy, and the other brave kids who had captured our hearts despite enduring pain. Legally, on the other hand, we couldn't do much more.

***

A FEW MONTHS after the interviews had been edited, we visited Pastor Nancy of Highland Church in Hollywood to ask her advice about distribution and publicity for our documentary. Dennis once attended her church services when he was homeless, and he recommended her for her expertise with faith-based projects as well as her unbounded enthusiasm for human interest subjects.

He wasn't exaggerating. The moment I met her, I felt an immediate spiritual connection as I shared my charity goals with her. Pastor Nancy suggested we get involved with a nonprofit organization to raise money for creative community projects. I followed her advice and started a 501(c)(3) called Haiti Kids Now. Later, we renamed it Global Kids Now to serve impoverished children worldwide, starting in Hawaii.

In 2009, through Nancy's connection, The Missionary Church International formally appointed and ordained me as the Reverend Okhui Lee, the founder of its ministry. Our mission was to motivate young people from underserved communities all over the world to take action on important global challenges.

But best of all, during that first mission, I saw a compassionate side of Dennis I hadn't seen before. In fact, by the end of his trip, he had given away all his belongings, including his suitcase, to the orphans. I told him, "I thought you were going to come back home with no clothes on."

Dennis chuckled and replied, "Well, I figured if I'm going to give away my belongings, I might as well go all the way! Besides, who needs clothes when your heart is covered with compassion."

I laughed with him. He'd never shown this side of himself before. And it suited him nicely.

***

THROUGH THE COMBINATION of our show business know-how and Dennis's Hollywood producer background, we humbly embarked on the journey of crafting Christian music videos for local community events, resulting in the gradual expansion of our presence and visibility. With the adept editing of Director Youngman's footage, we distributed these videos across social media platforms, leveraging them to generate funds for the betterment of underprivileged street children.

After viewing a rough cut of the completed documentary, Dennis found himself struck by a brilliant idea: why not kickstart his very own band to raise funds? Seeking guidance, we approached Pastor Kim of Korean Christian Church, who recommended a suitable worship band in Kalihi.

But first, we needed to finish the documentary.

HAITI EARTHQUAKE

WHILE DIRECTOR YOUNGMAN'S documentary neared completion, my focus turned to finding a catchy and marketable title. Marylin suggested "Innocence Abandoned: Street Kids of Haiti," which was perfect.

Unfortunately, tragedy suddenly struck just before its release. On January 12, 2010, CNN reported a devastating 7.0 earthquake in Haiti. Horrified, I saw the tragedy and tried to contact Wilner and Stephen Garrett, but all communication had been completely cut off. The death toll was reported to be as high as three hundred thousand.

Images of children buried in rubble flooded my mind, images they only showed glimpses of on television. I imagined those faces belonging to the children we had ministered to. My heart pounded faster. I called Director Young, who suggested we go to Haiti to follow up on the orphans. Dennis told me I should stay home in case any of the kids called. I sat by the phone during their entire one-week trip, nervously awaiting any news.

When communication to Haiti resumed, Jimmy from the Cité Soleil orphanage reported that eight of his nine orphans were safe, as well as our friend, Wilner. Unfortunately, the ninth orphan, a boy named Mario, had been killed in his home during the quake. He was only eleven years old.

With tears in my eyes, I immediately rewatched my only interview with him, taken during my last trip in 2009.

I asked little Mario, "What's your name?"

With great enthusiasm, he shouted, "Yes!"

I then asked, "How old are you?"

Again, he answered the question with an excited "Yes!" That was the extent of our entire conversation, but it was all we needed.

When Dennis finally returned, he showed me footage of the most horrendous devastation I'd ever seen. Dennis and I immediately organized fundraisers at local churches to provide relief. The poignant footage they had captured drew a flood of media attention. In response, numerous local pastors embraced us with open arms, showcasing a beautiful display of compassion and unity.

By the end of September 2010, I brought Wilner to Hawaii to help earthquake victims and raise awareness of Haiti's plight through the release of the documentary. I also told Wilner it was never too late to go back to school, and I pleaded with him to finish his education once he went back home. I promised him I would support him if he followed through.

Despite the efforts I made to support Wilner and Emmanuel's education, their former mentor made no effort to educate them despite having received nearly a million dollars a year in donations. As a result, neither of them understood the crucial role education played in their future. Emmanuel only went as far as taking photos of the school we sent him to. Wilner ended up dropping out after getting into some trouble with the law.

Haiti had become a huge part of our family's lives as we'd tried our best to help these former street kids. Over time, we came to accept that their lives were now in God's hands. The street orphans were now adults, and some of them had gotten married; some even moved to the United States. On the bright side, our efforts hadn't been wasted, as we'd touched so many young lives and taught them to have faith in God.

In 2013, *Innocence Abandoned: Street Kids of Haiti* won the Monaco Charity Film Festival Award.

FREE TO FOLLOW, THE BAND

CONTINUING WITH DENNIS'S aspiration to start a band, we followed Pastor Kim's recommendation to visit Full Gospel Emmanuel Church in the heart of Kalihi Valley. Located on the second floor of a dilapidated two-story building, I could smell *mandu* soup wafting through the hallway the moment Dennis and I walked inside.

I immediately felt at home.

The sanctuary, barely larger than the average living room, welcomed us into a tranquil atmosphere. A petite Asian woman sat on the floor engrossed in prayer and accompanied by her three feline companions. To our amusement, one of her cats had adorably placed her paw on the open Bible. As we made her acquaintance, the petite woman introduced herself as Pastor Hannah Haraguchi, a delightful soul possessing a special bond with her furry prayer partners.

Despite her last name, Pastor Haraguchi was Korean, having married a local Japanese businessman named Willard. With her dark hair, white complexion, and beehive hairdo, she reminded me of an Asian version of television hostess Elvira.

Within the half-hour, a small congregation entered. Chatting with this motley crew of misfits, I discovered many were ex-cons, each with their own unique quirks and stories. The toll of their past struggles with drug addiction was evident on their haggard and weary faces. However, despite their rough appearances, they had managed to put on their Sunday best, decently dressed for church. Each one of them perfectly captured the beauty of God's transformation in their diverse journeys.

After service, the band broke down their instruments while a heavy-set Hawaiian-Filipino guitarist introduced himself to us. He had a unique but memorable name: Mac Macadamia. With a genial smile, Mac introduced us to their band. I told him I was very impressed with his singing voice, though his bandmate, lead singer Harvey, was rather pitchy on the high notes—an opinion I kept to myself.

With a humble smile, Mac thanked me. "Music saved my life," he said. "Playing for the Lord gave me a second chance from a life of prison."

As we conversed about Dennis's musical background, Pastor Haraguchi asked if he wanted to join the band, believing he could help them improve. Dennis was more than happy to comply, and I was delighted to see him return to his first love of music. Although Dennis was an experienced performer, I realized he needed to be mentored by colleagues who had struggled to overcome their own addictions.

This would be a win-win situation for everyone.

***

BREAKING INTO THE Christian music scene was not an easy task. Compared to pop music, the audience was much smaller, and its marketing reach was narrower. Still, Hawaii has a unique Christian heritage, and unlike Christian music on the mainland, local artists infuse Hawaiian culture, especially hula, into their own brand of contemporary Christian music.

Dennis eventually replaced Harvey as the lead singer, something Harvey didn't take well to, and he walked out one day after service. Though I wished him well, I was glad Dennis had found a new life with this band, which they renamed "Free to Follow," because they were free from their addictions—free to follow the word of God.

Inspired by their rehabilitation, Dennis produced a testimonial video detailing his own struggles with drug addiction. Local churches started welcoming our band to their services to share their stories.

As their following grew, women from different churches offered to dance hula while the band played. Since colonial times, utilizing the indigenous Hawaiian dance for worship has been a long-standing tradition, and it has enhanced our church services dramatically. Soon, Pastor Haraguchi booked the band at different venues around the island and, eventually, produced a music video for their self-titled song "Free to Follow."

As a bonus, Pastor Haraguchi gifted me two dogs that had been abandoned by their homeless owner: a fluffy poodle named Mochi and a plump chihuahua named Laura. These adorable furry companions quickly found their place in my heart and became cherished members of our growing family.

Soon, the band played at church conferences, water parks, and concerts in the Philippines as well as in California, with crowds of as few as twenty or up to several hundred. But it wasn't always smooth sailing. During their concert in the Philippines, their drummer, Kimo, relapsed and tumbled off the stage, unintentionally dragging the drums along with him.

Minor problems aside, the band's progress climbed. Their popularity increased as they performed for other churches, prison ministries, and beach ministries to help the homeless. With our hula troupe accompanying us, we became a second family to them, as most of our hula dancers had come from broken homes and abusive relationships. Not only did these women support Dennis in his music endeavors, but they also helped me grow in my walk with God.

Working with the hula worship team encouraged me to focus our efforts on local venues, reaching out to the needy in our own backyard first. Feeling empowered within the local Christian community, Dennis and I co-created Cornerstone Multimedia, based on a verse in Acts 4:11, "The stone that you builders rejected has now become the cornerstone."

Our family's media company was born. Coupled with multimedia experience, our small church band grew to play bigger venues. At the time, we had no idea that media and the arts would play such a pivotal role in the human consciousness, especially how they influence our youth, sometimes in harmful and destructive ways. Many in our church believed it would require a spiritual battle to win back their souls.

In 2016, I was overjoyed when our music video for the single "Free to Follow" won a Battle of the Bands contest on FISH radio, resulting in the Free to Follow band earning a spot to open at the Neal Blaisdell Center for a nationally known Christian band called Mercy Me. They performed in front of a sold-out crowd of twelve thousand.

Dennis once told me that while living as an addict in Los Angeles, he cried out to God many times. Desperate to find answers, he would open his Bible to a random page. One time, he landed on Jonah's prayer: "In my distress, I called to the Lord, and He answered me. From deep in the realm of the dead I called for help, and You listened to my cry . . . I have been banished from Your sight; yet I will look again toward Your holy temple . . . When my life was ebbing away. I remembered You, Lord and my prayer rose to You, to Your holy temple."

Having gone through that ordeal, we both understood how fitting this prayer was. When he was at his lowest point, he confronted God as I had myself.

Over time, I learned how to communicate with our Father in Heaven, and I now see that the miracles in my life, which often guided me and saved me, could in no way be mere coincidences. They triggered the healing process for my son and me.

Prayer participation in fellowship at church and a genuine, loving relationship with God were the ingredients for true healing. As my son's faith began to grow, so did my own. A new journey for my family had begun.

A WITNESS TO ALOHA

JUST BEFORE CHRISTMAS in 2018, I had a dream in which I stood in the middle of a freshwater pool surrounded by rocks, whereupon a large, imposing Hawaiian woman wearing a flowing white gown sat oblivious to me at the pool's edge and dipped one foot into the water. Gleefully, she scooped up some water with both hands and held them up to heaven, perhaps as an offering.

By the time the new year began, my dream had turned out to be a prophetic one, as I would soon learn the identity of the woman in the pool.

Before missionaries arrived on the island, the plain south of Honolulu was barren, resembling a windswept desert. Amidst this landscape stood an oasis, now the location of Kawaiahaʻo Church. The word "kawaiahaʻo" translates to "the water of Haʻo" referencing a sacred freshwater spring once used for ceremonial purification baths by high-ranking chiefs and chiefesses, including High Chiefess Haʻo. While the spring has vanished, a fountain and a rock from its original site serve as memorials. I believe the woman in my dream must have been the chiefess.

Shortly after experiencing this dream, I got a call from Kahu (Pastor) Kenneth Makuakane from Kawaiahaʻo Church, the oldest Christian church in Hawaii. Kenneth was the writer of "Hula Girl" from Dennis's *Smile* album.

Through Pastor Ken, Dennis was commissioned by their church leaders to produce a documentary for the bicentennial of Kawaiahaʻo Church. While extensively researching and developing the documentary, we began to understand the true story behind the early Christian influence in Hawaii.

Under the title *A Witness to Aloha*, the documentary incorporated the history of Hawaii's first missionaries and included interviews with the church's congregation and staff. To a large degree, I felt this project would be spiritually connected to my son.

Dennis's biological father, Kim Gwangyeong, once portrayed one of the first Christian missionaries in Korea in the film *Martyr*, based on a New York Times Best Seller about missionaries who were executed during the Korean War. This upcoming documentary marked one of Dennis's forays into filmmaking, potentially carrying forward his father's legacy.

Through the documentary's filming process, Dennis met Marie, a talented pianist, and they married on March 30, 2019.

DEFEATING THE FAMILY CURSE

IN SEPTEMBER 2021, I faced an unexpected reality—a pandemic stretching into its third year, which hit Hawaii hard with fear and isolation. Despite the challenges, my faithful dog and companion Mochi joined me on morning walks, even though my neighbors stayed indoors.

As Mochi and I wandered through Manoa Valley, the scent of freshly cut grass brought back cherished memories of my first home in Denver, Colorado. Our peaceful moment was interrupted by quacking ducks, but I didn't mind Mochi playfully barking at them.

Sitting with him at a picnic table, tears mixed with rain as I contemplated the difficult decision ahead—saying goodbye to my beloved pet, who was battling advanced prostate cancer. It reminded me of life's fleeting nature, urging me to cherish every moment.

Following a brief stroll, we passed a Catholic Church on Lowrey Avenue, where I noticed the absence of young adults and children, raising concerns about the decline in spiritual beliefs among the younger generation. Despite these societal challenges, I always found comfort in prayer, knowing it connected me directly to our Heavenly Father, guiding me through uncertainty.

I often reflect on my great-grandmother's act of killing the snake, which brought only trouble. To break this curse, I had to seek a strong relationship with God because overcoming generational mistakes requires divine guidance. The process of learning to draw near to God is a personal and continuous journey. I recognize the significance of aligning with Him, as facing life's challenges alone is not a sustainable approach.

To be honest, there are times I feel a growing darkness surrounding me. Societal issues such as depression, homelessness, drug abuse, and war contribute to the challenges faced by every family, perpetuating our collective suffering.

Understanding the Lord's sacrifice is vital to addressing these problems.

Our daily connection with God has been a source of positive changes, particularly evident in the case of my son Dennis. Through this, we gain wisdom and inner peace. The solution lies in a profound spiritual change, achievable through rebirth to Christ. Miracles in mind, body, and spirit result from devotion, dedication, and prayer.

PASSING OF DEAR LOVED ONES

NOT LONG AFTER Hal walked out of my life, I started dating Roy Akaki. Ironically, it was Hal who had first introduced me to Roy back in 1987, just before we closed the Burgundy Lounge, my last bar. Roy and I got married in 2005, and in the years that I knew him, we shared an easy familiarity and sense of comfort that had been missing from my prior relationships.

Roy proved time and again that he was the kind of man with whom I could settle down. As a retired Air Force major, he generously helped shoulder my financial burdens, but most of all, I appreciated his companionship. Unfortunately, in 2018, he began suffering from dementia, and I eventually became his caregiver.

***

ON THE MORNING of March 29, 2022, Roy sadly passed away. He was laid to rest at the National Memorial Cemetery of the Pacific at Punchbowl. I honestly believed I would be better prepared for this day, but I immediately felt pangs of guilt, regretting all the times I could have been nicer to him.

Perhaps everyone feels some form of regret when their loved ones leave them. Without a doubt, Roy was a good man, and I knew he was with God now, golfing on the eighteenth hole in the landscape of heaven.

Over the last five years, one after another, my dear loved ones have continued to pass away. This series of tragedies started quickly on December 15, 2017, when my eldest brother Jeong suffered a sudden cardiac arrest and collapsed during his morning workout. Sadly, he did not survive.

Adorned with beautiful wreaths, his memorial service filled the entire sanctuary at First Korean Methodist Church on Keeaumoku Street. When I approached the casket, I noticed how he lay with a peaceful smile. I immediately recalled how, as a child, he refused to buy me a bus pass, forcing me to walk to school in the rain in my new uniform. I immediately forgave him for that and for everything else as well.

I found solace in forgiveness.

At the funeral, I saw many family members whom I hadn't met before, which made me realize that our family had grown significantly over time. I reminded myself that this remarkable expansion started with a life-changing choice when our family traveled on a steam engine train in pursuit of a better life. Those crucial moments have profoundly influenced our lives, and now, I am surrounded by the love and support of our thriving family.

As of this writing, only two of my brothers are still alive. Yeong suffered from leukemia and lived under hospice care. I took care of him until his last day. Yong and his wife, Carolyn, are retired and living in Honolulu, while Gyeong remains on the streets. My sister, Okyon, resides in a care home. Throughout this journey, I dedicated myself to my family, and I am thankful that my sacrifices benefitted them.

KOʻOLAU MOUNTAINS

WHEN THE EARLY morning drizzle stopped, I decided to tend to Mother's garden in my front yard. I dug into the warm soil, letting slimy worms crawl away. The musty scent of fresh dirt smelled good as I planted various types of flowers. Watching me at work, my new puppy ran up to me and licked my face.

Life always came full circle regarding my pets. After Laura and Mochi's passing, I promised myself I would never ever get another dog because I couldn't go through the pain of losing a little loved one again. However, one day, while shopping at the PX with my sister, we caught sight of a shaggy little puppy—a mixed terrier with sandy fur—displayed there by the humane society. The minute this puppy and I locked eyes, my heart melted, and I ended up taking her home. I decided to name her Sandy, as she reminded me of the dog from the musical *Annie*, and she has been a faithful companion ever since.

As Sandy chased a butterfly under the branches of Mother's willow tree, it reminded me that I should visit my mother. A soft wind touched my cheeks, and my eyes were drawn toward the blood-red Poinsettias on the porch steps. Brother Yong and Carolyn had sent them as an early Christmas present.

Within the hour, I picked up Sister Okyon from the care home, and we embarked on a visit to our parents' resting place at Kaneohe Memorial Park. As I looked up at the wispy clouds curling around the tops of the Koʻolau Mountains, I felt some comfort as we silently put a bouquet of flowers at the base of Mother and Father's grave plaques.

Okyon's joints cracked when she squatted on the ground beside me. Like generations of Korean daughters before her, she paused to carefully manicure the flowers of Mother's gravestone, working competently despite having experienced bouts of dementia over the past few years.

I recalled the last time I'd seen Mother in that same position in her garden. She had been trimming the grass around the bottle-brush tree that she'd planted on the day she told me her time had come.

My sister and I stood between the gravestones and prayed. In the midst of life's tumultuous journey, grappling with the void left by Mother's physical absence, I sensed a responsibility toward the rest of the family, a duty that compelled me to carry the torch forward.

On our way back home, we stopped by the beach where Brother Yeong's ashes had been scattered and dropped two purple orchid leis into the water. While we watched the waves carry the flowers out to the sea, I fondly recalled the day I had brought him and the rest of my siblings to America, and I comforted myself, knowing that although I could not change my past, I could acknowledge our gain in Christ.

As much as I wish it were not so, I am resolved to accept that it took me until the autumn years of my life to realize that something bigger than our individual selves exists—that our world isn't limited to what we see with our eyes, but what we can feel in spirit.

Prayer—a mother's prayer—is a powerful tool to communicate with God. I believe that it was our faith that carried our family through our trials and tribulations, many of which arose out of my own life choices. I learned that hiding from God as I had in the past led to my lowest breaking point, and by letting go of all the nonsense that once defined my life, I finally submitted to God.

As Mother once prayed for our family, I now pray for mine—my children, their spouses, and my grandchildren. If humanity were an ocean, an individual person would be akin to one drop of water among countless others. *Every* life is precious, and each of us should have the opportunity to live well and celebrate that life.

"But certainly, God has heard me;
He has attended to the voice of my prayer."

—Psalm 66:19 (NKJV)

ACKNOWLEDGMENTS

"Do not be anxious about anything, but in every situation,
by prayer and petition, with thanksgiving,
present your requests to God. And the peace of God,
which transcends all understanding, will guard
your hearts and your minds in Christ Jesus."
—Philippians 4:6-7 NIV

THIS JOURNEY IN writing this book has been life changing for my family and me.

I extend my deepest gratitude to publishers Bryan Heathman and Alice Kirkwood for their tireless effort, as well as to our editor, Emily Waltenburg, whose guidance was pivotal.

My heartfelt thanks go to the Free to Follow worship team for accompanying me on this spiritual voyage and special thanks to my eldest son, Dennis, who has been by my side every step of the way. His guidance and encouragement have made this storytelling journey not only possible but also a remarkable adventure in faith.

I am also grateful to my daughter, Marylin, for her understanding and encouragement, which have been pillars of support through life's journey. My son, Patrick, has been an incredible support over the years, always there for me as my youngest son.

My gratitude extends to my mother, Pong Hui, who has endured life's trials with unwavering strength. I know she watches over me with a smile.

I am thankful for Pastor Hannah Haraguchi and Elder Haraguchi, who have offered me encouragement and support while walking beside me on my spiritual journey. I am thankful for Joanne Kurata and Pastor Jimmy Yamada, who have offered us encouragement and support for Dennis and our family for many years. A special acknowledgment to Auntie Cynthia Mae Ho for her belief in me. She, in particular, has been a source of joy, frequently leaving food at my doorstep with a great smile, alongside Muffin, her dog.

With all my heart,
Mom